A FOOT IN BOTH CAMPS

Praise for *A Foot in Both Camps*

"In this lucidly written book, Marcus Ferrar bridges the gap between the two camps he was born into with scrupulous analysis and humane sympathy. His account of growing up and crossing post-war borders, his experiences over forty years as a European correspondent for Reuters, his travels to interview family members and other participants and witnesses make an absorbing story in themselves. His German relatives and friends were a cross-section of people at the receiving end of history, of Nazism and Communism especially. Their story and memories give a human face to the facts and statistics that are discreetly present in the background. Issues of responsibility are never far away, and are brought to a moving conclusion in a final chapter set in Dresden. This is an elegantly concise view of Anglo-German history set in the realities of personal and family existence." - *Professor Jim Reed, Emeritus Professor of German Language and Literature, University of Oxford*

"As the son of a German mother and an English father the author grew up with relatives in both countries and a knowledge of both languages before going on to an international career as a journalist which has taken him all over Europe. In this engaging book, Marcus Ferrar combines a personal memoir with a well-informed grasp of the history of both countries and their attitudes towards each other over the past century. Both his parents are still alive, his mother now in her hundredth year, and in this lively and personal account the author gives a vivid picture of what he has made of the challenges presented by both sides of his Anglo-German heritage during the past half century." - *Iain R. Smith, Emeritus Reader in History, University of Warwick*

Praise for *Slovenia 1945*

"It has contrived wholly to avoid all the clichés of the genre... it presents us with a range of individuals as vividly seen and as sharply characterised as the multifarious inhabitants of War and Peace or A Dance to the Music of Time." - *John Bayley, Book of the Year 2005, Times Literary Supplement*

"Extraordinarily interesting... heart-rending... particularly moving... it shows the resilience of the human spirit in a finer light than I can remember reading elsewhere." - *Nigel Nicolson*

'This book is inspiring. It shows how a few people with hearts and strong minds can help to transform tragedy into hope." - *Paul Oestreicher*

'This excellent book underlines the continuing need to get at the truth." - *Richard Bassett*

"Your work promises to contribute to our collective understanding of a terrible period of European history." - *Jack Straw, then UK Foreign Secretary*

"A valuable contribution to upholding the common values Slovenia and Great Britain share as partners in the European Union." - *Janez Janša, Prime Minister, Slovenia*

"A splendid book. It was an exciting and moving read." - *Michael Nelson, former General Manager Reuters*

"Your book is impossible to put down." - *Cardinal Aloysius Ambrožič*

About the Author

Marcus Ferrar was a journalist with Reuters for 18 years. In 1971/72 during the Cold War he was the only western correspondent in East Berlin. He subsequently lived in Prague and over three years covered all of Eastern Europe. He then reported the Portuguese revolution and served in the management of Reuters.

Now a writer and an award-winning communication consultant living in Oxford, he specialises in writing about WWII, Communism, Germany, and Eastern Europe, with special emphasis on peoples who have difficult historical heritages. He has an English father and a German mother. He is a fluent in German, French and Italian.

Together with John Corsellis, he wrote *Slovenia 1945*, which was published in English, Slovene and Italian. It recounted the flight of Slovene Catholics after World War II, the British Army's repatriation of 12,000 soldiers among them to ex-Yugoslavia, their slaughter by Communist Partisans, and the scattering of the civilian survivors around the world. In Slovenia, this book was a best-seller. In Britain it occasioned questions in Parliament and an expression of regret by a Foreign Office minister.

In Oxford, he is Chairman of the Friends of Summertown Library.

For more information, you can visit his website
www.marcusferrar.org

or read his blog
http://mferrar.wordpress.com/

or follow him on Twitter @mferrar or Facebook

Also by the Author

Slovenia 1945
I. B. Tauris & Co Ltd, 2005

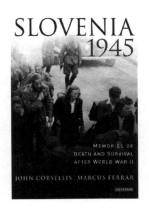

A FOOT IN BOTH CAMPS

A German Past
for Better and for Worse

MARCUS FERRAR

Ibla
DIGITAL

*The fate of democracy rests in
faith in history*

Ernst Reuter, mayor of West Berlin

Contents

Prologue

A MOTHER FROM HITLER'S GERMANY

Learn from yesterday, live for today, hope for tomorrow. The important thing is not to stop questioning – Albert Einstein

She sits before me with her legs slung playfully over the armrest of her chair like a little girl. But she is not young; she is in her 100th year and her childhood began before World War I. My mother lives in the most English of environments – an old people's home in north Oxford. But she is not British; she is German.

She does not quite fit with normal concepts. Nor do I. I was born 30 miles from London and have a British father, but through my mother have a link with Germany, over which a cloud of history still hangs. I see that country through the eyes of both peoples, which is both a gift and a challenge.

Understanding Germany has not been easy. I encountered contradictions. My German aunt wrote scathingly in her memoirs of the British as "the enemy" (they bombed her home). Yet a few years later she warmly welcomed us as "family" (we came to visit). So were we friend or foe? Or both?

I met prejudice. A Viennese living in England told me how an Englishwoman refused to talk to her, 63 years after World War II ended, because of her guttural German accent. In fact, she was a Jew and a *victim* of Nazi oppression, not a perpetrator. She had won the Order of the British Empire (OBE) for decades of public service in Stoke-on-Trent. She was a friend, not an enemy.[i]

I also had to deal with silence. Nobody wanted to talk much about the past. It was too painful; too awkward; too touchy. I grew up against the background of a fragmented past. I guessed it was dramatic, but large parts were left blank.

I was brought up in England speaking only English at home. I was proud that my father served in the war as a British officer for six of his best years. As a little boy, I crept into the spare room wardrobe to look at the insignia on his uniform. I devoured boy's war stories in which my compatriots shot down wicked Germans.

Yet I sensed this was not the whole story, all the more so since I soon became intimately familiar with Germany. Scarcely had the dust of war settled than my parents started taking me there on holiday – and I liked it. German cousins took me on long climbs up into the Bavarian Alps and swimming far out in lakes. An uncle found me a holiday job with a firm in Hamburg. If the cousins grew bossy, I relished the friendly tussles that ensued. With its cobbled streets, practical Volkswagens, cigar-smoke, *Wurst* and tasty beer, I felt at home in Germany.

As a teenager in the 1950s and 1960s, I compared my own country's economic disintegration and waning prestige with the vigour of a defeated nation starting out again from zero. The British lost an empire, went on strike and devalued the pound. The Germans worked hard, ran smooth railways, played sublime classical music and served cakes with whipped cream. For all this, I never abandoned the knowledge acquired as a little boy that in the greatest conflict of modern times the British were on the side of right and the Germans wrong.

I thus had a foot in both camps. With my compatriots, whose wartime heroes I admired with all my heart as I grew up, including my father, who risked his life for the sake of his country. But also with the homely, forward-looking Germans I got to know, including the odd ex-Nazi or two.

Despite the silences and contradictions, I kept my eyes and ears open, even as a small child. I spotted the gaps in what I was told and picked up hints. I became sceptical of common assumptions. I learned to speak German and studied its literature. I spent time as a journalist in Berlin when radical changes were taking place there. I frequented people who fought, survived and found new paths; people ready to challenge the old suppositions and look beyond national spectrums.

I was fascinated how people *made choices*, for bad and for good, en masse and as individuals, often confronting difficult dilemmas, following the stream or courageously swimming against it. The choices made over the last century by ordinary Britons and Germans influence the way we think and judge today. But the lessons the two peoples have drawn do not coincide. Having a foot in both camps, I abhor such divergences. My background prompts me to seek a single truth to which both peoples can subscribe, and lessons which are valid for us all.

Sitting now with my mother from Hitler's Germany, I am with a person who lived through much of this herself. She began life in a world much different from ours. If her parents wanted to go somewhere, they walked or harnessed a horse and cart. To keep warm, they lit wood in a tiled stove. Or rather a servant did, since plenty of cheap labour was available from the land.

When my mother was born in Germany in 1912, Europe was a proud continent. Memories of war were giving way to a belief in progress – economic, social and scientific. Towns were expanding, and flourishing industry was allowing millions to escape from scraping a miserable living from the soil. The new was built on solid foundations of the past. Culture had roots going back for centuries. In attitudes, standards and values, Europe set the tone for the world.

When she was two years old in 1914 and World War I threatened, British scholars wrote a letter to The Times of London protesting against the prospect of fighting with Germany: "We regard Germany as a nation leading the way in the Arts and Sciences, and we have all learned and are learning from German scholars."[ii]

However when my father was born in London barely a year later in 1915, all such solidarity had vanished. On the day of his birth, the number of *Killed in Action* in The Times outnumbered *Births* by half. Germans had started using poison gas and my British grandfather, a mild-mannered civil servant, had volunteered to fight them.[iii] Europe was tearing itself apart.

By the time my parents reached their early 30s, the old Europe was in tatters. Ideologies had ravaged the human basis of its civilisation. Tens of millions of people had been exterminated in two world wars. Others lived on in shame for what they had done themselves, or connived in as collaborators. Europe lost its moral leadership. From 1945, it became the terrain over which outside powers wrestled in their Cold War. Germany and Germans sank to the very lowest rung of respect, and Germans and British were enemies.

My parents, who married on the last day of 1938 after a chance encounter, survived the catastrophes, but thereafter lived under the shadow of this past. Being a German-British couple was awkward. They bestrode a great divide which still exists. But the challenge of surmounting this gap motivated them – and their children – to go beyond prejudice and acrimony.

My mother sits dangling her legs over her chair – with a foot in two centuries. With that background, her life could well have come to naught. Millions of others met violent ends, lost families and suffered humiliation and ruin during this time.

But here sits a survivor, smiling sweetly as her drifting mind alights on a piece of clothing, a colourful drawing, a passing car. She has had her dose of history and, with her mind emptied by extreme old age, she has put the past behind her.

She holds hands with me, her son, and looks into my eyes for an eternity. I look back, also for an eternity. Almost a centenarian, she is slim and graceful again, almost weightless. She is dressed neatly, and the carers have put her hair back in a pony-tail. She tosses her head with a light elegance.

I see a little girl. She is skating, racing over the frozen flood meadows of the river Elbe near Hamburg. Swish, swish, swish. Skating with her elder brother, their dog racing alongside.

I wonder whether she will ever be able to tell me anything any more. Then a sudden flash of lucidity takes us back nearly 100 years as I show her a family album. My mother points to a photograph of a house on the river bank and says: "That's the window of my bedroom."

Chapter 1

DYNAMITE

Probably my factories will put an end to war... on the day when two army corps may mutually annihilate each other in a second, probably all nations will recoil with horror and disband their troops – Alfred Nobel

My German grandfather, who lived in the house my mother was pointing at, made dynamite. That certainly made him interesting in my eyes. Was he one of those warmonger industrialists who were supposed to have pushed Germany into World War I in order to make money out of armaments? As a Briton, it was important for me to know, but the answer was not obvious. Dynamite can be used for both peace and war.

Its great innovation was that it did not explode too readily, unlike its volatile predecessor, nitroglycerine. It is stable to manufacture and transport. Dynamite revolutionised coal mining and the building of roads, tunnels, canals and the London Underground, but similarly facilitated the manufacture of munitions for waging war. Its inventor, Alfred Nobel, worried about the ethical aspects of dynamite, and calmed his conscience by investing the money he earned from it in the Nobel Peace Prize.

Friedrich Roewer, my grandfather, was more interested in the scientific implications and the chance to make an exciting career with something new. As a chemistry undergraduate, he realised dynamite could help him rise above his origins as the son of a shopkeeper. He came from Neustrelitz, then as now a sleepy town lost in the emptiness of East Germany. Having visited it, I understand my grandfather's desire not to spend the rest of his days there. He was lucky: Germany's expanding industry was opening up to lowly, ambitious young men with skills and knowledge.

My German grandfather (top left) with his family in Neustrelitz, late 19th century. Germany's industrial boom enabled him to escape a provincial town

Until the 1870s, war had been the norm in Europe, as inevitable as disease and death. Since then peace and prosperity had gradually taken hold, based on liberal economics and scientific advances.[iv] Germany in particular profited from this. By 1900, its industry had overtaken all other countries except the United States. In 1913 it was producing three times as much iron and steel as Britain. German technical high schools turned out well trained graduates, workers received social insurance, and Berlin became the fastest growing capital in Europe. After centuries of turmoil, history for once was moving Germany's way. Having become a united state only in 1871, it seemed poised to emerge as the continent's natural leader.

My grandfather was both a protagonist and beneficiary of this process. He spent a year in America, but unlike the five million Germans who emigrated there earlier in the century,[v] he decided to return.

Germany, and in particular dynamite, offered him better prospects. Alfred Nobel had produced the explosive for the first time in 1866 on a raft on the river Elbe at Krümmel, upstream from Hamburg. Nobel was obliged to move from his native Stockholm after his brother and several other people were blown up in an experiment. He discovered that Krümmel's fine, sterile sand mixed well with nitroglycerine to form a stable paste to insert into blasting holes. The result was dynamite.

Friedrich Roewer joined the Alfred Nobel Dynamit AG in Hamburg shortly after the founder's death in 1896. He subsequently became Director of the company's sole production plant, which had made all the money funding the Nobel Peace Prize. He was a scientist, manufacturer and businessman. As such, he was a man of his time.

Yet the Germany he lived in had not given up the idea of war. Despite the rise of men such as my grandfather, war remained on the agenda for the old military caste of land-owning gentry who exercised political power. When I look at illustrations of Germany at the time, soldiers are on all the photos, much as the British Royal Family spread over publications in Britain in the 1950s. They look stiff, superior and out of place.[vi] Despite the rapid modernisation of Germany, the military determined the country's political course. The years of peace had not changed their view that war was both inevitable and honourable. This of course was not unique to Germany. Similar trends could be observed in France, Austria, Greater Hungary, Russia and Italy. Britain too engaged in a series of colonial wars.

With the hindsight of a person brought up in peace, I find this obsession with war amongst all these powers absurd and repugnant. But if I look back at the Germany in which my mother was a child, it is evident that not just the diehard landowners entertained these martial assumptions. Many civilians thought likewise.

Even a reputable democrat such as journalist Sebastian Haffner went along with them in his youth. Later, he was perceptive enough to quit Germany for Britain because of the Nazis, and I came to admire the columns he wrote in the liberal London *Observer*. But in his autobiography, he admits yearning as a small boy for the "Final Victory" in WWI. He eagerly consumed army bulletins about ultimatums, mobilisations and cavalry. He scolded German housewives grumbling about food shortages and urged them to "hold out." None of his cultivated family or friends warned him that his belligerent patriotism might be wrong-headed.

When defeat came, Haffner was shocked that the military's boasts of imminent victory turned out to be hollow. He wandered the streets in a trauma feeling "a horror for life."[vii] So too did millions of other Germans who had allowed themselves to be duped.

My grandfather went along with this to the extent that he expanded production of explosives at the Nobel factory to meet the growing demands of the German Army. Employment soared from 600 to 2,700 during WWI.[viii] Friedrich Roewer doubtless had little choice but to supply the armed forces, and like millions of wartime munitions workers on both sides he probably thought he should do his bit.

But he was not a person to fall for the fairy tales of the military. Darwin was his hero, not because Darwin demonstrated that species fight for survival, which led others to justify human savageries, but because his theories explained life on the basis of science rather than myth. My grandfather had little time for God – and even less for the German officer class. This became apparent when his elder son announced plans to enrol as a military cadet. The father objected strongly and threatened to withdraw financial support. The son took heed and became a solicitor.

My mother, who was six when WWI ended, had no interest at all in the military, nor did she have second thoughts about what dynamite could be used for. What she liked was running wild in the beautiful German countryside around her home on the river Elbe. The memory of an idyllic childhood in Germany would remain with her forever and shape her attitudes to life. At a time when other Germans fought, suffered and despaired, she enjoyed a Golden Age of youth.

All this I know from the stories my mother told her children. When she was over 80 she also wrote a memoir conjuring up the world which inspired her.[ix] The enchantment did not however survive the passage of Hitler. When I was small, my mother told me Krümmel "does not exist any more." When I visited in 2007, I found the place was still there, but I understood what she meant.

In those years of a magic I could no longer feel there, she roamed the water meadows of the Elbe, full of wild flowers, frog spawn and dragonflies. She climbed trees, built huts, visited horses in stables swarming with swallows, tended her own garden plot, picked wild berries and mushrooms, and lay in the grass in the sunshine watching the clouds go by.

A stylish new Director's house and a dozen dwellings for employees made up Krümmel's self-sufficient community. Built in red brick, the house had four storeys and modern conveniences such as double glazing and central heating. It was a residence fit for a Director at the forefront of industrial innovation. It stands there today, looking much the same, but older now, no longer at the leading edge.

The garden supplied all the fruit, vegetables, salads, chickens, eggs and flowers the family needed. The father

*Running wild in the German countryside: my mother, just before
the end of World War I*

set up a bathing hut on a sheltered bay of the river for the
children to swim. A one-carriage steam train took them
to a nearby school, but by early afternoon they were back
to roam free.

In the North German climate of those last years of
World War I and the early 1920s, summers were warm
and sunny, with short, violent thunderstorms refreshing
gardens and countryside in the evenings. In the autumn,
fog descended and rain poured down in deluges. In the
long winters, snow covered the ground for months and
the Elbe froze over.

Her elder brother Walter taught her to swim, row a boat,
ride a bicycle and skate over ice. They ranged far and wide
on their bicycles in summer and glided over vast, frozen
water meadows in winter, as fast as they could, on and on
until they returned home panting and exhilarated. "I always
joined the boys," she wrote in a memoir 75 years later.

The children knew spring was coming when the ice started to craze over as they skated. Ice-breakers pushed slowly up the river three abreast, breaking through the ice with thunderous claps. Then the procession of Hamburg tugs pulling long strings of barges with goods for the German hinterland resumed. Those going the other way picked up dynamite from Krümmel.

Sights, sounds, smells – all left indelible memories of a German childhood which my mother later passed on to her own family. Her father was her guide to nature. She remembers him walking with his children through the ancient forests and heathlands, teaching them which mushrooms and berries to pick and how to spot wild animals. As the younger daughter, my mother hit it off with her father from the start. She noticed how women found him charming, and thought likewise:

"My special treat came in the holidays. I was allowed to fetch my father home from work. Arriving early, I sat in a big armchair, as quiet as a mouse, and watched him at work, conferring with his staff or his secretary, or on the phone, entirely happy in this men's world. The walls were panelled and when it was time to leave, my father opened one panel where there was a wash basin, a second panel to get his coat and walking stick, a third – and that's where the chocolate was kept. Outside we found our dog Prince waiting. He accompanied my father to and from work."

Who knows whether my grandfather did not also have a darker side? But my mother liked his enterprise, ambition and amiability, and she fed this approvingly through to me, the British grandson whom he never knew. His impact was not destructive, like dynamite, but positive and inspirational.

Not everybody experienced the family life as an idyll. The younger son Fritz spoke darkly later of *eiserne Disziplin* – iron discipline. There *was* a "dragon" in the family. She

Fredrich Roewer, Director, Nobel Dynamitenfabrik AG.

was not German, but Belgian. It was the mother. She had come at the age of 20 to interpret for her father, a Belgian Inspector of Mines, when visiting the Nobel offices in Hamburg. She, Gabrielle, and Friedrich, 38, fell in love at first sight, married in 1901 and had four children.

She was a French-speaking Catholic from a well-heeled Brussels family. She had grown up with frequent visits to Paris, arts, music, exhibitions, theatres, books and elegant shops. Marriage landed her in a Protestant backwoods far from culture, entertaining company or worldly refinements. She found life in Krümmel boring. She loved a German, but considered Germans to be barbarians.

Before World War I, Gabrielle and her husband went on holidays to Belgium, but during the war German troops slaughtered and deported thousands of Belgian civilians and wantonly destroyed homes. Afterwards, the Belgian family refused to see her again. Gabrielle must be shown that she had moved beyond the pale by marrying a German. When she returned for her father's funeral, her sister turned her back on her and said: "One does not speak with a Boche."[x] As a gesture, it was understandable but uncharitable. Europeans of a later era would prove more forgiving. For my own generation, which has grown used to mixing with other nationalities with ease, such vendettas are primitive and obsolete.

Grandmother Gabrielle

Gabrielle ruled the household absolutely, managing four servants, a nursemaid and a gardener. At meals, *eiserne Disziplin* ruled. After spending much of the day roaming around with the dog, bathing and climbing trees, the children had to clean and tidy themselves, comb or plait their hair, sit up straight, use perfect table manners and eat everything that was put before them. The Belgian mother had the demanding standards of a rigid, high-born cosmopolitan, which would do her no good in the Germany to come.

Eiserne Disziplin meant that when the father brought a colourful scarf back as a present for his teenage younger daughter from a business trip, the mother took it away as unsuitable for a girl. When the girl reached 21 and wanted to wear lipstick, the mother forbade her to do so until she married.

A kindly Methodist sister, *Schwester Käthe*, kept the family together. Employed as a nurse by the factory, she was also governess to the family, imparting good will, household skills and friendly advice. The Belgian mother took to her, and the children happily accepted her as a substitute mother when the parents were away.

My own mother chafed at the *eiserne Disziplin*, but accepted it as a price to pay for her wild freedom in the outdoors paradise. Germany represented delightful nature, joyful anarchy, a beloved German father and a kind German nurse. Ironically, it was the francophone Belgian mother who upheld the tradition of a tyrannical Germanic upbringing.

Chapter 2

PARADISE LOST

Etiam si omnes – ego non! – Matthew 26: 33

When the Treaty of Versailles imposed on Germany by the victors of World War I forced the Nobel factory to give up its manufacture of explosives in 1919, my grandfather was disappointed, but converted the plant to synthetic textile manufacture and got on with business. His family carried on much as before.

Millions of other Germans took Versailles much worse. Having mistakenly believed in the myth of German military invincibility, they blamed their misery not on themselves but on others: Communists and Jews who had "stabbed the nation in the back," or the foreign victors, who had tried to kill and starve them and now sought revenge and humiliation.

This facile blame of others not only differs from attitudes of Germans today, but offends the values which I and millions of other Europeans have in the meantime grown up to respect. Having covered a revolution as a journalist in Portugal in the 1970s, I can appreciate the Germans' disorientation as Communists threatened to seize power, millions of ex-soldiers were set adrift in a disintegrating society and hard-earned savings were destroyed by hyperinflation.

However the Germans were denying the reality that their armies had broken before the enemy and suffered defeat in a war they had embarked on only too readily. It was a delusion which would cause immense harm. I see no reason to believe that they were forced into this attitude.

Rather they chose it freely. It is not that they were incapable of doing otherwise: after World War II, Germans showed they could surmount self-pity and assume responsibility for a much worse catastrophe.

The victorious Allies similarly focused on blame and punishment. They imposed huge reparation payments, debilitating restrictions and territorial losses on Germany. The reparations would have lasted 40 years or more if they had gone their course. The frontier changes created a host of new minority problems and inflamed ethnic animosities. The Allies did not include the Germans in the Versailles conference. They summoned German plenipotentiaries at the end and enforced the outcome on them. The victors thus brought the war to an end in a spirit of revenge and hatred rather than reconciliation. They too did not *have* to act thus. They chose to. After World War II, in the period when I grew up, the Western Allies did the opposite: they *helped* defeated Germany rather than punish it.

When the democratic Weimar Republic allowed inflation to get out of hand in the early 1920s, Germans considered it as state-sanctioned theft and an attack on the German ethic of thrift. They were appalled – as I am today, having lived for 20 years in a country with a sound currency, Switzerland.

Not everybody however experienced the hyperinflation as a disaster. Sebastian Haffner's family learned to cope by spending monthly salaries within a couple of hours on all necessities for the next month. He himself found it "peculiar rather than unpleasant."[xi] The writer Stefan Zweig found most people got through somehow and old values such as friendship, work, art, nature and love came back.[xii] In my own German family, scarcely anybody ever mentioned hyperinflation, which was brought under control in a relatively short time. As an 11-year-old at the time, my mother noticed nothing. One of her in-laws remarked that businessmen and market women learned to

London Mytone — Pr. Ru

Pm. 17. 16·53 — 17·44.
          D.   A.
          17·24 — 18·11
          17·53 = 18·45
          18·21 — 19·00

cope very quickly. He remembered his director panicking over his clinic's debt, but by 1923 the clinic was already expanding again with a new wing.[xiii] The disruption and loss caused by the crisis allowed extremists such as Hitler to emerge, but they remained on the fringes of power.

The experience of hyperinflation can hardly be seen as a cause or justification for Germans' later plunge towards a second war and genocide. Over the longer term, Germans have reacted *healthily* to the phenomenon. Today's acute German aversion to inflation has influenced Europe's economy far beyond Germany's borders. I and millions of others have benefited from the resulting economic stability.

As for reparations, the Germans in the end avoided paying most of them, with the result that the cost of WWI was higher for the Allies than for Germans.[xiv] Versailles was a humiliation for Germans, but they were well on the way to assuaging its effects before Hitler came to power. It certainly did not stop my German grandfather from rebuilding a profitable new business.

Having seen Communists take advantage of the war to overthrow the old order in Russia, Germans wondered whether they too were in for a revolution. But the threat was short-lived. The little town of Geesthacht near where my mother grew up seethed briefly with disorder and was nicknamed "Little Moscow." Jobless workers marched and tried to occupy plants. Police were drafted in from Hamburg to break them up and ringleaders were sent to prison.

The prospect of revolution put fear into the upper and middle classes, but the Communists were too weak to succeed. In 1919, they did attempt an insurrection, but it was easily put down by the Social Democrat government aided by right-wing ex-soldiers. The Geesthacht upheavals did not reach my mother's settlement at Krümmel, where the dynamite workers were skilled and less radicalised.

In Würzburg, a relative remembered a general strike collapsing after one day, and street-fighting in Munich not lasting much longer. Even in Berlin, many people were little disturbed. János Plesch, a well-to-do Berlin doctor, wrote later that the unrest was "not very violent."[xv]

My mother (left) and her brothers and sister, growing up in Germany just after World War I

History books tell of dramatic events during the 1920s. The Weimar Republic has gone down as a time of extremes and instability. But for my mother's family, as for so many other German families, concerns were more prosaic. Schooling, illnesses, household affairs, the change of seasons, running the factory and occasional travel preoccupied them more than the distant noise of beer hall rampages and street fights. The converted Nobel plant gradually recovered as Germany got over the worst of its economic troubles. The horse and carriage were upgraded to car and chauffeur. The family went on holidays amid the windswept sand dunes of the Baltic Sea.

Others were living well too, even Jews. Jews were among the groups whom Germans blamed for the defeat of 1918, but that did not stop the doctor János Plesch from becoming a leading light of Berlin's social scene in the 1920s. Plesch was a Jew but identified with neither the religious nor racial aspects of Jewishness. As his son told me in England many years later, János Plesch brought up his children as Catholics, and considered himself a German, a liberal, and a cosmopolitan European.[xvi]

His Berlin apartment was decorated with Louis XV furniture, drapes from the Imperial Palace in Peking and chinoiseries from a Renaissance palazzo in Parma. The parties he and his wife Melanie threw attracted a brilliant array of artists, bankers and politicians. The guest lists included Albert Einstein (also a Jew), who once ate three kilos of strawberries at a sitting; Emil Orlik, the Czech writer who dressed shabby-smart and impressed girls with dramatic entrées at the Romanische Café;[xvii] painters Oskar Kokoschka and Max Slevogt; violinist Fritz Kreisler; General Johannes von Seeckt, monocled commander of the German army; bankers Rothschild, Bleichröder and Schacht; and French ambassador André François-Poncet, sporting a small painted moustache and "overtaken by events."

A typical menu consisted of spring soup, mushrooms in champagne sauce, Hamburg chicken, puff pastries, croquant, cheese and fruit, washed down with Tokay and Château Mouton Rothschild 1889, not to mention Geisenheimer Kreuzweg 1921 and Pomméry & Greno 1911. Melanie kept notes of the success or otherwise of each evening – "much dancing till half past two, red tulips on the table" or "danced till half past three, little atmosphere, I had flu."[xviii]

Jews were flourishing not just in Berlin, but in Vienna and Budapest too. Viennese writer Stefan Zweig described his Jewish parents as very rich "good Jewish bourgeoisie," dedicated to tolerance, conciliation and progress.[xix] In Budapest, assimilation was so thorough that by the end of the 19th century 25 Hungarian Jews were barons and one was even a Catholic bishop. Many Central European Jews went through life without knowing that they were such. American historian Fritz Stern, born in German Breslau (now Polish Wrocław), learned he was a Jew at the age of seven only because Hitler's coming to power caused his parents to talk about it. A German friend living in Berlin told me her 80-year-old mother revealed to her children that she was Jewish only half a century after the war ended.[xx]

As for my German grandfather, Friedrich Roewer, artificial fibres may not have been what he wanted to make, but it gave him a welcome chance to visit the United States again. He found it much changed since he was there 35 years earlier, but he still appreciated all that was "specifically American."

Travelling German businessmen, 1928. My grandfather (left) sailing for America

My grandfather at this stage of his career comes across like a German manufacturer of today – travelling the world on business, fluent in English, and with the war put firmly behind him. The letters he sent to his wife as he toured Du Pont plants all over the United States in 1928 were written on notepaper of the hotels where he stayed. At the top of each were printed pen-and-ink sketches of the skyscrapers in which they were located. "1100 rooms, 1100 baths" said the inscription on his mail from the Hotel Statler in Buffalo, New York, sent as he set out on a Great Lakes steamer to factories in Toronto, Canada.

Mein lieber Schatz "my dear treasure," he addressed her. In the last letter before boarding the *Deutschland* liner to return, he wrote of the holiday they will take together and how he longs to be again with "my treasure," signing off with "my dear, another lovely kiss!"

In many respects, it was a beautiful life. A few months later however, he had a stroke and was forced to retire. Two years later, the Nobel business collapsed in the Depression and the factory ceased nearly all its activities.

This was the roller-coaster Germany in which my mother and her siblings became young adults. Her two brothers and elder sister went to university, but my mother left school as soon as she could and entered an arts & crafts school, learning skills which would serve her well in the times of austerity she did not yet know lay ahead. As a young woman of the comfortable middle class, she had suffered no major upsets so far. That was not to last. At a time of massive unemployment resulting from the Depression, Hitler came to power in 1933, a few months before my mother's 21st birthday. It could hardly have been a worse moment to enter adulthood.

My mother could still celebrate in Paris with a French friend married to the Professor of Romance Studies at Hamburg University. But the Nazis stirred up animosity against foreigners, and the Germans began ostracising her Belgian mother. When the latter lived on her own in Bergedorf after the death of her husband, no one would do housework for her. A Catholic priest initially lent her

My mother turned 21 just as the Nazi's came to power

books from his library, but after a time he shut the door in her face.

SA storm-troopers with lists in their hands descended on "Little Moscow" Geesthacht, rounded up Socialist and Communist leaders and dispatched them to the new concentration camp at Neuengamme a few miles away[xxi] The people of Krümmel were, according to one boy growing up there at the time, 95% in favour of Hitler when he took over.[1] "Too many jobless, too many political parties, too much street fighting, too much bad behaviour, high time to change things, now we have the right man" is how he summed up the joint opinion of his father and the Krümmel primary school teacher.[xxii]

1933 changed everything, and some knew this straightaway, even though they were little concerned

---

1   Sebastian Haffner estimated the support for the Nazis then at 90%.

by politics. Years ago, I bought a record of tunes played in the 1920s by the Marek Weber dance orchestra at Berlin's Hotel Adlon. They were racy, provocative and cosmopolitan, as befitted the Berlin of that period. The record sleeve told how Marek Weber, a Jew, reacted on the night of 30th January 1933 when Hitler came to power. After he finished playing at the Adlon, he went straight to the railway station, still wearing his white tie and tails, and boarded the night train to Paris, never to return.

Dr János Plesch gave up his society dinners and left for England. He and Melanie gave a farewell dinner for 20 guests on 6th March 1933, with red tulips on the table for the last time. To save his art works from Nazi confiscation, he handed over his Berlin house to the *Institut Français*, but it was destroyed later by bombing. Nazi Foreign Minister Joachim von Ribbentrop expropriated the Plesch country house and made it a rest home for Nazis.

Plesch had contacts at the highest level in England and had accumulated enough wealth there to buy a large house outside London and send his sons to school at Harrow. The sponsors for the sons' British naturalisation were a former British Foreign Secretary and a high-ranking Royal Air Force officer.[xxiii] Plesch could react to the Nazi disaster with cool realism and decisive action. For his wife Melanie, the pain went deeper: she had to abandon the country where her family had lived for 600 years.

Alex Natan, who later taught me Goethe and Schiller in the English city of Worcester, was a member of the German athletics team which set a 4 x 100 metres relay world record in 1931. He too left in 1933 and the Nazis expunged his obviously Jewish name from records. He and I chuckled later as he recalled how records during the Nazi era showed that a three-man German team ran a 4 x 100 metres relay world record.

German Jew Marcel Reich-Ranicki, who survived the Warsaw ghetto to become a leading post-war literary critic, wrote in his autobiography that teachers and pupils at his *Gymnasium* school in Berlin at first treated him correctly – one teacher even made a point of raising his hat to Jews passing in the street – but then Jewish pupils began steadily disappearing, and his classmates accepted this as normal. In his German *Abitur* exam Reich-Ranicki received a mention "good" because, as his teacher privately explained, Jews were not allowed "very good."[xxiv]

The enlightened German culture personified by Lessing, Goethe and Schiller disintegrated as professors allowed associations of Nazi bully-boy students to dictate to them. Reason, tolerance and liberty were abandoned for romantic, bigoted concepts of German cultural superiority. Professors looked the other way as the Nazis organised public bonfires of books deemed degenerate. Learning and knowledge went up in flames, giving way to a doctrine of ideas, will and action. In the grandiose architectural plans for Berlin drawn up by Hitler and Albert Speer, there was a dome 300 metres high for 180,000 people, but no library.[xxv] Goethe's poetry still moves hearts, but nobody will ever forget how Germans sent their own culture up in cinders.

Academics and artists were expected to serve the Nazi ideology and many were flattered to be included: composer Richard Strauss, actor Gustaf Gründgens and writer Gerhart Hauptmann made themselves available.[2] Of course they kept quiet about it after the war. I knew these names and their works for 20 years before I learned that they had been compromised with the Nazis. At the notorious 1942 Wannsee conference which drew up plans to exterminate the Jews eight of the 15 people attending were academics with doctorates.[xxvi] Intellectuals who did not toe the line however were ruthlessly excluded: Thomas

---

2   As did writers abroad such as T.S. Eliot, D.H. Lawrence, Ezra Pound, W.B. Yeats and Wyndham Lewis.

and Heinrich Mann, Leon Feuchtwanger, Anna Seghers, Alfred Kerr and Albert Einstein were all deprived of their citizenship.

Professor Walter Küchler, head of Romance Studies at Hamburg University, was dismissed from his post and retired to the Bavarian Alps with his wife, with whom my mother had celebrated her 21ˢᵗ birthday in Paris. She was a Frenchwoman, so her husband was suspect for having married her. He was a translator of Rimbaud and Verlaine, at a time when the Nazis insisted that Germans reject foreign influences. To cap it all, he was known to be a *Judenfreund* – a friend of Jews. Küchler refused to bow the head, and had to go.

Joachim Fest, who became famous as a post-war biographer of Hitler, had a similar family background. The Nazis sacked his father from a post as a Berlin school-master. As Fest recalled, the father upheld "decency, manners, consideration" and publicly maintained his loyalty to the democratic Weimar Republic, which the Nazis were set on destroying. In this, he departed from the usual political apathy of German intellectuals.

"Etiam si omnes – ego non! – Others may all do this, but not I!" was Fest senior's motto. He was not prepared to bow to traditional German authority, nor swim with the tide. *Ich nicht* – not I – remained in the young Joachim's mind and was the title of the book he wrote about his own life.

The father's principled stand brought a crisis in the family. The mother pleaded with him to ignore his conscience and join the Nazis so that he could regain his job. He could just pretend allegiance: deception was the way small people traditionally stood up to the powerful.

"We are not small people, not in such questions," the father retorted. The mother countered that upholding principles only worsened the mounting pressures on their daily lives. Such was the quandary facing many other Germans.

As his two boys grew older, the father invited them to political discussions with him after the evening meal. He spoke to them openly and Joachim felt proud to be taken into his father's confidence. He became familiar from an early age with the questions of conscience Germans had to deal with.

The mother however was right to have misgivings. The father never regained his job, lapsed into bitterness, was conscripted into the war at the age of 60, and returned from Soviet captivity a shriveled old man, broken in spirit and scarcely able to hold himself upright. Joachim sympathised with his mother's pragmatic desire to swing with the tide, but his heart was with the father who in the end was crushed by Nazi tyranny.[xxvii]

Another who stood up to the Nazis was my mother. She was studying arts and crafts at a school of further education in Hamburg. Unlike the Fests, she was no intellectual and was apolitical. But she had inherited some of her Belgian mother's disdain for Germans. Petite, slim and stylish, she wore the used dresses that mannequins had modeled in Hamburg fashion shows. German women were too fat to fit into them, she would pointedly remark.

Fest's father threw out the *Hitlerjugend* – the Hitler Youth – when they knocked trying to recruit his two sons. He got away with it, as for a time did my mother, who refused to join the Nazis' equivalent for girls, the *Bund Deutscher Mädel*.

However the Nazis in my mother's school found out that she did not take part in Nazi rallies. Somebody denounced her. They gave her an ultimatum: go to the rallies or we throw you out of the school. She left the school rather than bend the knee. From her non-military father and her aloof francophone mother, she had a dose of scepticism rare among Germans. She let her instincts tell her what was right, what was wrong, and what she had to do.

What decided her was Hitler the human being. She could not stand him. She thought he was a wretched little man, coarse and vulgar. While millions of other Germans – and some foreigners – fell under his oratorical spell, she heard just fanatical ranting. While thousands of German women swooned in orgasmic arousal at his rallies, my mother was turned off by Hitler as a man. She did not have to *think* about Hitler: she knew.

János Plesch, the doctor, had the same gut feeling. When he attended a Hitler rally, he saw "a flabby, narrow-chested, unimpressive little man with furtive eyes." With his puffy face, little black moustache and cow's lick over his forehead, he seemed "a criminal type of low mentality."

Plesch was standing close and noted that Hitler was reading from slogan-like notes with extra large letters. His gestures were theatrical and he detected no real excitement or tension. Plesch felt sick just looking at him.[xxviii]

The ousted school-master, Fest senior, dismissed Hitler as "a foolhardy moaner," and "a born suicide," while Liselotte Kubitza,[3] daughter of penniless Communist parents in pre-war Berlin, was brought up from earliest childhood to consider Hitler as a criminal.[xxix]

So there was nothing about Hitler which made it inevitable he would be adored. Millions of Germans chose to do so, but others rejected him without any great mind-searching. It was the latter whom I admired. They taught me to think for myself.

British historians who published post-war analyses of Hitler saw him as obsessed with *Lebensraum* and anti-Semitism (Hugh Trevor-Roper), the logical outcome of centuries of irresponsible German behaviour (A.J.P. Taylor), an adventurer driven by a brutal will for power (Alan Bullock), and an "unperson" surrounded by increasingly fanatical careerists (Ian Kershaw).

---

3   Whom I interviewed in Berlin in 2008.

For Joachim Fest, Hitler was a guttersnipe. His biography was the first substantial attempt by a German to come to terms with the real Hitler and became a best-seller on publication in 1973. He acknowledged Hitler's forceful personality, oratory and ability to wrong-foot his opponents. As the son of a respectable middle-class dissident however, he expressed contempt for Hitler as the jetsam of Vienna working men's hostels – a seedy environment frequented by adventurers, gamblers, jobless and the indolent, where resentment festered, human solidarity counted for nothing and failure was the norm. Hitler comes across as a feckless, half-educated, neurotic swindler. At ease mainly in the lowly company of chauffeurs, maids and secretaries, his gifts were those of the underworld criminal: street-wise, manipulative and lethal.[xxx] As my mother did, Fest instinctively rejected Hitler as far below his own family's upright, middle-class standing.

So why did the pre-war Germans go for such a character, who would eventually drag them into the abyss? Why did they accompany him en masse into a world war which they must have known would be at least as destructive as the preceding one? The collapse of traditional values, fear of Bolshevism, the Depression, the attraction of forceful new ideas, and the weakness of Hitler's political opponents – all these were potent influences. However other nations went through similar difficulties to Germany after WWI and in the Depression. They too searched for new life concepts and even indulged from time to time in anti-Semitism.[4] But they did not create the mayhem the Germans did.

In the end it was a choice the Germans made on the basis of their values. They gave way to resentment and greed, indulging in hatred and excess rather than peace and moderation. They opened the door to the sort of low

---

4   My father remembers my English grandfather making occasional anti-Semitic remarks.

criminal that other nations kept in prison or far from the levers of power.

My mother was christened with the same name as her own mother – Gabrielle. From 1933 she began using the German spelling – Gabriele – to appear less foreign to officialdom. She and her sister had to fill out *Ahnenpässe* – ancestral passports certifying their racial origins. Without them, most professions, studies and even marriage were excluded.

These documents required individuals to give details of their ancestry going back to great-great-grandparents. The number of ancestors for which information was required was 31. It was tolerated that most people could not get that far, but every entry had to be certified by the competent registry office. The two sisters had to write to none-too-willing Belgian registry offices to extract the required confirmations. The Nazis offered help in research from a Reich Association for Kinship Research and Heraldry in Berlin.

It was all pretty subjective. One instruction in the *Ahnenpass* stated pompously but vaguely: "For marriage to a girl of pure German origin, it is self-understood that we prefer a fellow German to another Aryan of more distant racial relationship."

My mother's elder sister Luz by 1938 had 11 confirmed entries in her *Ahnenpass* and eight more awaiting ratification. She did not throw it away after the war, and in 1949 even completed it by entering the death of her mother.[xxxi]

By the late 1930s, the Nobel factory had reopened and was again producing dynamite. Germany's economy was on the upswing, for which the Nazis took credit. Germans did set to work with new energy, the Nazis did invest in job creation, and the order they brutally imposed did end disruption. However the world economy was moving into a recovery cycle in any case, and Franklin Roosevelt achieved the same results democratically with his New Deal in the United States.

As for my mother, she had lost a battle, but not the war. Of course, she did not know that at the time. After her open opposition to the Nazis, she had no chance of further studies or any worthwhile career. By the age of 24, she felt cast into the wilderness and depressed. Life seemed to offer no prospects.

She took to spending summer holidays with the similarly excluded Küchlers in the large house they had retired to in the Bavarian village of Benediktbeuern, a Benedictine settlement dating from 739 A.D. The house was an old glass factory with a stream flowing underneath to drive a water wheel producing electricity. From the windows they looked on to the majestic *Benediktenwand* mountain. On the edge of the village stood a Baroque monastery with the 13th century *Carmina Burana* script made famous by Carl Orff's music. As an exile, it had its advantages.

My mother mixed with the foreign students who came to learn German with the Professor and his wife. There were long hikes, picnics and fresh air to alleviate the learning. Unlike much of the rest of Germany at the time, it was a place where foreigners and Germans were encouraged to mingle easily.

There my mother met my father, Harry, a Cambridge University undergraduate studying Modern Languages. As he recounted to me at the age of 93 (but not before), my mother one day wandered into his room and stood on the balcony in front of him leaning back on the rail. In the light of his evident interest, she leaned back again. 70 years later they were still married and living under the same roof.

Chapter 3
PRECIPICE

Yes, we are barbarians! It is a title of honour – Hitler

I got the impression that here was a man who could be relied upon when he had given his word – Chamberlain on Hitler

Hitler could have been prevented from reaching power. He was widely disliked, but those who could have stopped him could never quite make up their minds that they wanted to. The old guard of the aristocracy considered him a petty rabble-rouser, but a useful bulwark against Bolshevism. The military disapproved of his penchant for violence and disorder, but thought they could manipulate him. Industrialists mainly financed the conservative *Mitte* party, but stepped in with funds also for Hitler's SA storm troops when the Communists gained seats in Parliament. The Social Democrats, who until 1933 were still stronger in Parliament, were disorientated by long years of compromises with conservatives. The Communist rank-and-file detested Hitler, but their leadership blindly followed the Soviet line that the Social Democrats were the enemies. Many people were against Hitler, but nobody rose to the challenge of eliminating him from political life.

Several times, Hitler seemed down and out. After the failed 1923 Munich beer hall putsch, he was brought to justice and sent to jail – a blow which would have ended the career of most politicians. It was clear rejection by the state. He struggled to re-assert himself in the late 1920s as Germany settled down and began to prosper again. Only the disaster of the Depression made his extremism seem relevant again. Even then, after a further electoral defeat in 1932, the Nazi Party practically ran out of money. That same year, President Paul Von Hindenburg briefly outlawed the Nazi SA and SS armed forces. Even the right-wing General Erich Ludendorff, hero of World War I, advised Hindenburg that if he appointed Hitler as Chancellor, he would bring Germany into "an abyss, an inconceivable misery." But nobody took the decisive step to remove him once and for all.

Foreigners hesitated too, half awed but half impressed by what Hitler represented. Roosevelt declared himself "thrilled" by the Führer's advent to power, and many others were attracted by what seemed an exciting novelty. At the 1936 Olympic Games in Berlin, the French and several other teams gave the *Heil Hitler* salute as they marched past the Führer. When Hitler visited the British Embassy in Berlin in 1935, the embassy children raised their arms and shouted *Heil!*[xxxii] A delegation of British Legion war veterans visited Germany to meet Hitler and Hermann Goering and see the Dachau concentration camp.[xxxiii] Western leaders were worried, but had no idea how to cope with a counterpart like Hitler, who blew hot and cold while craftily pursuing brutally selfish goals.

Britain's Neville Chamberlain, hoping to appease Hitler at their meeting in Munich in 1938, agreed to allow Germany to seize Czechoslovakia's Sudetenland border areas. Britain lost honour and credibility by this betrayal – Chamberlain acted over the heads of the Czechoslovak government. His deference to the dictator soon turned out to be humiliating weakness, as Hitler made clear he had no intention of keeping the "peace in our time" Chamberlain proclaimed on his return to Britain.

For generations of Britons henceforth, Munich has represented the dreadful consequences of failing to stand up to a dictator. Winston Churchill promptly denounced it as "a total and unmitigated defeat." In retrospect, the British felt ashamed for having gone along with Chamberlain's delusions, and proud that they eventually stood up to Hitler and won. Later British governments would invoke Munich to justify a series of further wars, such as the attempt to overthrow Egypt's Gamal Abdel Nasser at Suez in 1956, the reclaiming of the Falkland Islands from Argentina in 1982 and the invasion of Iraq in 2003. The shame of Munich remains engraved on the British psyche. It taught Britons, including those of my generation, that appeasement is wrong and belligerence right.

It is doubtful however whether a stronger British stand at Munich would have prevented the war. As became known later, Hitler was disappointed that the British yielded to his demands at Munich. He wanted to go to war, and felt frustrated that the British concessions thwarted him. "If ever that silly old man comes interfering here again with his umbrella, I'll kick him downstairs and jump on his stomach in front of the photographers," he is quoted as saying about Chamberlain afterwards.[xxxiv]

In 1939, the British were preparing also to offer him Danzig, a Polish city with a large German population administered under a League of Nations mandate. They hoped to stave off a German attack on Poland, which Britain was bound by a treaty to defend. But Hitler invaded Poland before they could make the offer. He was not interested in their concessions. He wanted war, not peace.[xxxv]

Munich also had a more positive aspect, in that it showed how reluctant Britons then were to start a war which they knew would be devastating. After a Great War of 1914-1918 which was supposed to end all wars, Britons were not just spineless in wishing to avoid a new one.

Watching newsreels of Chamberlain's declaration of "peace in our time", London cinema audiences sprang to their feet and cheered. The Royal Family invited him to appear on the balcony of Buckingham Palace. This doubtless represented a certain naïveté by an island people. But the famous Jewish writer Stefan Zweig, who had gone overnight from being a best-selling German author to an anonymous immigrant in London, felt touched by this British yearning for peace. Although he was himself a victim of Hitler, he wrote admiringly of "a feeling of new brotherhood which should now begin for the world... a day which gave wings to the soul."xxxvi When Britain finally took up hostilities with Germany, it was therefore as warriors who had tried in vain to avoid a war.

My father, 25 years old at the time, was not taken in by the prospect of peace held out by Chamberlain. He was then living in England with my mother without being married. Co-habiting with a refugee from Nazi Germany made his antennae more alert.

"I realised immediately the situation was getting much more serious, and war was likely. We couldn't have stayed together as we were. War would have obliged your mother to return to Germany or led to her internment in Britain," he said 70 years later. Before the year was out, they were married.

The thug at Munich of course was Hitler, not Chamberlain. Stopping Hitler moreover was not primarily the responsibility of the British. It was up to the Germans, and they could not cope with Hitler's deceptive shifts from soothing promises of stability to bold outbreaks of radicalism. He could "feel" his opponents and catch them off guard. German generals planned to remove Hitler through a coup as he prepared to launch war in 1938. But when the British stalled the outbreak of hostilities by ceding the Sudetenland, the generals lost heart and gave up.

The Nazis seduced the people by their energy and youthfulness – Josef Goebbels became *Gauleiter* at 28, Baldur von Schirach *Reichsjugendführer* at 26 and Heinrich

Himmler *Reichsführer SS* at 28. The Communists were grey and unimaginative by comparison.[xxxvii]

But Hitler also had his drawbacks, at least some of which must have been obvious before he came to power. He was given to lethargy and indecision, abandoning a regular work routine shortly after he became Chancellor. A day would typically consist of a speech in Munich, a funeral in Berlin in the afternoon and Wagner in Bayreuth in the evening. In between he indulged in Karl May Westerns and films.

He wrote down little. His speeches were vague and his political strategy undefined. He was practically never shown laughing or acting spontaneously. He did not listen, constantly interrupted and jumped from one subject to another. He once harangued Mussolini at a dinner for one and a half hours without a break.[xxxviii] Most noticeable of all, already in his early career as a rabble-rouser, was his lust for violence and aggression.

Knowing Germans of today, I find it hard to believe that they were taken in. In the history book of Geesthacht, the little town near where my mother grew up, the figures of the Nazi period of 1933-1945 look like characters from a comic opera. Their leather shorts, white socks and archaic emblems appear ridiculous today. It was a revolt against industrialisation, migration from the land to the cities, weakening of traditional authority, and the rise of science and democracy – in short, against the modern world of my German grandfather and of Germans today.

The Nazis seized upon the traditions of the 19th century Romantic German poets and the *Wandervögel* (Wandering Birds) movement of hikers, who forswore the modern world for rustic nature, legend and national mystique. The influence these movements had on German intellectuals was to distance them from the real world. They identified with the moral protest against worldly power and the aspirations towards the sublime and redemptive. In consequence, they retreated into their inner selves and left politics to traditional authorities, whose decisions they did not question.

150 years later, I remain moved by Goethe's galloping poem of a father vainly trying to save his son from the deathly embrace of the Elf King; by Joseph von Eichendorff's verse of his soul taking wing in response to moonlight filtering into fields and woods; and Heinrich Heine's evocation of the superiority of mountain-climbing over effete, worldly pretentions.[xxxix] I read them in my father's *Oxford Book of German Verse,* compiled in 1914 on the eve of World War I. The poetry can still inspire despite all that has passed since.

Also on my father's bookshelves I find a work of 50 years earlier by one of my family's English ancestors, the political philosopher John Stuart Mill. His austere, rigid prose is harder to digest than the poetry of the German Romantics. But he represents the intelligentsia as political thought leaders rather than dreamers. His bold campaign to extend the boundaries of 19th century liberty remains a foundation of political thought today.[xl]

It suited the Nazis that the German intelligentsia had abdicated from such a role. Few intellectuals resisted the Nazi insistence that serving the nation was a sacred calling to be followed blindly, that authority was absolute and not to be questioned, and that information should be channeled to the people through government-controlled media and mass events.

Nazi emblems recalled the animal spirits of pagan times. Their ceremonies took place after dark and torches created an atmosphere of apocalypse, with elaborate staging effects to stir up emotions. Funerals were staged as if celebrating death.

The Nazis relished the gloomy pessimism of the operas of Wagner presenting ancient sagas of Teutonic heroes betrayed by foreigners' tricks. All this represented a dark, warlike outlook on life that is alienating to those of us who grew up in post-war years. Needless to say, my mother detested Wagner.

At the time, these attitudes drew some seven million Germans to join the Nazi party, representing at its height over 20 per cent of the male population.[xli] The totalitarian state the Nazis created papered over many regional differences. The core of Nazism was in Bavaria, which until 1871 had a proud history of independence. Hitler and some other leading Nazis came from Austria, which until World War I was a Habsburg domain. My north German mother, taking her lead from the Lübeck writer Thomas Mann (and his novel *Buddenbrooks*), considered Bavarians coarse and primitive, Austrians schmaltzy and unreliable, and Berliners bumptious and sharp. Hitler and his fellow Nazis never felt entirely at ease in Berlin, all the more so since it was traditionally left-wing. Even today many Bavarians speak casually of Berliners as *Saupreussen* – Prussian pigs. However Bismarck in 1871, and later the Nazis, forged these variations into a monolithic Germany which was to cause untold suffering as a single national unit. It is this Germany that dominates our consciousness today.

To some Germans, the destructive elements of Nazism became quickly apparent, to others only later or not at all. Intellectual Sebastian Haffner believed he was clever enough to stand aloof from the mass euphoria. But after two months at a mandatory Nazi boot camp, he found himself enjoying the discipline, camaraderie and sense of purpose. He realised he risked moral dissolution and emigrated to Britain to preserve his integrity.

Dankwart Rost, a Siemens director after the war, admired his Nazi father, who was a schoolteacher and a piano player in the village in Pomerania in the northeast where he grew up. Other boys envied him because his father was popular. Another of his teachers was a part-

Nazi boot camp: work, discipline, doctrine

time SS – the regime's military elite. Dankwart joined the *Jungvolk* Nazi boys movement and liked the idealism, absolute values, obedience, code of honour, comradeship and sense of belonging to an egalitarian community. He was happy that the *Jungvolk* were preparing him to be a soldier, which he equated with chivalry. He felt engaged in an existential struggle for Germany's place in the world.

After the war, Rost expressed regret at what it all led to and his own involvement as a teenage soldier. But in his memoir, he wrote: "I was not a victim. I stand by my youth… My feeling of duty to others, comradeship and sense of service have remained."[xlii]

I met Dankwart through his English wife, with whom I once worked. Others I came across through an organisation which sends older people into schools and the media to talk about Germany's past. I found them through my old employer, Reuters. When I walked into Reuters Berlin office, I met a young journalist – German-born but educated at Oxford University – who understood immediately what I was trying to do.

"Go and talk to the *Zeitzeugen*," she said. Berliner Peter Lorenz was one member of this "witness to history" group whom I interviewed.[5]

For Lorenz, it was "self-understood" that he joined the Nazi *Jungvolk* and *Hitlerjugend,* since otherwise no other children would play with him: "It was an interesting time. We did military exercises with rowing boats and practice ambushes. It was fun, we sang and marched and camped in the woods. We learned a sense of community, but were not trained politically. What we sang was military, but we didn't think about it."[xliii]

As for Hans Werk (another *Zeitzeuge*), born in 1927 and later a teenage SS soldier, school taught him to shout *Heil Hitler,* sing "fatherland songs," and learn to read from a story about a dirty Jew pawing a blonde German woman in a butcher's shop. He picked up that Poles were drunk and lazy, French treacherous and Russians subhuman. Only after the war did he appreciate Moscow was not a gathering of squalid hovels but rather a city much like Berlin. He longed to serve in the military and thought it natural when he later witnessed German soldiers hanging three Poles as a deterrent to others.[xliv]

Rachel Seiffert, a novelist who like me is of mixed birth – she is German-Australian – described how people slipped passively into the Nazi way without feeling personal responsibility: "Someone else said it was the thing to do. Even if they didn't order it, not really order it, they still said it was the thing to do. So you weren't responsible, you see? And then you did it, even though they didn't order you to do it. So you did it voluntarily. And that way, the ones who gave the orders weren't responsible either."[xlv]

Others determined their attitude to the Nazis on personal considerations rather than principle. Professionals often could not carry on their careers without joining the

---

5   www.zeitzeugenboerse.de

Nazi party. In Cologne at the end of the war, 18 of the 21 operators of the waterworks were Nazis, as were 102 of Berlin's 112 doctors.[xlvi]

The professionals often found the Nazi interference unpleasantly disruptive. One surgeon, a distant relative of mine, complained that older doctors were being pushed aside by younger ones who formed cliques after the Nazis came to power. "The pleasant conditions in the university were disturbed," he regretted. At the request of a superior, he and other colleagues joined the Nazi Party, but he still had trouble: "Although I placed all my hopes in the Party and agreed with its programme, I still constantly had difficulties because the Party functionaries wanted to interfere in my work."

My mother's brother-in-law, Johannes, was one of those caught up in this process. His wife, whom I would later know as *Tante Luz*, described it in a personal memoir written many years later.[xlvii] Their children, who are my cousins, told the same story in talks with me.

Johannes did not have to join the Party in his first job in Heidelberg, but when he moved to a new post in Stuttgart, the professor was a Nazi himself and demanded that all his assistants join one of the Party organisations. Johannes chose the SA – *Sturm Abteilung* – which had started as Hitler's private army of street rowdies but later lost importance. At their height in 1932, the SA were 500,000 strong and had the same manpower as the German Army. They had louche connections to the underworld and many of the leaders around the commander, Ernst Röhm, were homosexual.

However once Hitler took power, he found the SA a nuisance, all the more so since Röhm was evidently using it to build his own power base. In 1934 Hitler had Röhm and his close associates arrested and shot. After that, the SA lost its raison-d'être. When Johannes joined in

1936, his most notable activity was as a camp doctor for labourers building a defence wall in the West, according to his son Fritz.[xlviii]

His wife Luz remembers being shocked by the Nazis' Crystal Night pogrom against the Jews in 1938:

"I was breastfeeding Fritz – suddenly there was a clatter in the house next door and vases, plates, even chairs were flying down from the first floor window, and there was shouting and cursing. I thought somebody had gone mad – but it was the SA men who had forced their way into the home of Jews and were ransacking it… An awful feeling seized me – it was as if war were in the air."

Luz wrote later that she was thankful that her SA husband Johannes was not involved. Many Germans helped themselves to the goods ransacked from the Jews. A few gave shelter to Jews on that night. Most stood by uneasily and kept out of it, my aunt included.[6]

Luz said Johannes never told her what he was up to at SA meetings. She knew they were drinking beer (except her husband who had no money) and assumed they were being politically indoctrinated. "In no case did he ever have any special 'operation' and never had anything to do with Jews," she remarked pointedly in her post-war memoir.

Could Johannes have refused to join the SA? Of course he could. However he would almost certainly have lost his job as an X-ray doctor, and would have had few prospects of continuing a worthwhile medical career. By that time the couple had three small children, and could scarcely bring enough money together for essentials such as a dwelling and food.

The Fests chose to stand by their principles, which resulted in a career brought to a halt, one son dead in the

---

6   Britain gave shelter to 10,000 German Jewish children and parents after the Crystal Night pogrom.

war, a father reduced to a wreck, and a surviving son who could hold his head high afterwards. Johannes chose the SA, the medical work for which he was qualified, and the means to support a young family through the trials to come – but got into trouble after the war. It was a typical choice for Germans at the time: between principles and the demands of day-to-day existence.

Later on, having a foot in both camps, I wondered which way I would have jumped myself.

Chapter 4

OUT OF THE FRYING PAN

I have only these few needs: to eat, to sleep, to hold in my head
the nerves of the battle, and to keep alive
— wartime letter from my British father

My German mother and British father had other
preoccupations. When they met in Benediktbeuern, my
father had just broken up with another woman, and my
mother had her eye on an American. After they parted,
my mother suggested both men to write to her. That put
the American out of the running: writing letters was not
his forte. But my father leapt to the challenge.

So my mother took the plunge and headed for England
in 1937, aged 24. Not only may the man of her life be
there, but it was a way out of a Germany where she had
burnt her bridges. Before she left, she went to her mother
and said: "If I can manage it, I am not coming back." Her
mother, the Belgian dragon, raised no objections, took two
precious rings off her fingers, gave them to her and said:
"I want you to have these." After all the *eiserne Disziplin* –
the iron discipline – this was a mother's classic blessing to
a grown-up daughter setting out into the world.

Arriving in England barely 20 years after a First World
War in which three quarters of a million British perished
at the hands of Germans was an uncomfortable prospect.
In the light of the vindictive Treaty of Versailles to which
Britain was a signatory, my mother could not be sure of a
warm welcome.

But Britons had rapidly felt a bad conscience about Versailles. It offended their spirit of fairness. As it was, my mother could not have been welcomed more warmly. My father invited her to a May Ball at Cambridge University. Spring burgeoned, the old colleges looked eternal, the lawns were green and nurtured, and she danced with the man she had come for.

In cosmopolitan London, taxi-drivers were charmed by a good-looking young woman who spoke English with an alluring foreign accent. They responded with the best Cockney wit they could summon. A couple of Australians – she a fashion buyer at Harrods – took her in as an au pair. My mother spent mornings wheeling their son in a pram through Kensington Gardens. London suited her completely. As she would learn later, not all England was like London.

When my father went away for nine months to work on his uncles' fruit and sheep farms in Australia – the voyage was a graduation gift from his parents – my mother met other men in London, and each time the fashion buyer said: "It's not you, Gaby." Now she was Gaby, not Gabrielle, and certainly not Gabriele.

In late 1937, her father suffered another stroke. The Australians paid her passage on a German liner to Hamburg to go to his deathbed. She arrived just in time for him to recognise her and say farewell. As she prepared to return, her elder brother who taught her to skate and cycle through the German countryside went down to the docks to see her off, and advised: "If you want to stay in England and get married, don't wait too long. War is not far off."

On his return from Australia, my father brought her an engagement ring set with a black opal from the Australian mines, paid for with earnings from his farm labour. It remained with her for 50 years until it passed into the possession of an English burglar.

My father took up a teaching post at the Catholic Oratory School at Caversham on the outskirts of Reading, where he was one of only two non-Catholic teachers (nicknamed "the heretics"). He liked the congenial atmosphere. One of his senior pupils was to be my godfather, but was killed in the war, as was the son of the Küchler family in Benediktbeuern.

Approaching was a time when many other families would be torn apart, but my mother was determined not to let evil ideology spoil her chance of a family. She and my father married on the last day of 1938. Four nationalities, including her Belgian mother and her younger brother Fritz, made up the wedding party for a traditional English service in a tiny church on a bitterly cold day. The bridegroom's parents threw a party in their London flat, and baked a wedding cake with all the trimmings.

My mother, photographed by my father after they married and she took British nationality.

My mother returned to Germany in early 1939 to buy furniture for their new home. Why Germany? The Nazis did not allow emigrants to take money with them, but they could take furniture and household belongings. She came back with an old ancestral chair, modern armchairs, a dining table and a sideboard. My brother, sister and I thus grew up in England amid North German 1930s pear-wood furnishings. Not that we appreciated it. We thought it was what everybody had.

Just before she went, my mother received a letter from a Jewish friend she had made at her Hamburg arts and crafts school. Telly had married a Jewish businessman from Berlin, and on the spur of the moment they had fled to Britain by plane, leaving everything behind. Telly was one of several Jewish émigrés my mother befriended as fellow victims of the Nazis.

Back in Hamburg, my mother made a rendezvous with Telly's brother. Nazi laws forbade Jews to enter a public place, so the two walked round and round the city under umbrellas, talking animatedly for two hours as icy rain poured down. The main purpose was to have a chat. But my mother was also making a small gesture against German repression of Jews, braving the disapproving looks of passers-by. It cost her little, since by that time she had British papers, but her Jewish friend must have welcomed the rare demonstration of solidarity. She was making a small stand for human decency.

My parents decided to spend summer holidays in 1939 in the place they first met. From Benediktbeuern they were about to go on to Vienna, when my father spotted ominous news in the German newspapers and called the British Consul in Munich, who told them to take the first train home. They emerged from their Bavarian mountain idyll to find the railways swarming with troop transports. After many delays, a last train filled with fleeing Jews dumped them over the border in Holland late in the evening. They had no Dutch money, but a hotel proprietor put them up for the night for free. They were thankful when they finally stepped off a ferry in Harwich.

When the war broke out a few days later, my mother went to the British authorities and asked if they would be interested in knowing the layout of one of Germany's largest explosives factories, which she knew from her childhood. She felt no patriotic loyalty any more to the Germany where she had grown up. As far as she was concerned, the Germans were to blame for a war which threatened her ambitions to create a family, indeed her whole life. However the British replied: no thank you very much, and sent her packing. Did they doubt her reliability as an enemy alien? Was she speaking to the wrong official? Or did the British miss a golden opportunity?

When I asked the Geesthacht museum director 60 years later, he said British intelligence already had plans of the Nobel explosives factory from World War I. He had been shown them at the Imperial War Museum in London. So the British knew where my grandfather went to work and where my mother grew up.

When my father was called up to the British Army in 1940, he became a private in the ranks. In Germany, soldiers were paid over twice as much as in Britain. Some soldiers' families lived better than before the outbreak of hostilities. That was one of the enticements for Germans to join the Nazis in their war of aggression.[xlix]

The soldier's pay of my British father represented only 38% of his pre-war salary. British soldiers were expected to defend their country as a patriotic duty, not out of financial incentive. Conscription thus resulted in an immediate drop in my parents' living standards, and my mother learned for the first time to set a coal fire and scrub clothes on a washboard. Using the skills she learned at the German arts and crafts school which Hitler would not let her continue, she made curtains, cushions, divan covers, bed-spreads and tablecloths for her new home.

My British father in 1940: a civilian called up to fight.

My mother became pregnant. Some may wonder that a woman may choose this dire moment to procreate. With a German invasion possible and her husband soon to be put in the line of fire, she was placing herself in a vulnerable position. But she was determined not to let the Germans destroy her chances of a family. It was an act of defiance towards the Germans, and also to death – if her husband should be killed, his child would live on.

Britain was in its gravest danger. By early summer 1940, France was defeated and occupied, the Battle of Britain was raging as the Germans sought to destroy Britain's air defences, and an invasion seemed imminent. Hitler gambled that Britain would make an arrangement with Germany once France fell. It was not obvious that the British would fight to remain free.

The main fear of Traudi Plesch, the Viennese Jew who had emigrated to Britain, was that the British would accept Nazi occupation. She herself had seen Nazis throwing Jewish babies on to the Vienna streets to be run over. The British on their island did not seem to perceive what was in store. "I heard a British woman at the Women's Institute say: 'If Hitler comes, all that will happen is that the rates (local taxes) will go up,'" she told me.[i]

The SS *Einsatzgruppen* (intervention groups) which were already ravaging Eastern Europes had in fact drawn up a "Black Book" of 2,820 people in Britain to be arrested and handed over to the Gestapo. Prominent Germans who had fallen out with Hitler and fled to Britain were on the list. For my mother, who was a marked woman in Germany, it would only have been a matter of time before the Gestapo came for her. In the kitchen, she kept a pepper pot at hand to throw into their faces. I was enormously impressed when she told me this as a little boy. It was the stuff of heroes, just like I had been reading in my British comics.

Within less than a year of the shameful Munich agreement of 1938, the British mood had taken a historic turn. Instead of passively hoping for peace, they had become fired up for war. Stefan Zweig watched Londoners digging bomb shelters, hoisting balloons and distributing gas masks and admired their "tough, sober determination."[ii] Chamberlain was discarded for Churchill, who made clear he would resist, rallying the nation with speeches about never surrendering, fighting on the beaches, fighting on the landing grounds, fighting in the streets, fighting in the hills. He even spoke of the possibility that the British Isles may be subjugated, in which case the fight would be waged from the Empire and the New World. The people had heard his promise of "blood, toil, tears and sweat" and did not flinch at this honest realism.

For Hitler, it meant the end of his strategy to win in the West, since Churchill with those words signaled that even invasion of the British Isles would not end British resistance. Hitler wanted to attack Russia in pursuit of *Lebensraum* in the East, but after failing to break British resolve, he was condemned to fight a war on two fronts. By the end of 1941, when the Soviet Red Army pushed the Germans back from around Moscow and the U.S. entered the war, all Hitler's chances of winning had vanished. Few knew this at the time, but from then onwards the German war was a futile exercise in annihilation and self-destruction.

My mother savoured Churchill's deliberate mispronouncing of the Nazis. Instead of saying *Nahtsis* as the Germans did, he called them *Nayzis*. Unlike with Chamberlain, there was also no *Herr* in front of Hitler any more.

The London taxi-drivers were not the only Britons to treat my mother kindly. The doctor who delivered her first baby waived his fee "as a contribution to the war effort." Her mother-in-law, an Oxfordshire villager, stayed with her after she gave birth to both her wartime children in the absence of my father, and brought up fresh eggs, fruit and vegetables from the countryside. My father's Oratory School colleagues, including a cheerful Irish secretary, came to help and counsel. Her British neighbours commiserated: "How dreadful that the war has cut you off from your family!"

Her Belgian mother fared differently in Germany. In December 1939, the mother wrote to a friend in Bavaria: "I feel only the deepest disgust for all these quarrels and crimes which I try not very bravely to avoid seeing. Let us try to search for what nobility and beauty humanity can still have... in this arid desert in which we live."[lii] As a foreigner, the Belgian was considered a second-class citizen and a potential enemy once the war broke out.

Gabrielle, my Belgian-born grandmother. She tangled with the Gestapo.

German neighbours in Bergedorf refused to greet her on the street. Women dumped their rubbish cans in her garden and scrawled abusive slogans on her walls. She wrote that she felt "terribly alone."

One of her German grandchildren took the uncharitable view that the headstrong old woman brought this misfortune upon herself "because she couldn't keep her trap shut." The mother did indeed write to her friend: "I have serious reason to be on my guard. I cannot tell you more... It suffices that my outbursts do not go unnoticed. Who cares? A little devil must be sometimes pushing me to say things which would be better kept quiet."

She took to visiting French forced labourers working nearby, and read to them in French from her bible and prayer book. Doing this certainly courted trouble, but it was also an act of humane defiance. She stood by her principles.

She was arrested several times, but acquaintances intervened to secure her release. Doubtless the Nazis did not want her soldier sons to find their mother in prison when they came home on leave. Public humiliation was the Gestapo's usual punishment for those who consorted with forced labourers, and that was what the Belgian mother got.

Germans readily turned against neighbours in Nazi Germany. The Gestapo spent most of their time sorting through voluntary denunciations by people who were often not even Nazis. The Gestapo discovered 80% of political offences in this manner. It was a society of spies, who mostly thought they were performing a worthy service.[liii]

My mother found this behaviour disgraceful when she heard about it after the war. For her, the Belgian mother's treatment indicated the difference between the German and British peoples. It strengthened her anger against Germans and appreciation of British values.

My mother did cross swords with the British too. When she ran out of coal during the war while nursing my infant elder brother, she telephoned a merchant who said a consignment had just come in. He told her to come down a long, steep hill to Reading station and drag the coal back on her bicycle. She flew into a rage and the next day the coal was on her doorstep. Then a hard-drinking BBC woman[7] billeted on her brought a man home to the sitting room one night and set fire to the carpet with cigarettes. My mother threw her out, the BBC tried to send someone else, she refused, and the Army sent her a well-behaved female captain.

By this time, my father was stationed in Northern Ireland, coming home twice a year for leave. She recalls

---

7 The BBC had a listening station on the outskirts of Reading.

At home in Reading, with her husband away in the British Army.

him turning up unannounced on a motor-cycle. For the first three years of the war, like much of the British Army, he did no fighting. The British were too weak to challenge the Germans in Europe. So the bulk of their forces were bottled up in the British Isles doing endless drilling and marching around the countryside. He became deeply averse to the rigid discipline, the rough Army ways and, to his eyes, the mind-numbing pointlessness of it all.

Then, in 1943, my father was posted to a unit preparing officers to be sent overseas. My mother wanted another baby, but only on his final two-week embarkation leave did my father make my mother pregnant with me. I know: I checked the dates (so did he). He was issued with a tin trunk. Tin – that meant the tropics, probably Burma, where the British were fighting a nasty jungle war against a Japanese army trying to push into India. But he was not told anything, so when my mother stood with my two-year-old brother Paul to wave him off as he loaded the trunk into a taxi, she did not know where he was going, let alone whether she would ever see him again. She described this as her very worst moment in the war.

As for my father, he admitted later he was full of foreboding that "this was it." From a peaceful career as a teacher and several years of military training, he was heading into mortal danger. Ahead of him lay a perilous voyage through U-boats in the Atlantic, and in Burma combat under the grimmest of conditions. The Japanese had driven the British Army back to Burma's frontier with India, and the British knew that the Japanese were disemboweling and mutilating wounded British soldiers they came upon. Hot, sticky, unhealthy and dangerous, Burma was one of the worst assignments of the war – nearly 30,000 British soldiers died there.

My father was a university graduate fluent in German and familiar with Germany, but the British Army never gave him any mission involving Germany. Did it not occur to the Army that he had something special, did they want to spare him because he was married to a German, or did they distrust him? He never found out.

My father felt he had been sent to fight the wrong war, and the longer he was there, the angrier he got. He wrote to my mother: "It annoys me that I, who could have been so useful in France and Germany, and who understood better than a good many how essential it was to fight the Germans, should not have been allowed to do so, but have been one of the unfortunate minority sent out to this distant, gut-rotting sphere to fight for a good many things I do not believe in. It is a bad show when you get called up to make Europe safe for democracy, and then get involved in putting Asia back under British rule... I have seen quite a bit of the British Empire since the war – Ireland, West Africa, India, Burma – and believe me, it stinks."[liv]

I found the letters he sent to my mother when I cleared out their home in 2010 after they moved to a nursing home. I spotted a shoe box nestling in a corner of their bedroom and guessed immediately what it contained.

My father, with the British Army in Burma.
He would have preferred to fight the Nazis.

"Should I read them?" I wondered. They were tied with string in neat bundles, each with a label showing the dates. After six months hesitation, I asked my father's permission to read them. He granted it. I undid the bundles and noticed that each envelope was stamped "Passed by Censor." Everything he wrote had been read by a military censor. The officers took it in turns to perform this duty. In the jungle, my father acted as censor too, reading through the letters of his comrades-in-arms. In the army, intimacy was shared around. I was peering into a privacy which had long ago been breeched.

Until hostilities were practically over, he could not mention any military actions, nor say where exactly he was. His letters arrived with a "Field Post Office" stamp and she could write back to him at "H.Q. 82 (WA) Div,

APO. 6130." He wrote of sweat, rashes, boils, septic wounds, eye inflammations, belly palaver, poisonous snakes, mosquitoes, sand flies, biting ants and tropical lassitude.

"I carry my few spare clothes and washing kit on my back. I have nothing else except a blanket and ground sheet. By day I am soaked with perspiration, and by night damp with dew," he wrote in March 1945. "I have only these few needs: to eat, to sleep, to hold in my head the nerves of the battle, and to keep alive."

My father once hitched a lift in a military postal aircraft, and found it could scarcely take off because it was crammed so full with mail going to and fro between Burma and Britain. The planes lumbered through tropical storms over mountain ranges to keep the soldiers together with their women.

One such aircraft took a letter from my mother before my birth in July 1944 suggesting that I should be named Mark Alexander. Another took my father's reply that perhaps it should rather be Mark Timothy. Back and forth went the discussion via the heavily-laden transports week after week – the soldiers could write one air mail letter per week – until finally they settled on just Marcus. "One day my son will appreciate being able to write a signature as elegant as Marcus Ferrar," he wrote, settling the matter for good.

What the censor read most frequently was how these two young people in their 20s loved and yearned for each other and swore chastity until they met again. For the six years of his military service, during which they only rarely met, they wrote in order to preserve the hot desire of their first marital bliss. The letters served to stretch it out for as long as the war would last.

He was on the high seas from Nigeria, where he had stopped over to pick up local soldiers, when I was born on the 12th of July 1944. I was a month old by the time he received a cable in India announcing my birth. It hinted vaguely at problems, and his ensuing letters betray the frustration of a man separated from his wife at a key moment of their life as a couple.

An elderly Irishman was one of the few doctors left at the overcrowded, under-staffed hospital in Reading. My mother had given birth to my brother by caesarean, but she did not have this option for her second child. She lay on her own for the best part of a day, struggling to give birth to me. The few nurses were short-tempered, and only the anesthetist calmed her by whispering: "Don't worry. We're going to get you through this." I finally emerged, head bleeding from a forceps wound, and my mother collapsed in exhaustion.

A war child. It made a difference from being a baby-boomer. I was born out of wartime hardship, fathered by a soldier leaving to fight for his country, conceived in defiance of war and death. In my own mind, I stood apart from the children begotten when it was all over and everybody relaxed. I first saw my father when he returned in 1946 and I was nearly two.

By that time, Britain was plunged into economic hardship felt bitterly by a young couple struggling to put their lives back together. The first flush of love was replaced by the less romantic solidarity of a couple struggling to cope with post-war hardship. Who was to blame? The Germans of course, according to my mother, and my father did not quibble.

Chapter 5

INTO THE FIRE

*Clung around by demons, a hand over one eye, with the
other staring into the horrors, down she flings from despair
to despair – Thomas Mann, Dr. Faustus*

In Germany, my mother's family fared no better. Despite
relief about economic revival, restoration of order and
diplomatic successes, few Germans welcomed the outbreak
of actual war. There was no cheering on the streets, as in
1914. For my mother's sister, Luz, it was definitely bad
news. She had three small children and another was on
the way.

On 25th August 1940, Luz was in a Stuttgart hospital
waiting to give birth to my cousin Roland, when the
British launched their first bomb attack on the city.
Nurses panicked, dragged her out to a corridor and left
her. No doctor came, the menacing drone of "enemy"
bombers drew closer, flak opened up with mighty crashes,
and she was in such pain "that I didn't care if I died from
the bombs." Several hours later the all clear sounded and
she promptly gave birth. Her husband could not come to
visit her for several days because the surrounding grounds
were littered with unexploded bombs. Back at home, she
grew used to breast-feeding her baby in the cellar.

As I read through the memoir in which she described
this, I had the impression my German aunt experienced
the war as an outside affliction such as illness or famine.
She may have had private thoughts about how the
Germans got themselves into it, and for the feelings of the
people they were fighting against. But her memoir conveys

no sense of co-responsibility as a German. What comes through overwhelmingly is the sheer stress of the daily struggle to survive, which seems to have precluded any wider questioning about the morality of this war which Germany had started.

In 1941, Johannes applied for a job as an X-ray doctor in Łódź in western Poland. His relations were tense with his boss, who was a convinced Nazi, interfered with his work and kept summoning political meetings. Daughter Hilde remembers Johannes telling the family: "I've said something wrong, I have to go." Łódź gave him the opportunity to get away, and his X-ray skills were sorely needed.

Luz was horrified. She was expecting a fifth child and dreaded coping on her own. She urged him not to go, but he wrote to the hospital there saying he would come to see. "I still today see myself putting this fateful letter into the post-box. I had a terrible presentiment," she wrote. On his return, he told her he had accepted. She said she would not accompany him. Johannes could make his contribution to the war effort, and like other soldiers' wives she would stay at home with their family.

Her foreboding was well founded. Terrible things were taking place in the East. By 1941, news was filtering through to Germans back at home about mass killings by the German occupiers of Poland. Some six million Poles perished as a result, three million of them Jews. Practically all were civilians. German soldiers were indulging with impunity whatever lusts they had for torture, killing and stealing.

These were the lands that Hitler and Himmler had earmarked as *Lebensraum* for German settlers. They imagined re-enacting the conquests of the Teutonic Knights in the Middle Ages. Germany's frontiers to the East had never been clear, and German settlers had long been pushing into Poland and the Baltics. But it was never obvious that Germans were really destined to live in large numbers in the East. Himmler settled 500,000 Germans in Poland over five wartime years, but 575,000 Germans had already left Poland between 1918 and 1926 and there had been another big exodus in 1937/38. On Polish lands, Germans faced a permanent struggle to establish themselves. It was not a place to prosper and live easily.

The Nazis sought to change this by brute force. As German "supermen," they treated Poles and other Slavs as subhumans only slightly better than the Jews. Slavs should exist only to serve the interests of Germans, who were free to seize whatever they wanted. Professors and other intelligentsia were sent to concentration camps. Germans reduced schooling of Poles to a few basics and raised the minimum age of marriage to limit births. They forced Poles out of the cities to make room for German settlers who took over apartments and stores – Łódź lost 150,000 of its 585,000 population within a few months.[lv]

Poland was where the Germans exterminated the Jews, principally in the death camps of Auschwitz, Treblinka, Sobibor, Majdanek and Chełmno. Łódź itself harboured one of the largest Jewish ghettoes. 160,000 were crammed in there from 1940, and the Germans considered it initially as a model arrangement which they were proud to show off to visitors. Model or not, it lacked running water and a sewage system and was inhumanly overcrowded. Some 40,000 of the inhabitants died of illness, cold or starvation. The others were forced to make uniforms, boots and munitions for the German military. Eventually the Nazis dispatched the remaining Łódź Jews to be murdered in Chełmno and Auschwitz.

The devastation the Germans wreaked in the East of Europe far exceeded anything they did in the West. In the Soviet Union over 16 million civilians perished. By contrast, Britain suffered some 350,000 dead in total.[lvi] An assignment to occupied France was seen as a holiday by most German military. Until the Germans started deporting French as forced labourers towards the end of the war, neither they nor the French sought conflict.

Himmler tried to ensure that the persecutions in the East were kept secret, but so many Germans were involved that word inevitably leaked out among the German population at home.

Hence Luz's foreboding. Johannes was the sole X-ray specialist serving three hospitals. The old French machines kept breaking down, he was overworked and lonely, and he appealed to his wife to join him with the family. He had been offered a comfortable five-room apartment in a villa sequestered from a Polish industrialist. Luz delayed until she had given birth in 1942 to her fifth child, my cousin Marie-Luise. Four months later, she reluctantly moved with family and furniture to join her husband in Łódź.

It was a disaster from the start. Her newborn infant landed in hospital with diarrhoea and vomiting brought on by the stress of the laborious move. Luz had been told not to worry about moving to Poland, as German armies were deep inside Russia. But after two months the German Sixth Army capitulated in February 1943 at Stalingrad, and nowhere in the East was safe any more. "I felt thoroughly miserable in this godforsaken Poland," she wrote in her memoir.

The downtrodden Poles were sensing however that God had not forsaken *them*. With German armies in retreat, Luz found she had the enemy right in her home – the Polish kitchen maids.

"I was astonished at the Poles. They were supposed to be a defeated people? They carried their noses high and my kitchen maids, first one then another, who could speak some German, were insolent and tried to sabotage… Every morning I knew that I would have to go through a struggle with the maids."

Luz no doubt understood at least partly why the Poles should behave like that. But her personal concerns were so acute that she had no room for the interests of other peoples. According to her son Fritz, who was there, she feared the Poles might enter their home and kill her children. In the apartment below lived a police major from Hamburg called Stolpmann. The German Army had its command in the villa opposite. A one-legged German sentry checked people going in and out of the compound.

Johannes was exhausted from work and little at home. Between her seventh and ninth birthdays, daughter Hilde recalls seeing her father there only twice. She was sent to a school for incoming German settlers, where she found the other children stand-offish and the teaching cruel and humiliating. At night, Luz watched cockroaches roam over the kitchen and the bedclothes of her sleeping children.

Hilde and her younger brother Fritz, then six, remember traveling in a horse-drawn carriage and a tram along the fenced off street running through the middle of the Jewish ghetto. On a bridge connecting the two parts of the ghetto, Hilde spied men with tall black hats and asked her parents who they were. "Jews" was the reply, but no more was said. Fritz does not remember receiving any answer. "I did not ask more. We were not much used to questioning our parents," Hilde remarked later.

Luz discovered she was pregnant again – with a sixth child. It was mid-1944, and the guns of the Red Army could be heard rumbling outside Warsaw 50 miles (80 kilometres) away. Worn out and desperate, she suffered a miscarriage. An X-ray assistant took their two little boys to a friend who sheltered them in a village near Giessen in western Germany. As panic spread among the Germans in Łódź in August, Luz joined the rush to get out with her three remaining children. She decided to head for Stuttgart, the home city of her husband's family. As they crowded on to a train crammed with Germans fleeing the

Ukraine, she heard that Stuttgart was ablaze after a bombing raid. As night fell, they were left standing for hours waiting for a connecting train at Schweinfurt, which was also a prime bombing target because of its ball-bearing factory. After a 16-hour journey, the train came to a standstill in Würzburg. She staggered with her children into a refugee shelter and collapsed on a heap of straw, bleeding from the after-effects of her miscarriage.

She left her youngest daughter with doctor friends in Würzburg, found a place for the two others in a children's home in the Allgäu in Bavaria, and then, after an injection to stem her bleeding, traveled 600 miles back to her husband in Łódź. Like other Germans, she was sensitive to the concept of the *Dolchstoss* "the stab in the back" which supposedly cost the Germans WWI. She did not want to appear to be a deserter. Only back in Łódź did she go to hospital for the operation she needed to treat the after-effects of the miscarriage. At Christmas 1944, she and Johannes received a message that their youngest in Würzburg was down with scarlet fever.

Within weeks Luz was fleeing again, first in a horse-drawn coach with a Polish driver, then waiting in Poznań, half way between Warsaw and Germany. The city was in uproar, with long processions of carts dragging German refugees from further east, crammed with old people, children, bedding and cooking pots. From Poznań's castle, smoke and ashes rose to the sky as the German *Gauleitung* – the local government – burned documents day and night.

"Tears came to me; I was not aware they were rolling down my cheeks. I only noticed it from the mocking grin of a Pole I encountered. At that, I pulled myself together," she recalled.

Her husband refused to leave Łódź, but a woman who put her up said: "Now you have to get out of here yourself. From tomorrow no more trains leave here. You have five children and you shouldn't wait any more here for your husband."

It was 17th January 1945 when Luz, on her own, took a train which dumped its passengers at the old frontier between Poland and Germany. She walked three miles through a cold starlit night to join a throng waiting at another station for a train to turn up. Eventually she shoved herself through a train window, arrived in Berlin, and threw herself straight into an underground shelter as bombs came raining down. Exhausted, she fell asleep on a table.

A day later she was in Stuttgart, tramping through the ruined city centre to find to her relief that her parents-in-law still had an undamaged house in the suburbs. An elderly aunt had joined them after losing her home in Würzburg, where the old city centre had been wiped out by a firestorm created by the British Royal Air Force.

She was away from the horrors of the East, but Johannes was missing, the two smallest children were in a home in ruined Würzburg, two others were up in the hills of the Allgäu, and the elder son was lodged with a family near Giessen, a town of 47,000 inhabitants which had been bombed 27 times since September 1944.[lvii] The family had lost all their belongings in Łódź. In Stuttgart, low-flying British and American fighters constantly strafed anybody they caught moving on the streets. Occasionally survivors ventured out to eat sausages of blood and husks in public kitchens, or picked wild nettles and dandelions to make soup.

A few weeks later Johannes turned up. One of the last German military vehicles leaving Łódź gave him a lift out, but much of the way he had walked. In February 1945 he was ordered back to Dresden. The British had just made one of their biggest firestorm bombing raids, which had killed up to 25,000 people, and an X-ray specialist was needed in the field hospitals set up outside the city. To the horror of *Tante Luz*, her husband returned within range of the advancing Russians.

Alone again, Luz realised the Americans and French were about to occupy the Allgäu region where two of her small daughters were sheltering in a home. She went to Stuttgart station to catch a train in the evening. It sat there for hours as sirens wailed and rumours spread the French were already there. Eventually she got to the village, found her children and settled down to wait amid a late-winter snowstorm, steering a wide berth of the occupying French Moroccan troops.

Peace came in May 1945, but she and her children were blocked at the top of the valley for several weeks, wondering if they were going to be raped or otherwise maltreated. Hilde remembers the dark-skinned Moroccans sitting on a green meadow in a circle and singing. Her only footwear was made of cloth and wooden soles. Eventually they could make their way back to Stuttgart and rang on the door of her parents-in-law. A side window opened, and out popped the head of Johannes. With the help of farmers, he had escaped at night from the Soviet-occupied zone around Dresden. Gradually they retrieved their other children from Würzburg and Giessen. Seven-year-old Fritz slept with his father in a wood on the way back.

In the midst of this personal turmoil, the whys and wherefores of the war had been long forgotten. Hitler and the Nazis had become an irrelevance, as had the identity of the "enemy" and the reasons for the fearful attacks they were launching. Bringing her family safely through the war was Luz's supreme task. In the battle for survival, my aunt focused on safeguarding her children, staying alive to care for them, and hoping her husband would return safely. The events which led up to the war, and the German role in making it happen, all seemed distant, overtaken by a final catastrophe which overwhelmed other considerations by its painful immediacy.

My German family, together with the rest of the German nation, had reached Hour Zero. The torment was over – or so they thought.

Chapter 6

ON THE OTHER SIDE

Death is a master craftsman from Germany – Paul Celan

When it comes to war, each soldier has to fight bravely for his country and cannot be blamed that war is devastating. That was the attitude Germans generally took as they became embroiled in the conflict. Implicitly it excused much of their violence against other peoples. From the point of view of those whom they opposed however, that missed the point, which was: why did Germans go to war in the first place?

Today I can scarcely conceive that a European nation should feel justified in invading most of the rest of Europe, coercing the inhabitants by force of arms, seizing much of their wealth, slaughtering millions as "subhumans" and forcing millions more into slave labour.

But that is what the Germans did. Besides genocide and untold physical suffering, they destroyed the cores of societies through drawing millions into shameful collaboration, and turning one person against the other. Remembering his desperate months in the Warsaw ghetto, Marcel Reich-Ranicki wrote that he felt deeply ashamed of himself, because at times he inadvertently survived at the expense of others. He added: "More terrible than the hunger was the fear of death; more terrible than the fear of death was the constant humiliation."[lviii]

The Germans did all this with minimum questioning whether it was right. Millions went along with the Nazi view that Germans needed to make up for the wrongs of the past by imposing their supremacy. They readily accepted that nations needed to compete for survival by subjugating others.

Only years after defeat did Germans become dimly aware that this warped philosophy caused extreme resentment. At the time, they were oblivious to the likelihood that such wholesale cruelty would one day be paid back.

When the soldiers of the Red Army exacted terrible retribution on Germans on the Eastern Front, most Germans accepted the Nazi propaganda that the Soviets were cruel Asiatic hordes. It did not occur to them that the Germans had let three million captured Soviet soldiers die of thirst, starvation and exposure earlier in the campaign, and that the Red Army knew this. Or that the German Army in the Soviet Union had slaughtered Jews, Partisans and political commissars indiscriminately, raping hundreds of thousands of women and killing children in front of parents.[lix]

In the war on the seas, U-boat commander Herbert A. Werner boasted of slipping among columns of hapless merchant ships like a wolf in a flock of sheep, sinking several ships with a single salvo of torpedoes. At the end of the war, he complained bitterly at being "reviled" by the victors, ignoring that he had sent hundreds of their civilian seamen to drown in icy seas.[lx]

In countries where they had no particular quarrels to pick, and where their "New Order" ideas even attracted some sympathy, occupying Germans antagonised the locals with gratuitous cruelty and intolerance. In Slovenia for example (then part of Yugoslavia), much of the population had enjoyed good relations with their German-speaking Austrian rulers for centuries. Within weeks, the occupying Germans turned them into enemies by degrading them as Slavs, dismissing them from posts of authority, deporting tens of thousands and confining the rest into a slice of territory surrounded by barbed wire. As a result, the Partisan resistance movement grew rapidly in Slovenia, and Slovene Partisans fought with particular ferocity.[lxi]

In France, even the Jewish writer Irène Némirovsky at first found the polite German officers more attractive than the seedy ruling French classes she was familiar with.[lxii] But by 1944, Germans in France, angry that they were losing the war, were throwing their weight around with ever increasing brutality. Némirovsky ended up murdered in Auschwitz, and her son was still being pursued from one hiding place to another all over France long after the D-Day invasion. German massacres of French in Oradour-sur-Glane and of their erstwhile Italian allies in Civitella della Chiana, Sant'Anna di Stazzema, Castelnuovo dei Sabbioni and Marzabotto in Italy were as sadistic as any in the East.

This selfish miscalculation on the part of the Germans was another huge mistake. They were either locked in their own anguish as the war turned against them, or took refuge in the excuse that all wars were terrible – ignoring that there would have been no war at all if they had not started it.

My *Onkel Walter* won an Iron Cross for bravery in Germany's conquest of France[lxiii] and later served on the Eastern Front – a photo shows him in uniform on a horse – but nobody recalls him telling what he did. He held himself like an upright Prussian soldier, but never mentioned the war. As an uncle to me, he later performed a rite of manhood which belongs more to peace than to war – he took me at age 18 to his local tavern for my first glass of German beer. I savoured it as a kind, family gesture.

The younger brother, my *Onkel Fritz,* spent the whole war in a coastal battery far to the north of Norway. His mother wrote that he was sometimes on top of a mountain overlooking a fjord and at other times on an island out

My uncle Fritz: conscripted to a coastal battery in Norway.

in the Atlantic. It was cold, lonely and boring, with little scope for heroics or atrocities. His elder sister Luz found him nervous, irritable and permanently changed after he returned.

Both brothers no doubt spent some of their soldier's pay on local goods to send back to their families at home in Germany. There were few ways of spending it on themselves, and that seemed a constructive contribution amid so much suffering. But that too, unbeknown to the soldiers, was an activity selfishly benefiting Germans at the expense of the local populations of the countries they occupied.

The German military occupation costs, including the wages of the German soldiers, had to be paid for by the countries concerned. German finance ministry officials manipulated exchange rates so that the soldiers could buy local goods cheaply. Soldiers such as my uncles sent home butter, coffee, cocoa, chocolate, herrings, meat, tobacco, soap, female underwear, jewelry, and carpets. This created shortages and inflation in the occupied countries. In Germany however, the goods arriving from the front plugged the gaps in supplies and dampened popular discontent and rising prices.

The funds extorted by the Germans from the countries they occupied (including provision of gold teeth) were not just used for the Army's local upkeep. The money taken from the French also financed German air attacks on Britain from French soil, and construction of U-boat pens and bunkers on the coasts. In Belgium, one third of the sums exacted were used by the Germans outside the country. In France and Norway, where my uncles served, German levies represented one third of national income.[lxiv] In the East, the practice went to extremes: the genocide of millions of Jews, Roma and Slavs, as well as the mass starvation of Soviet prisoners-of-war, freed up food for Germans. Only in the last months of the war did Germans suffer significant food shortages.

Before they were sent to death camps, the Jews were robbed of their belongings, and the Germans offered a sop to local populations by allowing them to share in the spoils, which they mostly did.[8] However the Germans made sure that most of the proceeds ended up with themselves. Thus in Hungary, the Hungarian government used revenues from selling confiscated Jewish property to help pay the imposed costs of the German occupying army. The Germans used this money to pay their soldiers' wages and the Hungarian bauxite and oil they needed to pursue the war. In Greece, gold confiscated from the 49,000 Saloniki Jews deported to their deaths was used to finance the Germany Army's operations against resistance fighters in

---

8   Belgian officials were a notable exception in refusing to collaborate in depriving Jews of their assets.

that country. At home, the Nazis gave German Jews state bonds in compensation for their seized property, but the Jews were not allowed to sell the bonds.

The Nazis did all they could to keep Germans loyal by maintaining a reasonable standard of living. They promoted an egalitarian society in which all classes were treated the same. The poor benefited from low tax rates. That was the socialist element of their philosophy. The nationalist element, fostered in particular by Hitler himself, determined that the prosperity of Germans could and indeed *should* be secured at the expense of other nations. In effect, the Nazis bribed Germans with assets stolen from foreigners. Britons and Americans subscribed voluntarily to state war bonds, but Germans were never asked to do so. Robbery was an easier way to maintain German morale and internal financial stability.[lxv]

Forced labour was another. Some seven million foreigners were rounded up and deported to Germany to work in German industries in place of Germans serving in the German army. At first, some workers came voluntarily because of hardship elsewhere in Europe, in particular the Soviet Union. But as the war drew on, recruitment was done by force and the workers were in effect slaves. Some were paid wages, but deductions were made for food and lodging, and they could buy nothing since they were given no ration cards. For others, their wages were paid into the *Reichsbank*, which then arranged for families in the home countries to be paid an equivalent in local currency. However those payments were accounted as German occupation costs, so the government of the occupied country had to reimburse the German authorities. The country of origin thus ended up paying for the work of its enslaved citizens in Germany. Some other forced labourers were paid in vouchers they could exchange for buttons, soap and safety pins in their barracks.

In addition, Germans forced 1.8 million prisoners of war and 1.65 million prisoners in concentration camps to work for the German war effort. Of the latter, only 475,000 survived. None of these were paid anything at all. [lxvi]

The Krümmel dynamite plant, which my grandfather had managed until his retirement in 1928, depended largely on forced labour during World War II. With over 9,000 workers, it had become one of Germany's largest munitions factories, located partly underground. [lxvii] In Germany as a whole, 30% of the workers in munitions factories were forced labour, but in Krümmel they were a large majority. A third were *Ostarbeiter* – "Eastern workers." As Slavs, they were usually treated particularly badly – even those from countries such as the Ukraine, which had initially welcomed the German invasion as liberation from the Russians.

Conditions were worst in the production plants of V-1 and V-2 rockets, where 60,000 slaves had to carve underground factories deep into hills and work day and night without ever seeing daylight (one third of those died). In Krümmel, it was not so harsh, but only relatively speaking. When I visited, I found a dispute still rumbling on about how hard it was. Word was spread after the war that it was not so bad. The wartime Director was said to have protected the foreign workers to some extent. There were no uprisings, no sabotage and no escapes.

This was challenged later as a white-wash – an attempt to avoid wartime guilt. In 2005, a local pamphlet published testimony by Ukrainians who had worked there. [lxviii] In a foreword, Geesthacht Museum researcher William Boehart wrote that the lesson from it was clear: "The attempts to depict forced labour as harmless (for example as 'foreign labour') during the Second World War are in view of the present-day state of research about Nazi rule – including in Geesthacht – to be considered as unacceptable apologetics."

The survivors' accounts tell of being rounded up at gunpoint and shipped to Germany in cattle-trucks, shivering with cold and half starving during journeys which lasted up to six days. In Krümmel and nearby Düneburg, where there was a gunpowder factory, they were put into camps surrounded by barbed wire and watch towers and set to work for 12 hours a day. It was much the same as being in a prison or a concentration camp.

The age of the slave workers varied between 14 and 22. The work was heavy and at times dangerous. Some wrote of being burned, and another of crippling his hand. All spoke of exhaustion, strict discipline and gnawing hunger, with food consisting mainly of root vegetable soups and scraps of bread. They worked partly underground and slept on straw mattresses or bare boards. Anybody who made trouble was sent for a spell in the Neuengamme concentration camp or disappeared altogether. Over 100 forced labourers paid with their lives when the factory was finally bombed.

Yet the accounts also contain remarks such as… "Medical treatment in the sick room was good… the German doctor was a good man who tried hard to cure us as quickly as possible." – "Sometimes German workers would secretly slip us a piece of bread or a bit of milk" – and – "The German workers often brought their children's bread, clothing and shoes for us… this friendly behaviour was strictly secret." One told of a club room for young people to frequent until 9 p.m. and another of being allowed out of the camp for six hours on Sundays in the last year of the war.

These few anecdotes do not belie the cruelty of the German forced labour regime. But they do show that a few Germans here and there chose to behave decently. One Ukrainian family of forced labourers found itself united in misery with the German farmers to whom they were sent from Krümmel. The German wife was distraught with grief because her 17-year-old son had been killed as soon as he arrived on the Eastern Front. Then the Ukrainian mother received a letter from home saying her husband was dead and her brother had lost a leg.

"Mother wanted to die, but the farmer's wife comforted her. Both wept over the terrible war," wrote the Ukrainian survivor.

When the Ukrainian forced labourers of Krümmel were liberated in 1945, the Soviet authorities obliged many to serve in the Soviet military. Some only returned to the Ukraine in 1950. After examination of the testimony in the early years of the 21st century, the German authorities gave the contributing Ukrainians "plausibility declarations" entitling them to German government compensation payments. It came 60 years late: all were aged by the time, and many were living in poverty. It was however a gesture.

One wrote: "I thank you very much for your great interest and sympathy for the fate of the *Ostarbeiter*... may God now give you peace and happiness."

Chapter 7

FROM MIDDLETON STONEY TO OSTKREUZ

The flak, the guns, the lights, the search lights... I was really, really, really frightened – British airman

Middleton Stoney, the Oxfordshire village of my British grandmother, has a fine old English church surrounded by a graveyard of uneven earth, tilting headstones and swaying grass. A patch on one side stands out. It is neatly mown, the white gravestones are identical and they all stand straight. These are for the boys who flew from nearby airbases to bomb Germany into submission and died of their wounds on their return.

Age 18, New Zealand... 22, Canada... 19, Australia... 20, Britain... 21, Britain... They were boys who died men's deaths. Missing is the name of a Middleton Stoney ancestor who would have been an uncle of mine if he had not been shot down over Cologne a year before I was born. Henry Elliott Gaskell came from my grandmother's family in Middleton Stoney. His remains are not here. He never came back from his last mission over Germany.

Some of these boys were blown up in midair as German anti-aircraft batteries hit the bombs in their planes' holds. Others were trapped in burning aircraft which curved downwards to explode into the ground, or were thrown out of stricken planes sent spinning through the sky like Catherine wheels on fireworks night. Some parachuted to the ground but were lynched by the German civilians they were bombing. Yet others were dragged lifeless from damaged planes which had struggled back to their home bases. The survivors saw only too clearly how their comrades met their fates.

Book after book continues to be published in Britain about the bravery of the bombers who went through this ordeal. For the first years, the British Army was mostly confined to the British Isles and the British Navy had its hands full protecting convoys from U-boats and penning German battleships in their home ports. Only the Royal Air Force Bomber Command could take the battle to the heart of Nazi Germany. The bombers were generally volunteers and, as soon became painfully obvious, their chances of completing the regulation tour of 30 sorties were slim – statistically they had only a one in six chance in 1943. 55,000 of them were killed, representing a loss rate of 44%.

In the first two years of the war, casualties mounted but the authorities mercifully hid from the British crews that the damage they were doing to German targets was modest (even if they did disturb my *Tante Luz* giving birth in Stuttgart).

A ferocious battle of technology and wits developed between attackers and defenders. The Germans developed an integrated radar system guiding fighters to the bombers as they approached the continent. The British flew crooked routes into Germany, so the defenders could not guess which city they would attack. They invented special radar to direct them more accurately to their targets, and grouped bombers in broad, deep streams several miles in size so as to offer fewer flanks to the fighters. Then the Germans equipped fighters with guns which could fire diagonally upwards, so they could creep up unseen underneath bombers and destroy them unawares.

Above all it was a battle of terror, in the air and on the ground. British airman Harry Irons remembers on his first flight looking out of the mid-gun-turret as they approached Düsseldorf:

"I was absolutely shocked by what I saw. I could not believe my eyes seeing what was in front of me. The flak, the guns, the lights, the search lights. It was incredible and I was really, really, really frightened. The plane was bouncing about… On my left I could see an aircraft on fire and one below us I could see exploding. And I thought to myself: 'We're in for something here.' I could not believe that we were going to fly through this huge explosion. But we went through it."[lxix]

Pilots learned how to slip through small gaps in the flak. But some became trapped in the "cones" of massed searchlights beaming on to one plane. The crews sat in a cold, bright light which invited their killers to destroy them. Few survived that experience. People on the ground saw the flak get closer and closer until the plane was enveloped in flames and exploded. Like the British flyers, the German anti-aircraft gunners were often teenagers. The future anti-war writer Günter Grass, then 15, remembers his pride at shooting down a Lancaster bomber and finding the "rather charred" bodies of its Canadian crew.[lxx]

After the raiders bombed, German fighters still lurked on the return routes to Britain, waiting to infiltrate and destroy. The British aircrews knew the statistics were stacked against them, and discussed the odds of survival amongst each other ad nauseam.[lxxi] Two weeks after Harry Irons' maiden flight to Düsseldorf, his 21-year-old skipper was dead.

Why did they volunteer? Some for patriotic reasons, some because they wanted to change the world or were combative by nature, and others because as young men they found it hard to envisage death. Flying the powerful machines was in itself thrilling at a time when hardly anyone could drive on land for lack of cars and fuel. Most bombers soldiered on to complete a single tour, forming tight-knit communities with the rest of the crew for the duration. They could select whom they flew with and stay together. Some airmen volunteered for further tours, but a few cracked up in mid-tour and were moved to other services. The Royal Air Force shamed them in front of their fellows in order to encourage the others to remain strong.

Gradually the British Royal Air Force, together with the U.S. Air Force from 1942, found the means to change Germany forever. A few years ago, I found in a Trieste antiques fair a book of German town centres published "in the war year 1940." The Germany I got to know after the war bore little resemblance. In the book were 1,000 years of history. By the time I got there, the historic cities had been reduced to rubble, joining the ashes of German books sent up in smoke by the Nazis in 1933.

My never-to-be uncle, 407711 Sergeant Henry Elliott Gaskell, had a hand in this massive retribution. He died on one of the raids launched against Germany's industrial heartland in the Ruhr. He was an Australian, son of my great Auntie Ame from Middleton Stoney, who had emigrated to Australia to marry an Australian soldier whom she had nursed in England after he lost an eye in World War I. Gaskell was seconded from the Royal Australian Air Force to take part in the British bombing offensive. My father remembers him coming to stay in our home in Reading a few months earlier when they both had leave. "We left together to rejoin our units and after we parted to take different trains, I never saw him again."

Sergeant Gaskell was second pilot in a crew of seven on a Lancaster bomber which took off from Coningsby air base in England just before 1 a.m. on 1st August 1942. They were carrying an 8,000lb bomb they were to drop on Düsseldorf, but were shot down on the outskirts of

Cologne and all the crew perished. 5,000 other Australians seconded to the Royal Air Force met the same fate during the course of the war.[lxxii]

Six months later, British and American leaders meeting in Casablanca gave a directive to Allied bombing fleets: "Your primary object will be the progressive destruction of the German military, industrial and economic system, and the undermining of the morale of the German people to a point where their armed resistance is fatally weakened."

The last part of that order meant that the British Bomber Command should no longer target just military and industrial objectives, such as my uncle Henry did. The bombers were doing increasing damage, but such targets were numerous, well defended and replaceable. It was hard to deal decisive blows, and the Royal Air Force was suffering considerable losses.

At the end of the war, only 20% of Germany's industrial plant was found to have been destroyed. The Nobel explosives factory which my grandfather used to manage at Krümmel was bombed for the first time only at the beginning of April 1945. Photographs taken afterwards show only moderate damage, and if the war had not in the meantime ended, it could doubtless have been restored to working order in a few weeks. A bust of Alfred Nobel was found undamaged in the rubble.

In response to the order to undermine enemy morale, the Royal Air Force began mounting single raids against whole cities. Newer bombers were available in greater numbers, Pathfinders improved the marking of targets, and Cologne was the city in the front line nearest the British Isles. It had already been traumatised the previous year by a raid which razed 900-year-old churches and reduced bridges to stumps sticking up in the river. The attack left the city without power, water or transport and one fifth of its inhabitants in flight.

The British had no intention of leaving it at that. 608 British bombers set the rest of the city ablaze during 90 minutes on the night of 28th March 1943. They had learned to make firestorms. For that, they needed an old centre, in which houses were crowded together, preferably some of them wooden. They first dropped high explosives to crack the buildings open, then tens of thousands of incendiaries to set the wreckage on fire. For it all to come together, they needed the right weather combination, in particular wind, with little cloud obscuring the target. In Cologne, the square outside the black Gothic cathedral was the target.

On that night, nine months after my uncle Henry crashed on its outskirts, 4,377 inhabitants of Cologne came to a fiery end. It was a record death toll scored by Bomber Command. Conditions for the attackers were right, and quickly the individual fires joined into one vast conflagration, sucking oxygen from the air, throwing people to the ground with violent winds and burning them alive where they fell. Many of those who took refuge in cellars were entombed, suffocated or scalded by burst hot water pipes. 60% of the total 20,000 killed in Cologne during the war died in shelters.

The British followed in the next few days with three more raids on this city, which had been a bishopric since Roman times. By the time they moved on elsewhere, the population was shocked, despairing and physically at the end of their tether. It was, as future West German Chancellor Konrad Adenauer sadly put it, a ghost city. He had been its mayor until 1933, when the Nazis deposed him and set in train the infernal cycle of horror for its citizens.[lxxiii]

To the Germans, the bombing seemed to be indiscriminate, but the British airmen were on tenterhooks to know ahead of each sortie where they were headed. Occupied France was a "milk run." Hamburg had an easy approach over the sea. The Ruhr was close but heavily defended. The big prize was Berlin. The British and Americans attacked it again and again in the hope of landing a decisive blow as in Cologne. But Berlin was the most heavily defended target and the one the Allied airmen most feared.

Erich Honecker, who later ruled Communist East Germany for 18 years, watched in Berlin as "the whole area from the Alexanderplatz (in the east) to Lichtenberg (in the west) sank in rubble and ashes." The Nazis had locked him up as a Communist leader, but let him out to repair roofs as he was an apprenticed tiler. The day grew dark with the billowing smoke and he felt he looked like a coal miner. He seized dozens of incendiary bombs which came clattering down on to the roof of a women's prison and threw them to the ground. In between he found solace listening clandestinely to Radio Moscow – and the BBC.

But neither the British nor the Americans could ever create the firestorm which would consume Berlin and perhaps end the war. The city was laid out too spaciously, and fire could not easily leap from one building to another. The Berlin tenement buildings proved sturdy and did not readily collapse.

The Nazis sent children out into the countryside – anywhere but stay in the cities under constant attack. But nowhere was really safe any more. Erdmute Behrendt, who was later my assistant in the Reuters bureau in East Berlin, was dispatched at the age of six to East Prussia, when it was about to be overwhelmed by the Red Army. She watched a German farmer whipping a Russian woman who slipped into a hut to breast-feed her new-born infant. Then cart after cart of wounded German soldiers came trundling past westwards, and soon she was on her way back – not to Berlin, but rural Thuringia in central Germany.

The Thuringian countryside seemed picturesque to the city girl, all the more so since she was among brown-skinned men in turbans – Indian prisoners-of-war were located in the vicinity. Out of one of these turbans, the daughter of the farmer where she was billeted made a dress.[lxxiv]

As for the time Erdmute did spend in Berlin bomb shelters, she found it rather fun. The grown-ups took trouble to amuse her. My cousin Fritz on the other hand, also six at the time, was terrified at having to run under attack into basements, and became a bed-wetter. Most felt the same terror as Fritz. The shelters were squalid and overfilled. They shook and crumbled for hours on end, and the people inside constantly feared a collapse which would crush them or trap them inside with no escape.

Anneliese Bodecker, who wrote a book about her wartime life, remembers the children running out of the bomb shelters after each raid to see who could find the largest bomb splinter. But she still panics today at the memory of her trembling mother grasping her hand when they were cut off for hours in a caved-in shelter.[lxxv]

In the last days of July 1943, the British turned their attention to Hamburg, the proud, Hanseatic city near where my mother grew up. It was a city of hard-working, Protestant traders, who were open to foreigners and felt much in common with the seafaring British.

The British felt no such affinity. They destroyed Hamburg and 40,000 of its population on 28th July in an attack code-named Gomorrah. They calculated the cocktail of high explosive and incendiary bombs just right, the houses were close together, and summer temperatures were unusually high. The firestorm sprang up almost immediately, sucking away the air and roasting people alive on the streets. Iris Buhl, who emigrated to Britain after the war, remembers spending the whole night in a canal, clinging to her mother to avoid the fire. Afterwards she watched a young boy scoop up the charred remains of his brother and pack them into a box. She was 18.[lxxvi]

The death toll was shockingly massive, foreshadowing the even greater casualties of the atomic bomb attacks on Hiroshima (140,000) and Nagasaki (80,000). 7,000 of the Hamburg victims were children. Rescuers had to wait 10 days before the ruins cooled enough to be cleared. 900,000 inhabitants fled into the countryside. Women crazed with shock and grief clutched suitcases containing the charred remnants of their babies and refused to let them go. Thousands came to the little town of Geesthacht, near my mother's former home, and camped in makeshift refuges until the end of the war.

On 1st August 1943, armaments minister Albert Speer told Hitler six more attacks like that would mean the war was lost for Germany. Speer was wrong. The Germans fought on, but were increasingly helpless to defend their cities against the aerial onslaught. Of the estimated 500,000 Germans killed by wartime bombing, more than half lost their lives *after* the 1943 Hamburg raid.[lxxvii]

In a book called "The Fire" published 50 years later, German historian Jörg Friedrich characterised the British bombing campaign as "a war of extermination." He wrote vividly not only of the fearful human casualties but also of the destruction of Germany's cultural heritage. His outraged account touched on a question which the British too had been tussling with. Was the bombing campaign moral?

When the British became aware that they made the greatest impact through firestorms, the inevitable consequence was that they would target civilians. The closely packed housing they needed to set alight uncontrollable blazes could be found only in cities packed with civilians. So the purpose became spreading terror as much as achieving military advantage.

Insofar as they could bring themselves to think about this amidst their own fears, a certain number of British crews felt squeamish. Others were unmoved, knowing that the Germans had been the first to bomb civilians, already from 1940 onwards, in London, Coventry and other British cities. The war had in any case acquired an inhuman logic which escaped the judgments of ordinary individuals. Arthur Harris, the head of Bomber Command, knew what damage and suffering he was causing, but felt it was the best way to win the war. He argued doggedly with his chiefs for permission to attack more and more cities in order, as he hoped, to achieve victory by a collapse of morale.

The Germans never did give up until their whole country was occupied. They fought on tenaciously, doing their best to kill and maim Allied soldiers long after it was obvious that defeat could be the only outcome. British historian Ian Kershaw asserted this was because the Nazi leadership grew more fanatical in the face of defeat, and imposed ever more dictatorial controls.[lxxviii] Many Germans however still saw nothing morally wrong in pursuing their cruel war of aggression, and bolstered this obstinacy with a naïve belief in the imminence of "wonder weapons" which Hitler promised. They continued to dream of a world finally subjugated by German victory. One way or another, morale did not collapse, and the carpet bombing of cities cannot be said to have ended the war early. Air power contributed to victory in two ways. Bombing of German troops and defensive lines paved the way for infantry to advance, and attacks on German fuel supplies seriously reduced the enemy's ability to respond. In the end however, victory was largely won by huge armies of infantry with massive firepower slogging their way forwards.

More important was the psychological impact of the bombing on German minds after the war was over. The Allies forced the Germans to surrender unconditionally, so that they would not imagine they could have fought on, as after the armistice of 1918. The British and American bombing brought home to all Germans that they had been utterly crushed in defeat. They had no scope to persist in the attitudes and ideologies which had led them into war. As such, the bombing of their cities prepared Germans to adopt healthier values. It was a lesson painfully learnt: half a million paid with their lives for the moral turnaround of the survivors.

The gravestones in Middleton Stoney churchyard remember the young airmen on the British side for their bravery and sacrifice. In 2008, I sat in the living room of an old Berlin woman who as a little girl lay quivering under the bombs rained down by my uncle's British comrades. Liselotte Kubitza has no trouble recognising German war guilt. She comes from a Communist family who regarded the Nazis as criminals from the start. She knows perfectly well why she was bombed and believes Germans deserved what they got.

Frau Kubitza lives in Berlin-Ostkreuz, a dilapidated part of Berlin around a railway junction constantly targeted during the war. The railway tracks were always repaired, but big empty spaces remain where surrounding homes were razed to the ground. She spent the first years of the war with her twin sister on a farm on the border with Czechoslovakia and Poland, struggling to a Polish school in winter up to her waist in snow. At age 11 in 1944, she was back in Berlin, and war from then on meant endless planes and bombs.

Frau Kubitza is devoid of self-pity and used to confronting life's tough challenges. But as she tells me her story late in the evening, her voice quavers and her hand trembles. I see tears in her eyes as she recalls the traumatic final months of the war when Berlin was bombed two or three times a day.

She looks at me, the Briton with German relatives, and for a moment sobs. I look back and say nothing, but she knows she has touched me. Our spirits briefly fuse. For a few instants, I come between Middleton Stoney and Berlin-Ostkreuz and feel the breath of war as if it were today. I feel for my relative, the brave boy who took the battle to the German enemy who had attacked his kin, and I feel for this German woman, ready to assume collective guilt but still trembling with unbearable terror.

Henry Elliott Gaskell was treated decently in death by the Germans he came to kill. They gave his body a funeral and a grave at the Rheinberg War Cemetery, visited after the war by his parents. The parents found comfort in the knowledge that the enemy had treated his remains humanely. It was already a small gesture of reconciliation, a rebuilding of common human values.

I myself had to visit Dresden to fully understand this grim part of history shared by British and Germans. That was where it was hardest for me to stand with a foot in both camps.

Chapter 8

STARTING AGAIN

I have nobody who helps me – Job 5:7

Berliner Peter Lorenz, aged 16, knew that World War II was finished because silence came over the city. He was in hiding, because he had received his call-up papers for the army and did not want to die for a lost cause. Suddenly, there were no more shells. The next thing he grasped was that he was free. The third: that he was individually responsible for everything he did. All of this was quite new to him.

"We were used to obeying all rules and laws. Everything which was not ordered was forbidden. Now we lived without laws, in freedom. It was fantastic. The old was gone and the new was not yet there. For the first time I experienced personal responsibility for my actions," he told me in Berlin in 2008.

A change in sounds was the signal for Liselotte Kubitza. Instead of the roar of bombers overhead, she heard the rumble of Soviet tanks. At the end of her street, she could see them gingerly advancing up Berlin's Frankfurter Allee. Half-Jew Ruth Kitschler, aged nine, heard a knock on her door in Berlin-Spandau and someone shouted *Hitler kaputt!* She looked out of the window and saw dead soldiers and weapons strewn all over the street. "But I couldn't rejoice. As a half-Jew, I had been so frightened throughout the war and I was scared the Russians would leave again."[lxxix]

A few diehards could not bring themselves to abandon the fight they had sworn to continue. In the north German town of Ratzeburg, a sergeant insisted he would carry out orders to blow up the causeway between the town's two lakes. The local council formally summoned him to desist, rang a bell and sent over a couple of watchmen, at which point the sergeant agreed to "cede to greater force."[lxxx]

Some German soldiers found the transition to peace was the most dangerous moment they experienced in the whole war. Until the last moment, they risked being summarily executed by Nazi court martial if they showed any wavering in their desire to continue the fight. Even if they could avoid being killed by their own side at the moment of surrender, they risked being shot by a nervous enemy caught by surprise.[lxxxi]

Dankwart Rost stopped believing in the war a few months before it ended. Sent into active service in 1944 at the age of 18, he quickly perceived that his fellow soldiers had lost faith in the Nazi regime which inspired his boyhood. The soldiers resented the Nazis' political indoctrination, false promises and selfish fanaticism. The tide of opinion had belatedly turned. The ideals for which Dankwart had been fighting were shattered, along with a whole way of life. What he thought he knew and believed in collapsed. No more ennobling dedication to duty. No more chivalry in arms. No more German superiority. No more respect for leaders. Nothing ahead but defeat, humiliation and disorientation in a new world emptied of familiar values.

"Bit by bit the whole extent of German crimes against Jews, Gypsies and other peoples filtered through and, after initially rejecting the news incredulously as war propaganda, we sank into abysmal depression," Dankwart wrote of his last days of warfare. When peace came, he had practically no money, food or clothes. He wore underpants made of sugar sacks. Back at school shortly after, he found himself incapable of putting any thoughts to paper when a teacher set an essay on "home, homeland, fatherland." His mind was blocked and his hands were covered with warts brought on by stress.[lxxxii]

Eighteen-year-old SS soldier Hans Werk was luckier than his father, who was killed in Poland on January 1945 trying to flee. As the Red Army arrived, his younger brother watched a German farm-owner and his wife commit suicide and Russian soldiers rape German women in a field in front of him. However Werk himself was fighting in the Ardennes in the west and was taken prisoner by the Americans rather than the Russians, who would have executed him on the spot. In the prison camp, 12 died of hunger and three were shot for trying to escape. Fellow-soldiers started cutting out the blood groups tattooed on their arms, which betrayed them as SS. But then U.S. General George S. Patton ordered the release of all underage SS, and he was out.

Until he joined a trade union as a tram-driver in 1951, he thought stories of German atrocities were lies invented by the victors. "In the trade union, they started to educate me in democracy. A friend in the union opened my eyes. I realised that concentration camp inmates were not criminals. Many were socially-engaged citizens. I was ashamed."

For some others, acknowledgement came much, much later. Writer Günter Grass could not bring himself for over half a century to talk of his final weeks of wartime combat. At 17, he saw comrades torn limb from limb in front of his eyes, came close to death several times himself, was wounded in his arm and thigh and finally collapsed unconscious from exhaustion and pain. As a best-selling post-war author, he complained vehemently that Germans had failed to acknowledge their ugly past, but only in 2006 did he admit that he himself had served with the *Waffen-SS*.

When he finally owned up, he was lambasted for the hypocrisy of blaming others for failing to assume guilt while concealing his own past. Joachim Fest said he would not buy a used car from Grass. Chancellor Angela Merkel remarked tartly that she would have preferred to know of his SS service sooner.[lxxxiii] As for me, I felt a bit sorry for him. I understood his silence as part of the collective trauma of the German nation. Even the man who spoke loudest of conscience could not face his own. It showed how unstable Germans' view of their history still was. That his most famous novel, "The Tin Drum," recounts wartime history through an insane dwarf with a piercing shriek only served to reinforce this opinion.

So much for the soldiers. The German women faced a reckoning in the form of rape. In the American and British zones of occupation, this was relatively limited. The Americans had consumer goods such as cigarettes, nylons, soap and food which they offered as presents. Some American soldiers were shocked to see the devastation of Allied bombing, and felt sympathy for the German victims. The German women were short of male company, since many German men had failed to return from the war. So sex occurred on a more or less friendly basis.

If there was a problem in the American zone, from the point of view of the U.S. authorities it was fraternisation, not rape. The American military government forbade fraternisation, but their soldiers took little notice. In the months after the end of hostilities, 20% of the occupying American soldiers caught venereal disease, requiring an emergency airlift of penicillin in November 1945.

The Russians brought no gifts. Marshal Zhukov, the conqueror of Berlin, issued an order that "we shall get our terrible revenge for everything."[lxxxiv] They came to kill, burn and loot, in particular watches and bicycles. Americans came from a bright new world of promise, the Russians from darker reaches where poverty left no room for sympathy and primitive customs prevailed. They expected to enjoy victors' spoils, in the form of material goods and women. Pillage of the defeated was for them entirely normal. So too was rape, which went further than indulging forcefully in illicit pleasures. It was a way for the winners to possess and humiliate an enemy who had looked down on them. Rape expressed who was on top.

The Russians violated any woman they could lay hands on, from young girls to women over 80. When asked by a Westerner why he was set on an ugly old German crone, a Russian soldier replied: "Woman is woman." They set about rape systematically and became skilled in ferreting out victims. German women tried to save themselves by dirtying their faces to look old or hiding in wainscotings or remote tenement courtyards. The Russians knew most of the tricks however. The only safeguard which occasionally worked was to withdraw to the highest floors of a tottering, bomb-damaged building. Many Red Army soldiers had never lived in anything but a single-floor dwelling and were scared to climb rickety stairs.

In a later book, a German woman journalist described anonymously what she went through. In the final two weeks before the Russians arrived, Berlin received 40,000 shells and three quarters of the dwellings were made uninhabitable.[lxxxv] She and her fellow Berlin women were running out of food and water, and electricity failed. "We are going backwards to past centuries and becoming cave-dwellers again," she wrote in her diary.

For several weeks thereafter, she and her neighbours were raped repeatedly by drunken Russian soldiers. Some women were left bleeding and covered by bruises. One had jam and ersatz coffee smeared into her hair. Only 12 days after the Soviet occupation of Berlin did the author spend one night alone in her bed. Eventually she found a Russian major who protected her from his men and procured scraps of food in exchange for sex whenever he decided. In her desolation as German society collapsed around her, she felt the women would "forever live like rats haunting ruins." Her Russian major varied between extremes of cruelty and tenderness. When he left, she confessed to a few warm feelings for him, but without him she was again unprotected and thrown on her own meagre resources.

Children went out scavenging. Young girls felled trees in parks for burning. Other inhabitants sat around listlessly in shock. The few remaining German men were youths and old men of the *Volksturm,* the "Home Guard." They looked on apathetically, fearing for their lives if they risked intervention. The German journalist's own male friend rejected her with disgust when he returned from captivity and realised she had been having sex with Russians. Within a few weeks, these women lost respect for male authority in general. "One day the German women will present the bill to their husbands," she remarked grimly.[lxxxvi]

The book was first published in 1954 in English in Britain, then four years later in German in Germany. It attracted little notice. In my early years, I remember no one talking about rapes of German women, even though it subsequently emerged that possibly as many as two million were violated. The Germans I knew then must have been too pained to talk, felt complaining about the victors was counter-productive, or considered a young boy should be spared such horrors. Fresh memories of German war crimes outweighed any sympathy foreigners might have felt. What was probably the largest mass rape in history was judged as normal reprisal. War had brutalised minds to accept it thus.

Only after the death of the author in 2001 – it emerged that her name was Marta Hiller – did her testimony strike a chord with the German public, all the more so since it was told dispassionately and without self-pity. On being re-published in Germany in 2003, it became a best-seller. It was then also published in other languages, and foreigners such as myself, who had ignored the issue for decades, were likewise touched. Attitudes had changed.

Back in 1945, the Red Army felt no compunction to be merciful. They had lost millions of soldiers reaching Berlin. Millions more had been left to die by the Germans earlier in prison camps. Most of the rapes and plunder took place in the first weeks after the German surrender, but they only tapered off when the soldiers were sated. Not even a direct order by Stalin to desist could stop them in their tracks. [lxxxvii]

The shock of Soviet occupation led to mass suicides – tens of thousands among the raped women – but also in Neustrelitz, where my grandfather's family once ran a grocery shop. 737 Germans drowned themselves in the nearby lake. In the cemetery surrounded by towering Mecklenburg lime trees, where my German relatives have family tombs surrounded by wrought-iron fencing, there is a discreet monument to this act of despair. Discreet, since neo-Nazis have sought to exploit the act to portray Germans as victims rather than perpetrators. The extent to which Germans may feel sorry for themselves remains a delicate issue.

Back in 1945, few in the West felt inclined to criticise the behaviour of the Red Army. The Western public still considered the Soviets as allies. They admired them not only as comrades-in-arms but also for their politics, which promised a new and better world. The young British soldiers who risked all for victory were in no mood to bow their heads to the old guard of conservative politicians back home, not even Churchill.

A photograph of my father with his fellow-officers in Burma after victory depicts determined young men set on making a better new world. In a letter to my mother in July 1945, my father wrote: "I have become, I think permanently, politically conscious, which is a thing I never was before... My judgment is hardening and I am beginning to know my own mind... I am surprised at the mental vigour and determination that I feel in thinking how to tackle the problems of our new life."[lxxxviii]

My father and millions of other British soldiers took their futures into their own hands that summer by voting in a Labour government which began nationalising as zealously as any Communist regime.

"I would, reluctantly, rather be like Russia than America," he wrote explaining his decision to my mother. She however, rejecting extremes as a refugee from totalitarianism, voted middle-of-the-road Liberal.

In Germany too, Soviet Communism seemed a potential alternative to both Nazism and the conservative politics which had failed in the Depression. At the moment of Nazi collapse, the Soviet Union stood a good chance of winning the hearts and minds of Germans. With Communists in France and Italy riding high for having resisted the German occupiers, the whole European continent could have swung to the Soviets.

The mass rapes in Germany, which went largely unpunished, put paid to any chance of willing acceptance. By letting their soldiers rampage, the Soviets lost their opportunity to be liked. German women in particular were left with a deep loathing. They could not talk about it much, but the horror and disgust remained embedded in their hearts. Gradually it became known that the Red Army had also committed wholesale rape and plunder in Poland, Hungary and other countries they occupied. This was no longer a question of punishing the Germans. It was more like a descent of barbarians threatening the whole of Europe. The Soviets and their German Communist protégés would continue to seek ways of finding true popularity. But from the time of the rapes, they could only keep the upper hand in their zone of Germany by force.

To begin with, German soldiers felt shocked and bitter about their defeat, regardless of whom they surrendered to. Soon they understood that their fate varied sharply depending on which victor they submitted to. The Russians in Berlin robbed the trousers and shirt off Joachim Fest's grandfather dying in hospital, and he was buried in a paper bag. Joachim himself had a hard time for a few weeks in an American prisoner-of-war camp, but then an American captain befriended him and relaxed the conditions of his captivity. After his release later in 1945, he still felt "disenchantment, shame and defiance," but he was free to make a life as he wished.[lxxxix] Since German soldiers had done their best to kill them until the bitter end, the Western Allies were remarkably gentle with their captives.

In the east, Germans paid for the war not just through rape and pillage, but also mass expulsions – from Poland east of the Oder, Czechoslovakia, Hungary, Romania and Yugoslavia. Millions were forced out. Large numbers perished on the journey, packed into cattle trucks or walking, slaughtering horses for food, and collapsing asleep on roads through exhaustion. The deportations were agreed by the Soviet Union, the United States and Britain at the Potsdam conference in summer 1945. Churchill expressed reservations about the inhumanity of moving such large numbers, but this had no effect: half way through the conference he was replaced as Prime Minister by Labour's Clement Attlee, who disliked Germans from his WWI experience.

Poles had to leave the east of their country, which was ceded to the Soviet Union. Pushed to Silesia and Pomerania in the west, they seized the homes of Germans, who in turn were forced to flee to Germany. In Czechoslovakia, Czechs drove out the Sudeten Germans. President Edvard Beneš declared: "In this war, the German people have ceased being human or humanly tolerable, and they appear to us now only as a great human monstrosity ... we have said to ourselves that we must completely liquidate the German problem in [our] republic."

My *Tante Liselotte,* wife of my mother's younger brother Fritz, was one of those driven out of the Czech Sudetenland. We knew this in the family, but neither she nor any of us ever discussed it. We saw it as a fact of post-war life rather than an injustice to be shocked about. When I was a Reuters correspondent in Prague in the early 1970s, the issue of the deportees was in the air as Willy Brandt negotiated treaties of reconciliation with the Soviet Union, Poland and Czechoslovakia. But he did not push for redress: he knew this would have torpedoed any chance of rapprochement with the former enemies.

Now that the old German lands in these countries have been definitely signed away by united Germany, there has been a revival of interest in the plight of the expelled. It is safe to express sympathy more widely, since nothing can be changed any more. What seemed normal before now comes across as cruel. As peace has come to seem more natural, the inhumanity of war is judged more severely.

It was ethnic cleansing, of the kind which in the 1990s Western Europe and the United States decided (after some hesitation) they would not tolerate in Bosnia-Herzegovina and Kosovo. By that time, it was expected that people of different ethnicities in Europe should be able to live peacefully alongside each other. In 1945, hearts were harder because of fresh memories of the ravages of war. Even today, I find it hard to imagine how the Slavs whom Germans had mistreated and massacred during the war could have lived together with Germans in the aftermath. In retrospect, it can even be said that the deportations, harsh as they were, laid the foundations for a more stable Europe.

The western zones of Germany became severely overcrowded, not only with the deportees, but with the tens of thousands of German refugees who had fled their homes in the east before the Soviet advance in early 1945. They straggled over icy roads on foot, by bicycle, on horseback and in carts loaded with half-frozen women and children. The towns and villages on the way gave what care they could – a night in an improvised shelter, identity papers, a meal and delousing. Then the refugees had to move on further west, dumping their dead on the edge of cemeteries for the locals to bury.[xc] Every home had to take refugees in. My Belgian grandmother, having cleaned away the insulting slogans scrawled by Germans, sheltered some in her Bergedorf house.

My future East Berlin colleague Erdmute Behrendt remembers shouting *Papi!* as she opened the door to a gaunt figure returning unannounced from Soviet captivity in late 1945. Fellow Berliner Anneliese Bodecker saw scores of returning young prisoners shuffling along like old men "pale, worn down, reduced to skin and bones, discouraged, bowed."[xci] German Communist Wolfgang Leonhard, flown in from Moscow with 15 other comrades to set up a Communist regime in East Berlin, was shocked at "sights of destruction, hopelessness and misery... despair and suffering." My godfather David White, in the military government, wrote of a shattered capital with a population close to starvation.[xcii] Berliner Liselotte Kubitza slept for two years on the floor, sheltering under an umbrella because there was no roof. Their home was ridden with bugs, lice, fleas, mice and rats, and her sister almost died of typhus.

British historian Alan Bullock walked through the industrial Ruhr region and observed: "There wasn't a single smokestack. There was silence everywhere. There were no cars. No trains. Long lines of foreign workers wending their way home... civilisation was destroyed."[xciii]

Only 5,000 of the 90,000 soldiers of the German Sixth Army who surrendered at Stalingrad came home. The rest died of hunger, cold or mistreatment in Soviet captivity. In 1949, the villagers of Bayrisch Gmain gathered to welcome one of them back. They tolled the church bells as his train drew in at the railway station. A haggard man in military uniform climbed from the train, mounted the church steps to put the five Deutschmarks of repatriation pocket money he had been given into the collecting box, and went home in silence. He told his daughter, who was six and had never seen him until then, that he hoped to live only another four weeks. He lasted for many years more, but he was plagued by nightmares and refused to say a word about his experiences. He just told them never to waste bread or cake.[xciv]

My cousin Hilde, 10 years old in 1945, remembers the war as a time of constant dislocation. "We were constantly moving around from place to place, where people spoke German with different dialects. I felt homeless and hardly had any schooling. At the children's home in Allgäu in the last year, I was given a slate and chalk, but I could scarcely write more than A and B by the time I went to the Gymnasium [secondary school] in 1945," she said, all of which did not prevent her from subsequently qualifying as a doctor.

The occupying powers ruled by military government, but it was up to the Germans themselves to rebuild. Here too the German women were to the fore. Their men were mostly dead or in captivity, so the first images of post-war reconstruction are of women passing bricks and rubble hand to hand in the ruins of their cities. Erdmute – she who found nights in bomb shelters entertaining – also liked the brick work. It gave her something to do and was paid. Anneliese Bodecker found the rubble work dirty, dusty and strenuous, "but we laughed and lived." Money had been absent for months, and its gradual return through labour amid the ruins was a first step to making new lives.

My cousin Fritz, seven when the war ended, walked diagonally through what had once been buildings on the way to school in Stuttgart. His elder sister Hilde remembers a sea of small mauve flowers which sprang up over the razed ground in the early summer. Her father pointed out where the streets and house numbers of relatives had once been. All was flat. Bodecker's way to classes in Berlin took her over rubble as high as a one-storey house along the Friedrich Strasse. Once she came across a corpse wearing police trousers floating in a pool.[xcv] In the British zone of occupation, several children in a family shared one pair of shoes, and parents carried the small ones to school on their backs.[xcvi]

Fritz's younger brother Roland, born under the bombs in 1940, rode around in jeeps with American soldiers who gave him cigarettes. His mother forbade him to do this, but he took little notice. Cigarettes were a valuable currency (1 cigarette = 10 marks = one egg = 10 grammes of coffee grains). Moreover he was a bit of a rascal, and the Americans liked that.

Peter Lorenz in Berlin also liked escapades. From 1943, he and his teenage friends risked their lives listening to American jazz broadcast by BBC London. In May 1945, he found the American soldiers had opened a jazz cellar in Berlin, and he got in for one piece of coal. He was fascinated by the white laces on the glistening boots of the American soldiers. One of his friends asked "which train goes to America?" The boy's Nazi education had left him ignorant that there was an ocean in between. As he left the cellar to go home, Peter stumbled over German helmets and Russian corpses in the dark street outside.

Johannes, father of my cousins Fritz and Roland, worked up indignation over American pilots using one of the few remaining church steeples in Nuremberg for bombing practice. To no avail. He was in trouble with the Allies. He had to be "denazified." He had been a member of the SA, and the victors were intent on re-educating Germans to change their attitudes. The Americans classified 3.5 million Germans in their zone – about a quarter of the population – as chargeable. Not all were brought before tribunals, but Johannes was, and it was no trivial matter.

The impeccably democratic post-war West German Chancellor Konrad Adenauer considered "denazification" a waste of time. In his view, the Germans as a whole were not responsible for the crimes of the Nazis, and it was time to move on. Embarrassed by the shame of wartime collaboration, many west Europeans felt the same. This later led to the widespread belief that the Western Allies were soft on "denazification" because they wanted to use ex-Nazis against the Communist threat in the Cold War.

In fact, they could never have found enough non-Nazis qualified to provide Germany's basic administration.[xcvii] As for the Germans themselves, it was psychologically too early for them to acknowledge guilt. With Adenauer's tacit encouragement, Germans disdained the "denazification" questionnaires the Allies forced many of them to fill out. They widely disbelieved information spread by the Allies about German war crimes as enemy propaganda.

Johannes was arrested by the French authorities in Stuttgart and held in the Hotel Silber, the prisons being full. He was given nothing to eat, but his family could bring him the few pieces of bread and roots they could spare from the own sparse rations. Some of those arrested were taken off to prison camps as war criminals, and after two weeks the Americans took over from the French as occupying authorities. Luz went to the investigators to explain her husband's arrest must be a mistake:

"When I excitedly began my speech in bad English, the very arrogant Jewish officer interrupted me and said in German: 'your husband will be able to defend himself' – and that was all. I could do nothing for him." Indignantly she wrote in her memoirs that he was the last to be released, without any charge.

Although these interrogations established Johannes was not a major offender, he still had to fill out a long questionnaire for further investigations. During the year-long process, he and 1.9 million other Germans undergoing the same process could only engage in manual labour. Together with four other academics, he helped repair a damaged church building. Occasionally he scrounged a pound of peas, a few cabbages from farmers or left-over bread from a baker, but he was not paid.

Luz had sheaves of ration coupons, but the shops were empty of the food to which she was entitled. She found herself cold-shouldered by the neighbours, "who naturally had never had anything to do with the Nazi Party." Her seven-year-old son Fritz found that none of his class-mates admitted to parents in the Nazi Party either. In fact he knew perfectly well that many, including those of his best friend, had been dedicated Nazi supporters. The self-serving lie still disturbs him today.

Johannes paid the full price for his sidestep into the SA. He was eventually classified as a "fellow-traveler," which was the lowest of four categories of incrimination. When he could resume practice as an X-ray specialist, other younger doctors were already established. The only location he could find for his surgery was on the third floor of a block of flats in central Nuremberg. Doctors hesitated to refer patients to him because of the long walk up the stairs. With a family of five to look after, it took him 30 years to pay off the debt he incurred to buy X-ray equipment. Until his retirement, he struggled to make ends meet.

In the British zone of occupation, those awaiting "denazification" risked losing everything: jobs, homes, furniture, ration cards and the right to study at university. The British judiciary tended to consider all Germans guilty unless they had been active resisters. Even the Bishop of Münster, whose anti-war sermons had been scattered as leaflets over Germany by the Royal Air Force, had to be "denazified." Churchill, then in opposition, wondered how many British might have become Nazis sympathisers if invaded. He protested in Parliament that the British were demanding too much: "I thank God that in this island of ours, we have never been put to the test."[xcviii] The Communist East German state formed out of the Soviet zone of occupation in 1949 insisted that it had made a clean break with Nazism, which it argued was a direct result of capitalism. However this was not entirely true: the East German state subsequently employed 520,000 former Nazis.[xcix] When I arrived to take up my post as Reuters correspondent in East Berlin in 1971, my first interview was with the head of the government press office, Kurt Blecha, who joined the Nazi Party in 1941.

Britain had been reluctant to go to war, but finally fought from beginning to end. It emerged with a glowing reputation but drained financially – the American wartime loans needed to be serviced and repaid. It had insisted on unconditional surrender, and now was responsible for the defeated German people in its zone of occupation. With the German government broken, it had to establish a military government of its own. With the German economy at a standstill, it was obliged to provide for the immediate necessities of the people. By 1947, Britain was spending $317 million per year on sustaining Germans at a time when its own economy was on its knees.[c] This led to sour jokes about Britain paying reparations to Germany. It was the opposite of Versailles. Instead of punishment, a helping hand. Rebuild, not run down.

However it did not start like that in 1945. While the Russians raped and pillaged and the Americans combined sweets with re-education, the British treated the defeated Germans with cold dislike.

From his dug-out in the Burmese jungle, my father wrote to my mother at the end of March 1945: "Remember that train journey [of ours] back across Germany in 1939. Remember the place names. München, Augsburg,

Nuremberg, Frankfurt, Koblenz, Köln, Venlo. Now we are coming back, in the persons of our soldiers with tanks and steel. I wonder what the arrogant [German] people who sat with us in the train are doing now?"

In Ratzeburg, later the home of my cousin Carl, a British major gave a lecture on democratic practices to locals selected to set up a new local council, and ended with the words: "Gentlemen, I don't think I trust you even 50%."[ci]

This hostile attitude was comprehensive. An official handout to British Occupying Personnel read: "You are going to a strange people in a strange enemy country." A policy paper by British Labour government minister Richard Crossman asserted that all Germans were guilty and potentially dangerous, and there should be no fraternisation. A research paper on the German character described them as fanatical, gloomy, morbid and manic[cii] A.J.P. Taylor, a star Oxford professor, published a vitriolic analysis of German history beginning: "The history of the Germans is a history of extremes. It contains everything except moderation... the Germans have never found a middle way of life."[ciii] Robert Vansittart, Britain's senior diplomat, argued that Germany was intrinsically aggressive, and urged that it be stripped of all its military capacity and heavy industry.[civ] The British historian Sir Lewis Namier forecast at the end of the 1940s that Germans could well produce a new Hitler by 1959.[cv] British newspapers remained largely negative about Germany until Queen Elizabeth visited Germany in 1965. The *Daily Express* for many years after the war had an editorial policy expressly forbidding complimentary coverage of Germany.

The British showed little concern for the effects of their carpet bombing. What remained of my mother's old haunts in Hamburg was now put at the disposal of the conquering compatriots of her husband. While the

Hamburg locals set about rebuilding the 6,200 acres of housing which had been destroyed (compared with 600 acres in London), the British authorities requisitioned the homes of over 50,000 Hamburgers for their own personnel, who enjoyed facilities for dining, swimming, boating, dancing, sports and cinema which they could not expect in post-war Britain.

After the German refugees from the east had moved on, my Belgian grandmother, by then exhausted, depressed and nearing the end of her life, had a British officer billeted on her in her Bergedorf home. Of Cologne, which was 85% destroyed, a British housing officer of 1945 wrote callously: "Cologne proved to be one of the most interesting places you could see if you wished to see bomb damage to houses at its best."[cvi]

By end of 1946, the British Control Commission had five times as many staff as their U.S. counterparts. The British indulged in extensive black market operations, and did their own share of looting: two million Deutschmarks worth of property was missing when the British moved out of the Krupp family villa in 1952. One British businessman tried to extort the 4711 eau de cologne formula from the German woman who owned it. But she had committed it to memory before destroying the paperwork, and refused to divulge it. British car-makers passed up a more legitimate opportunity to acquire the Volkswagen company. They judged its technology to be too poor.[cvii]

The British also started removing German industrial plant, including most of what was left at the Nobel dynamite factory in Krümmel which my grandfather used to manage. To them, it was a modest recompense for the war the Germans had imposed on them. The Germans however saw it as a ploy to prevent the German economy from reviving. Demonstrations broke out in the industrial Ruhr area. In the eastern zone, the Russians were dismantling even more and shipping it to the Soviet

Union, but the menacing presence of the Red Army discouraged open dissent.

By the bitter winter of 1946-47, Germans in the western zones of the country were in dire straits. Many were close to starvation, men dropped at machines, signalmen fainted on the railways, cups of tea and ink froze, Hamburg was deprived of electric light from 7 a.m. to 10 p.m. In one newspaper there was only one light bulb, which the responsible British officer jealously guarded.

In Ratzeburg, the earth froze in the cemetery and coffins had to be piled into a room: the British were denazifying the explosives expert and did not allow him to blast graves.[cviii] Conditions were dangerously ripe for insurrection.

Chapter 9

WHAT BRITAIN?

"I have no easy words for the nation. I cannot say when we will emerge into easier times" – British Prime Minister, Clement Attlee, 1947

Millions of Britons celebrated VE Day – Victory in Europe – in May 1945. The war had been tough but Britons had won through. As a nation they could hold their heads high, Churchill was the hero and it was time to relax and party. My mother did not however. Her husband was still battling his way down Burma to defeat the Japanese.

The soldiers of the Burma campaign never quite overcame their bitterness at being a "forgotten army." Their battlefields were on the other side of the world in a country which few Britons could imagine. Not for them the cheering crowds who greeted liberating troops in Europe. Burmese disliked the British and showed it openly as the war-weary British Army gradually rid their country of the Japanese invader. Churchill, stung by the easy surrender of British troops in Malaya early in the war, felt progress was slow, and refrained from the heroic accolades he gave to other forces.

My father would change his tune somewhat in his late 80s, but what his family heard of his wartime service in the years immediately afterwards was firstly not much, and secondly largely negative. After a period of combat service, he was designated an intelligence officer. It was a promotion, but meant crawling out into the jungle to find dead Japanese soldiers.

"I spent Easter Saturday wresting secrets from dead men," he wrote to my mother in April 1945. "A dusty track, on either side the green jungle pitted with trenches, shell-holes, splintered trees, and the corpses, some half-buried with their boots sticking out, others just lying with the flesh rotting – black with flies. Equipment littered everywhere, bandages, blood, decaying food, dead mules, gun ammunitions and dank squalor… I poke methodically around among the corpses and empty trenches, collecting maps, diaries, identity discs. I appear nonchalant, but as you may imagine I don't like it at all – I who have fainted before this at the sight of blood. It took me nearly till this evening to wash the smell from my hands." To set off any explosive booby traps the Japanese might have placed under the bodies, he tied a string to a limb, retired to a distance and tugged at the corpse.

Worse still, my father could not return when Japan surrendered and the war came to an end in August 1945. As Britain slowly reasserted its rule over the parts of the Empire it had lost, he and more than a million other British conscripts had to serve on into 1946. Long after the war which they had been summoned to fight against hostile powers had been won, the Army kept them stranded thousands of miles from their families.

He was set to interview Japanese prisoners and Burmese politicians. When he asked Japanese generals why they thought they lost the war, they replied: "Circumstances changed." When he asked Burmese politicians what sort of government they wanted, they answered: "Without the British." This occupied him for eight months before he was demobilised and could take a ship home.

In that time, he drew his own conclusions about what he had achieved as a soldier: "One wonders if one is really doing the Burmans a good turn. Since this campaign, I have walked through quite a chunk of Burma, and after careful observation, I feel that they are only a little better off by becoming our subjects again. In some areas, the Japs treated them badly, but in others they appear to have treated them quite well. And under neither of us are they free subjects, politically or economically."

By the time he got back to England in May 1946, no one was interested any more in giving a returning soldier a hero's welcome. My mother noticed he had weeping tropical sores all over his body. He spent 10 days in a special hospital in Southampton before rejoining his family. My brother and I were five and two. We must have wondered who he was.

Over the years, the obituary columns of British newspapers have testified to the numerous acts of conspicuous bravery by which British soldiers distinguished themselves. But my father was not the only Briton to be disenchanted. On D-Day, British deserters had been sitting 10 to a cell in a Glasgow prison.[cix] Those who fought their way across Europe after the landings often did so circumspectly, preferring to occupy territory after superior weapon power had flattened resistance rather than fight their way through on foot.

Their generals were anxious to maintain a fighting spirit, but they did not expect their men to sacrifice themselves in suicidal onslaughts as in World War I. U.S. General Omar Bradley was particularly careful with the lives of his soldiers.[cx] Supreme Commander Dwight Eisenhower agonised on the eve of D-Day as he inspected first wave troops he knew were likely to perish. British General Bernard Montgomery likewise confessed in his diaries to worrying about casualties on the eve of the Battle of El Alamein. He wore simple battle-dress like ordinary soldiers and lived close to them in a caravan. These were generals who had learned compassionate lessons from the heartless waste of lives in the previous war.

My demobilised father traveled around the country seeking a teaching post. The best had already gone. He found a job in Worcester (taking the place of a teacher seconded to Berlin) and lived for six months in bachelor lodgings while he searched for a home for his family still living 80 miles away in Reading. With peace, life had become worse, not better.

As the winter of 1946 drew in, the same severe cold that wore down Germans also gripped Britain. Electricity was cut because frozen coal could not be delivered to power stations. Trains were dirty and late. Food was increasingly rationed. No wonder my father refrained from telling his children of his wartime exploits. They brought him no reward. He had not wanted to go to war, had done his duty as a conscript, but now felt anything but a winner.

The winter of 1946/47 was the nadir for Britain and Germany, and indeed for much of the rest of Europe. Our family lived in a house with water heated by a coal stove, an unheated kitchen on a sloping floor of rough cement, and draughty rooms heated by a few electric fires which we could only use sparingly because my father could scarcely pay the bills. Frost formed patterns overnight on the window panes.

In Germany, millions remained close to starvation. My cousin Hilde remembers hunger drove her to nibble chunks off the bread her mother sent her to buy for the whole family with ration stamps. She is eternally grateful that her mother pretended not to notice. Anneliese Bodecker in Berlin lived off roast barley corns, ground up to make soups tasting like sawdust, and semolina cooked with marjoram in pots fashioned out of soldiers' steel helmets.[cxi] The British tried to swallow Woolton pie, made of potatoes, turnips, parsnips and carrots. Despite the end of hostilities, the torment dragged on.

At this stage came a change of tack which changed mindsets permanently. The United States realised that the Soviet Union would henceforth be its rival, not ally, and set on a policy of containment to safeguard the West. Instead

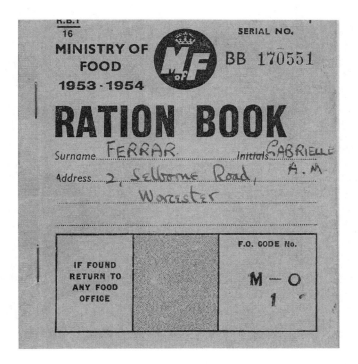

Victory came with hardship: the ration book my family needed to buy provisions after the war.

of leaving Germans to suffer their just deserts, and the rest of Europe to struggle on in misery, the U.S. decided to help. It launched the Marshall Plan of economic aid for European countries, including both Britain and Germany.

Despite the self-interest, this was a radical departure from the more punitive regime pursued by the European victors after WWI, and to varying extents by all the occupying powers immediately after 1945. It was a policy of healing through kindness. This novel approach marked the spirit of a whole generation and established a positive ethical benchmark. The Soviets could not compete with it. If I and my German cousins have lived well since then, it is in no small way thanks to the Marshall Plan. Not only did it benefit us materially, but it set an example of reconciliation which influenced our relations with each other.

The British too recognised that they had to change their approach. The Manchester Guardian wrote in August 1946 that the British were now hated by the Germans, having squandered previous goodwill by dismantling German industry. By 1947, the British had softened their occupation regime and were treating the Germans more as "people like us." Officials began inviting Germans socially and educational workers struck up good relationships with new German teachers.

British journalists built up new German media under British military control.[cxii] Among them was my future boss at Reuters, Gerald Long, then serving as a military officer in the Intelligence Corps. They were very young. Rudolf Augstein, 22, founded *Der Spiegel* with British Major John Challoner, 23.[cxiii] The British could not run the media themselves, as they lacked the language, so they sought out Germans such as the young Axel Springer who were both capable and untarnished by Nazi connections. The British concentrated on filtering out ex-Nazis and setting editorial principles.

Most candidates with the right professional qualifications had been involved with the old regime. There had been no opposition press. So the British let through journalists who belonged to the Hitler Youth, but tried to keep out the heart-and-soul Nazis. No candidate admitted to that status however, for obvious reasons. They appeared with "whitewash certificates" purporting to anti-Nazi credentials. These included endorsements from reputed German politicians, academics and artists, and occasionally even letters from refugee Jews who had been eminent in pre-war Germany.

George Clare, a Viennese Jew who escaped to England and later became an author, spent several weeks interrogating a candidate who continued to swear innocence despite being confronted with an increasing amount of incriminating evidence. Only when Clare, who was serving with the British Military Government, brought forth the man's signed National Socialist Party card with a photo did the candidate give in and sign a confession. He was one of 12 former Nazis excluded from the new *Nord-West-Deutscher-Rundfunk* broadcasting station. Six months later he had a job with another broadcaster.

Clare's boss, Hugh Carleton-Greene, later a Director-General of the BBC and then broadcasting Controller for the British zone, believed the filtering process was not a waste of time. "We did not attain our ideal, or, if we did, only for a fleeting moment. But we did wrench German broadcasting away from both its Weimar and its Nazi roots and we did provide a new structure."[cxiv]

The new structure was notably liberal. Carleton-Greene allowed his broadcasters latitude, and in newspapers German journalists were allowed to publish their own critical editorials underneath the official British ones. The Germans were astonished. They had been defeated and the new rulers were exposing themselves voluntarily to a free flow of diverse opinion. The British took the risk and it paid off by allowing new standards of objective journalism to take root in Germany.

At Göttingen University, British education officers found the students had childlike minds and were ignorant of anything but Nazi propaganda. The British authorities invited Germans to seminars on democracy, post-war reconciliation and conflict-resolution at Wilton Park in Britain. They picked Germans they thought would be influential in post-war society, and the Germans taking part valued the experience highly.[cxv]

In the political field, both Americans and British took an enlightened path by establishing strong institutions of government at grass roots and regional levels. Both

Allies now focused on avoiding the mistakes of Versailles. They provided help instead of humiliation, reconciliation instead of revenge.

When Hugh Carleton-Green died in 1987, German television paid him the compliment of a 90-minute documentary on his life and work. By that time, the German media had taken the lead in convincing reluctant Germans to acknowledge the crimes of the Nazi period. The tribute was a tacit acknowledgement of the inspiration for their newfound honesty and independence.

I myself grew up as a boy consuming publications which showed no such tolerance to the defeated. Like most of my male school-mates, I devoured comics and war stories rejoicing in the downfall of the German enemies. The British soldiers and airmen had handsome faces and were level-headed and brave. The Germans were hysterical and exuded hatred. The British won and the Germans were crushed. This reading inspired me to draw pictures of pilots firing guns into Germans. Today I find this shameful, but then it seemed normal. I learned that defending the right requires fighting, that the military represents the national spirit, that grown-ups go to war, and that Munich was disgraceful appeasement.

Until the age of 15, I wanted to make a career in the Royal Navy. I took a training cruise on a ship of the Royal Naval Reserve and practised firing shells across the Bay of Biscay. I paraded in uniform every Saturday morning in my school's Combined Cadet Force. A former Guards sergeant-major inspected the barrel of my rifle, the blanco on my webbing and the shine on my hob-nailed military boots. The rifle was a WWI model, but when I fired it on Field Day, its heavy bullets tore the target to shreds. I was being taught to kill.

Once a year, the whole Cadet Force paraded past a monument in front of Worcester Cathedral remembering the dead of two World Wars. Nobody questioned the warlike nature of our activities. The Saturday morning parades were compulsory. For 10 years after the end of the war, my father received letters, even from his own father, addressed to Major H. Ferrar, as if the military rank he held in Burma were still relevant.

The British, who had been reluctant to contemplate war in the 1930s, now seemed sceptical about peace. They had saved the world through force of arms, and should be ready to do it again, by developing nuclear weapons for example. When Europe began a rapprochement based on Franco-German reconciliation, the British stood aside, which made me wonder which side *I* should be on.

When the headmistress of my primary school invited pupils to her study to watch the televised coronation of Queen Elizabeth in 1953, I found it natural that the monarch should be attended by long columns of marching soldiers. They gave force to the sense of sacred duty the young Queen radiated. My kindly female teachers taught that we British had a responsibility to other peoples. Once a year, we collected money for poor little black boys in Africa, to be administered by Church of England missionaries.

I identified with the muscular nobility of this concept, but even at that early age I had a niggling feeling that something was suspect. If Britain did rule supreme, why did my father's *Times* bring a steady flow of news about colonies winning independence? If the Biggles of W.G. Johns' war stories was so complete a British hero, why did the pink parts of the map denoting the British Empire shrink with every new atlas? Talk of a "Commonwealth" did not fool me. We were losing power and respect. Furthermore, why did my father have to stop smoking his pipe for a month to save up for the family to take a Sunday coach-trip to pick bluebells? Why did winning a war leave us badly off?

I needed to go to Germany to begin to understand.

Chapter 10

REBUILDING

But do you LIKE Germans? – question by my mother

The ship wallowed in the choppy waves of the North Sea. The whole family had been seasick during the night, since this was a cargo boat adapted for just a few passengers. A kindly steward in a white jacket was on hand to convince us we were enjoying the voyage and restore appetites for breakfast. "Land ahead," I shouted, aged six, staring ahead over the bows. Heligoland passed, then the broad estuary of the Elbe taking us slowly up to Hamburg. It was 1950, and we were starting our summer holiday in Germany.

Holidays abroad then were cumbersome, to say the least. They started with an early-morning taxi to the station. Then all day on steam trains with long waits for connections, ending at nightfall in an English harbour. We trundled with suitcases through customs sheds, waiting for officers in black uniforms and white hats to chalk crosses on them, and then up the gangway on to a ship towering in the darkness. The next morning, we eased into a continental port where workers speaking foreign languages scurried to their jobs, fresh and vigorous after their night's sleep. It was a passage from one world to another, to a melée of different tongues and smells and sights. Salty breezes introduced me to my mother's country of origin.

Nobody else in my Worcester school went on such holidays. When the teacher asked my class where we went on holidays, the rest said Wales, Cornwall or the Lake District. I replied "Hamburg." He heard the Humber, and asked why I went to this industrial region of England. When he grasped I had been to a German city, he paused, said nothing and passed on. Germany? A holiday?

That's what my parents had decided. Or rather my mother had, for this was part of her game plan to show that the Nazis could not get the better of her. Not that she explained the plan to us then, but gradually over the years I grasped what she was up to. The war started by the Nazis had separated her family, and now she was demonstrating that *her* concept of life was more durable. That meant renewing contact with her German family and behaving as if the nasty business in between made no difference. It was an admirable act of defiance, but it did imply that certain matters went unmentioned, such as my uncle's membership of the SA.

At age six however, I had my eyes open, as befitted a future foreign correspondent. As the train rumbled very slowly over a Rhine bridge, I noticed flattened ruins as far as I could see, with an enormous black Gothic cathedral rising over the wreckage on the far side of the river. Cologne, my father said. Bombed. He told me nothing else, but I knew who had done it. We had. It was beyond me to consider what happened to the people on the ground or to the airmen dicing with death above. But I did know our side had caused this wreckage, and I did not feel displeased. I had those little shivers of excitement that a little boy feels when he sees other boys' toys broken in the sandpit. At six, it was good to be on the winning side and righteously mix patriotism with superiority.

Arrival at the home of *Tante Luz* and *Onkel Johannes* in Nuremberg required an act of mild schizophrenia. No more relishing in destruction, nor even patriotism – it did not fit. A modest sense of superiority was still useful, as my five cousins were all older than me, which needed careful handling by a six-year-old. However as it turned out, I did not need to bristle. Even though we were crowding into a flat they had only just occupied, the German family made us warmly welcome. *Tante Luz* was as comfy as an aunt should be, and *Onkel Johannes* offered the solid hospitality of a good middle-class home. The smell of brewing coffee and drifting cigar smoke was seductively exotic.

Onkel Johannes may have been hard up, but cigars were part of his daily life, as they were for many other German men of his generation. By 1950, Germany's industrial output was one third higher than it had been in 1936. Its collapsed economy had been resurrected by bold reforms enacted by leaders who dramatically broke with convention – and inspired me as I grew up.

In June 1948, the western military governments introduced the new D-mark currency in their zones, changing it one-for-ten against limited quantities of old Reichsmarks. At the same time, West German economic chief Ludwig Erhard unilaterally scrapped all rationing, price fixing and other economic controls. The currency exchange soaked up surplus money, and the Erhard reforms created a free market economy such as Germany had never known.

American administrators complained about Erhard to General Lucius Clay, the American military governor. By liberalising the still vulnerable Germany economy, they feared he would cause a catastrophe. Clay called Erhard in and accused him of changing regulations which the U.S. had imposed.

"I did not change them. I abolished them," Erhard replied coolly.

"My experts tell me your reforms will fail," countered Clay.

"My experts tell me the same thing," said Erhard, at which point Clay instinctively decided to back him all the way.[cxvi] They were right. Germany's course took a decisive turn for the better thanks to these two characters who were strong and bold enough to think differently.

It was a historic moment. A West German leader had stood up against the occupying authorities on a constructive, peaceful issue and won. It gave confidence to the German people that at least on this point they were recognised as right. As for Clay, he had shown courage, not in resisting but in giving way. He chose to be soft when his colleagues in the U.S. military government wanted to be hard.

Hoarding ceased overnight, and shops filled with food, schnapps, chocolate, cigarettes and toiletries which people thought they would never see again. A shop which one day had no spare parts to mend a bicycle the next day had 60 new bicycles for sale. "Suddenly, there was everything" or "it was like seeing a Christmas tree" – this is how Germans today remember an undertaking which they count as the most important post-war event alongside reunification. [cxvii] After a brief surge of unemployment as the tightening money supply took effect, conditions were established for the German economic miracle, combining a sound currency with growth, profitability, rising consumer purchasing power and a negotiated peace on the labour front.

While the British economy grew by 30% between 1945 and 1951, West Germany's grew by 300%. The number of nylon stockings sold in West Germany rocketed from less than a million in 1950 to 58 million by 1953. [cxviii] By 1958, West Germany's economy was bigger than Britain's and in 1960 its growth was still roaring away at 9%. Britain's trade with Europe in 1950 was still less than in 1913; it devalued the pound in 1949 and again in 1967. [cxix]

I could see the economic miracle with my own eyes at the age of six in 1950. Five years earlier, 521 bombers of the Royal Air Force had destroyed the medieval heart of Nuremberg, including the castle, the city hall, almost all the churches and about 2,000 ancient houses. The RAF campaign diary described it as "a near-perfect example of area bombing." [cxx]

In 1950, builders outside my relatives' flat in the central Königstrasse were hammering at a new department store that grew daily in front of my eyes. The whole city was a vast rebuilding site. Many years later, my male cousins told me they clandestinely crept out on to the roof to get a better view of the workers banging away opposite. This was needless to say strictly *verboten* by my aunt, but I cannot quite forgive them for excluding me.

Between the currency reform and the economic miracle came the Berlin blockade imposed by the Soviet Union in retaliation. By 1948, Germany had become the focus of the Cold War developing between the Soviets and the Americans. The wartime victors divided conquered Germany into zones of occupation, with the Soviets taking the eastern part where Berlin was located. Berlin however, because it had been the German capital, was subdivided into western and eastern zones. This complicated arrangement was not intended to be permanent, but Cold War rivalries prevented any agreement that would allow Germany to come together as one state. The arrangement was inherently unstable and resulted in endless tensions and flare-ups, in particular over Berlin, isolated deep within the Soviet-governed part of Germany.

The Soviets realised the currency change effectively divided the western zones of Germany from their own. They still entertained ambitions of swinging a united Germany into their camp, and did not want the West to get away with it. By blocking land access to West Berlin, they reckoned they could exploit the West's soft spot. West Berlin was isolated inside the Soviet zone and could never hold out if essential supplies could not get through. So the West would either have to back down over the currency or give up West Berlin.

The Soviets believed they held a winning card, and many on the Western side thought so too. Again, the intervention of a handful of inspired men who went against mainstream opinion achieved a victory which was crucial for the whole of Europe. General Lucius Clay was for a second time the prime mover, and this time he was the hard man. Against most military and political advice, he devised a plan to supply West Berlin by air for as long as it was needed.

Many on his own side thought this preposterous and favoured accommodation with the Soviets, but other courageous free-thinkers gave him support. West Berlin mayor Ernst Reuter, a Social Democrat, rallied 80,000 Berliners and proclaimed the city's determination to hold out. He urged the West not to leave. His words inspired his fellow-Socialist, Britain's Ernest Bevin, who argued as Foreign Secretary for resistance to the Soviet blockade at a time when British opinion was still hostile to Germany.

Clay won the backing of U.S. President Harry Truman, who declared: "We are going to stay. Period." Reuter then rallied a further 300,000 Berliners and declared: "We cannot be bartered, we cannot be negotiated, we cannot be sold... Whoever would surrender this city, whoever would surrender the people of Berlin... would surrender himself."

That shamed those in the West who had been thinking of doing precisely that. They were remarkably bold words for a German at a time when his people were still treated as pariahs. A German with little or no power asserted himself as a democrat, and won. The massive airlift, which cost the lives of hundreds of Allied airmen in accidents and included drops of sweets to Berlin children, bonded West Germans with the Western occupiers. Instead of weakening the West's presence in Germany, it strengthened their popularity and showed the Soviets in an oppressive light. After a year in which the airlift went from strength to strength, the Soviets backed off.[cxxi]

The West German economic miracle was free to take off. Soon I saw Germans traveling all over Europe, first in Volkswagens and then in Mercedes. German goods became bywords for reliability and functionality, to the point that one manufacturer could successfully sell cars in Britain with the German slogan *Vorsprung durch Technik*. On my first visit to Germany in 1950 however, I threw up after eating a *Nusstorte*: I was defeated by a German cream-cake. The economic miracle was a bit too much for me, but not for long.

Germany offered not just a bountiful future, but also a pastoral past. When the little steam train from Munich squealed to a stop in Benediktbeuern station, a cart drawn by oxen was waiting to pick us up. As dusk fell, we trundled slowly along a rough track, our luggage swaying from side to side with the bumps until we reached a sprawling old house, the *Glashütte* – the converted glass factory. I was fascinated by the stream flowing underneath it to drive the wheels of the electricity plant. This too was exotic. On the horizon rose the majestic *Benediktenwand,* a mountain higher than anything I had seen in England.

Our encounter with the Küchler family who lived there was another part of my mother's post-war strategy. The *Herr Professor* was a fellow-victim of the Nazis, the *Frau Professor* a Frenchwoman delighted to welcome my father, a teacher of French language and literature. The common European background took precedence over our different national provenances. At age six, I learned this was the natural way of things.

Then on to a farm up in the Bavarian Alps which took us in as paying guests. I can still see the courtyard with happy chickens scratching away, and a cock on the dung heap. I can sense the cows munching in the stable, smell the sweetish odour of freshly-drawn milk, and taste the honey from the beehive on homemade butter and newly-baked buns. I can hear the crashes as thunderstorms broke over the mountains. I can feel the sway of the carriages with wooden seats and outside platforms in which a little railway engine pulled us up towards turquoise pools of glacier water where we bathed. I can see the German soldier's helmet which I brought back from the nearby woods. This did *not* fit with my mother's post-war vision, and I was told to take it back smartly.

I was tantalised by the sense of latent violence Germany conveyed. The stories my mother told me as a small boy about Auschwitz caused me to fantasise that she was a Jew herself, which she was not. For years I associated the sandy soil and dark fir forests of North Germany with images of thousands of dead bodies. The pleasant porch of my uncle's comfortable villa, the blackcurrant bushes laden with fruit, the leafy surrounding trees and the cobbled road outside. All seemed decent and quiet, but I felt something sinister in the air.

On a later visit in 1953, I spent long hours as a nine-year-old watching trains passing on the nearby line between Hamburg and Berlin. Only one train, the "Flying Hamburger," went through across Communist East Germany to Berlin. All the rest were local steam trains going only a few miles further to the zonal border. I could feel war not far off: the Cold War. Those early experiences of Germany helped me develop a journalist's instinct for trouble.

In 1953, my mother was able to lay her hands on the remnants of her German father's inheritance, 16 years after his death. He had invested his savings in German state bonds, advising his children that these were the safest. In later years, we mocked his judgment – the war had wiped out much of their value. The legacy in any case went quickly on hospital bills for my elder brother, who nearly died from peritonitis on this visit. German doctors saved him with penicillin, first produced in Britain 10 years earlier. My mother used the last few D-marks of the inheritance to buy a seemingly indestructible *Mädler* suitcase and a heavy-duty, steel bean-slicer.

In these early stays in Germany, I picked up a few indirect remarks indicating my father took distance from *Onkel Johannes* because of his SA past. That did not stop him from sharing *Onkel Johannes'* cigars and hospitality and there was no discord on the surface. Doubtless he wished to avoid difficulties with my mother, who was set on acting as if this was no longer relevant. The man thought of principle and the woman of family harmony. I was split between two viewpoints, already as a small boy.

My father knew that there was nothing he could do about *Onkel Johannes'* past. There was no chance of an open, man-to-man conversation at the time. My father did have such a conversation 35 years later, and its outcome surprised him. Then it was all too fresh. I myself could not ask questions. Nobody told me not to, but I sensed this was forbidden ground. Likewise, nobody ever said anything about the war service of my mother's two brothers. My mother chose to turn her mind away and focus on family life as usual.

The enforced silence went far beyond *Onkel Johannes*. Ex-Nazis were prominent in all walks of life. It was impossible to exclude more than the most deeply involved, since there were too few qualified people without a Nazi past. Living in denial and taking strength from their numbers, most did not acknowledge any wrongdoing, let alone apologise.

The western Allies after a time discontinued re-education as not worth the trouble, or even counter-productive. They wanted the Germans on their side in the Cold War. So ex-Nazi Kurt-Georg Kiesinger could be Chancellor from 1965 to 1968, ex-Nazi Reinhard Gehlen could be spy chief (as he was under Hitler) and ex-Nazi Wernher von Braun could head the American space programme. This led many foreigners to question whether Germans were really being made to learn anything from the war. In hindsight, it was psychologically unrealistic to expect Germans to change their fundamental attitudes in a few short years. That however would come later.

With the world watching them like a hawk, Germans had to keep their heads down. They had to learn to be quiet rather than loud, meek rather than domineering, and cooperative rather than pushy. This left little room for lofty ambitions – except in the field of material success. In the post-war years, Germans acquired a reputation as businessmen devoid of polish and humour, but patently working like furies.

"We were materialists. We did not want to have anything to do with politics, the military or weapons. We were angels of peace," said Berliner Peter Lorenz of his early 20s at that time.

I experienced this work ethic in Germany in my teens. When I stayed one August with the family of a Hamburg import-export manager, the husband was supposed to be on holiday. He and his wife referred to it as *Erholung* "recuperation," in other words preparing to work even harder. During his *Erholung* he was constantly on the telephone to his office. His wife clucked, but tacitly approved. Her spouse was putting his shoulder to the wheel in the only way Germans were allowed.

When I took a holiday job as an intern at Deutsche Shell, my middle-aged boss was literally breathless with industry every day. Business, I learned from these Germans, was a hectic rush and unrelenting hard work. Work, in fact, was the principal purpose of their lives. When I spent a year in Communist East Germany, a country far less efficient than West Germany, I found Germans there too took pride that they were deemed the best workers of the Eastern bloc. In Britain by contrast, ostensive striving was considered vulgar. It was better to appear to be achieving effortlessly.

I was 16 when I first struck out into Germany on my own. Again, I set out on the steam train to London, the underground to Liverpool Street Station, a boat train to

Harwich, an overnight sea crossing, a night train across Holland, and through passport and customs checks on to Frankfurt. There I changed trains, already smitten by love. I had fallen into conversation with a German girl from Fulda, who also had to wait for a connection in Frankfurt. We had coffee in the station buffet. I offered to pay, but she patted my hand and said: "Thank you, but keep your money for yourself."

Due to another part of my mother's post-Nazi life strategy, I was ill-prepared for this encounter with the other sex. When I was 15, my mother wrote to my headmaster forbidding that I attend sex lessons which had just been introduced in my English school. Such matters, she insisted, belonged inside the family, the unit which the Nazis had done their best to undermine. The other boys in my class (there were no girls) knew I was not exactly an innocent – I too had consumed the illicit sexual literature circulating beneath desks for the past year. I kept face by teasing them about looking pale and shaky at the knees when they came out of the session.

Family instruction however turned out to be a slim, uninspiring manual laid on my desk by an embarrassed father as I struggled with maths homework. It did not help me much in dealing with girls, and even less with the maths homework. I struggled to grasp the technical parts, and the emotional aspects were daunting. As for my mother, she never told me anything at all about the subject.

I therefore found myself on uncharted ground a year later in 1960 with the *Fräulein* from Fulda. After some hapless stuttering, I was left to cherish her sweet smile in my befuddled mind as I tackled the last part of the journey to Nuremberg, on modern track over which the electrified train glided at a speed I had never experienced before.

My German cousins were engaged in advanced scholarly studies with Latin-sounding appellations, but none of them could manage much in a modern foreign language. So during my six weeks of swimming in the Starnberg Lake, climbing to mountain huts and sleeping in the hay with my youngest cousin, I never spoke a word of English. When I passed through London's Paddington station on the way back, I met a former class teacher from Worcester and could hardly blurt out a word in my mother tongue. At home, I prattled on enthusiastically about everything I had done, and my mother asked:

"But do you *like* Germans?"

"Well, yes."

"Oh!" was all she could say.

Chapter 11

COMING OF AGE

We knew nothing of what went on inside – German aunt

By the 1960s, neither the British nor the Germans felt satisfied with the status quo. The British abolished compulsory military service for young men, and one of the most popular radio shows, *The Goons*, mercilessly poked fun at British military pretensions. *Oh, What A Lovely War* did the same in the London theatre. The one-sidedness of British wartime stories made us teenagers suspect we were being manipulated for character-building purposes.

Television, theatre and cinema took up against the whole British way of life: the self-satisfaction, the sense of duty, the rules of behaviour and the post-war stodginess of slow decline. At 18, like many of my age, I felt part of a movement sweeping away the old to make place for new thinking and new values. I listened to the Beatles in a damp cellar, discussed experimental theatre, canvassed for the Labour Party and took part in student protest rallies in Paris.

My schoolmates and I felt part of a vanguard, and in this we were egged on by the German Jewish teacher in my Worcester school. Cosmopolitan and provocative, Alex Natan inspired dull boys to win university scholarships and encouraged free-thinkers to think with even greater abandon. When not teaching history and German, he played opera to sixth-formers. In his spare time, he wrote sports commentaries for German newspapers. My mother disapproved of his racy German style, full of American idioms, but I relished it. In this small, provincial town of the West Midlands, he made us feel like world citizens.

Refugee Jewish intellectuals were transforming English culture during that period. Writers Arthur Koestler and Martin Esslin, poet Michael Hamburger, publishers André Deutsch and George Weidenfeld, film-maker Alex Korda, philosopher Karl Popper, social scientist and music patron Claus Moser, conductor Georg Solti, opera impresario Rudolf Bing and art historian Ernst Gombrich – all left indelible marks on the English cultural scene, drawing it out of its pre-war insularity. At the time, it would have been relevant to ask who in this field was *not* a refugee Jew.[cxxii]

My parents befriended Natan because he was a fellow exile from the Nazis. He became godfather to my younger sister. One Christmas he brought a goose to remind my mother of Christmas dinners in her German childhood. In Germany, the goose would have been fattened for weeks. In post-war austerity Britain, it was thin and scraggy, but a goose all the same. Natan was not universally popular at my Worcester school. From comments by boys, it was clear many were unaware he was a Jew who had escaped from the Nazis. They heard his accent and assumed he was a German: the enemy.

From my mother I had learned about the German slaughter of six million Jews long before the Holocaust was made famous by an American television film of 1978. However, I started to question the ease with which she took up again with her German family, and her readiness to sweep unpleasant facts under the carpet. If *Onkel Johannes* had belonged to a Nazi organisation, why could this not be openly discussed in our Anglo-German family? Did my mother have double values?

I felt similarly when a German aunt, *Tante Anneliese*, drove me around the picturesque *Vierländen* area near Hamburg and we came upon the former Neuengamme concentration camp. The aunt said: "We knew nothing of what went on inside." Was this true? Possibly, but why? Was she too overcome by grief that her young husband had been killed in the war? Or did she not care to look?

If she *did* know, why did she need to pretend otherwise? She could hardly fear I would despise her – we got on well together. Or did she feel shame, because what happened offended her own principles, but she had done nothing to stop it?

Subsequently I found out that in April 1945 the inmates of Neuengamme were driven on a forced march that stopped over in Bergedorf, the small town where my aunt lived. This mass of distressed wretches had been halted right nearby. I sensed that this was not a simple matter, but I was at an age where I wanted real answers, and I did not receive them.[cxxiii]

A new generation of West Germans was meanwhile also challenging the refusal of their elders to acknowledge what they had done during the war. Like me in Britain, young Germans chafed at the stifling silence surrounding the subject. The young, who had not been involved with the Nazis themselves, demanded a change. Concentrating on material success was no longer enough. The media set up under liberal British influence began to militate for Germans to acknowledge war crimes more openly. Educators did the same, and in 1963-65 the judiciary held a series of "Auschwitz trials" of 22 SS extermination camp guards, at which 273 witnesses attested to the sadistic torture and slaughter of millions. Few Germans until then appreciated the extent of the depravity, because they had preferred not to inquire.

For those pushing the trials through, often against public indifference or hostility, they were a rite of passage for eventual re-admission to the community of nations. Unlike the Nuremberg Trials of 1945, Germans conducted these trials themselves. They were assuming responsibility for war crimes. As such, the "Auschwitz trials" of 1963-65 were a first step to regaining true independence. Most of my British friends considered the trials merely proved how repugnant Germans were. I myself, with a foot in both camps, saw them as a move towards normality.

The young German generation swung to the left, as in Britain and France. These new thought-leaders interpreted the Nazis in terms of Marxist class conflict, and narrow-mindedly attributed the rise of Hitler to the scheming of German capitalists. They opposed the West German-American alliance as a capitalist arrangement benefiting ex-Nazis. They scorned democracy as a sham covering up the past, and consumerism as mindless. It was an uprising of young hotheads against their elders. This came to a dramatic climax in the late 1960s and 1970s when the fanatical Baader-Meinhof movement began murdering leading protagonists of the democratic state, particular those prominent in the free market economy.

They were obviously seeking to provoke the West German state into violent retaliation. It was an attempt to create war, not peace. In a still unstable Germany, the pendulum had swung to the opposite extreme. This offended a person such as me, conditioned to moderation by my past and my background. If there was to be a deep-seated change in attitudes, it would not consist of exchanging one regime of murder for another. For me, even though I was of the same generation, the extreme leftists were too much like old Germans – unbalanced and destructive.

Moreover, if the West German leftists were correct, conditions in the Communist part of Germany must by comparison have been better. By that time, I knew this was clearly not so. The German Democratic Republic in the east had been established as an entirely new state representing a clean break from the Nazi regime. That may have impressed the new young thinkers in the West, but the price the Easterners had been paying in the meantime was oppression and dictatorship.

Neither the Soviets nor the Western powers ruled out Germany one day reuniting. Indeed they all claimed this was their aim. But Stalin only wanted a socialist Germany. Russians were used to absolutism, but Germans would never willingly accept such compulsion when a democratic alternative was working well in the West.

Stalin carried on with reparations from the Soviet zone of Germany for far longer than in the Western zones. In his hardened mind, this was a just recompense for Soviet losses, but it did nothing to enamour East Germans to the Soviet cause. He sent Walter Ulbricht from the Soviet Union to head the new East German state. Ulbricht, as I was to experience personally some years later, was an unpleasant man with an irritatingly grating voice. He survived Stalin's purges of the 1930s through ruthlessly betraying his comrades. That may have been necessary in Moscow, but certainly did not qualify him to be popular in Germany. Ulbricht knew that, and by the time I made my first visit to Germany in 1950 he had established a dictatorship in the eastern half.

The more unpopular he became, the more the Soviets were obliged to support him by military power, with the result that their own chances of appealing to Germans throughout the country diminished. The Soviets disliked him, but needed him. Stalin commented that Ulbricht's fist was larger than his head.[cxxiv]

In Ulbricht, the eastern part of post-war Germany thus had a leader who incorporated the most unfortunate character traits of Germans the world had learned to hate – he was bossy, selfish and prone to violence. A nasty German was back in power. This was clear to me as a boy in England just looking at his picture in newspapers. On the day of the foundation of the German Democratic

Republic (GDR) in October 1949, the regime's *Freie Deutsche Jugend* youth movement marched down Berlin's Unter den Linden street with burning torches – much like the SA did in Hitler's time. A year later, Ulbricht had 50,000 *Volkspolizei* quartered in barracks. West Germany was also beginning to rearm within the NATO alliance, but Ulbricht's was then the largest armed force in Europe apart from the occupying powers.[cxxv]

In June 1953, East Berlin workers rioted against higher work norms on building sites, and the East German regime immediately tottered. Its socialism was supposed to appeal to the Germans' best side, but the idealism had already been squandered. It was supposed to be a state for workers, but the workers did not want it. For all their numbers, the new *Volkspolizei* lost control. The Soviets had to bring out tanks to crush the revolt. Although some West Germans imagined this was a fight for German reunification, it is unlikely the rioting workers thought so far. They wanted less work, more money and less harassment. But the violent repression of their protest put paid to any dwindling Soviet hopes of reuniting Germany under their own type of socialism. No Communist regime in Europe ever found a way to be popular. In the final analysis, it was a type of government sustained only by diktat, and in East Germany that meant the Soviets, or rather the power of the Red Army.

When I visited Hamburg again as a nine-year-old in 1953, a few weeks after the Berlin uprising, it was clear only one part of Germany could be frequented – the eastern part was out of bounds. Throughout my boyhood in England, I identified East Germany, like Hungary, Poland and other east European countries under Soviet sway, with grainy images of unrest and repression cropping up in newspapers and on television. This distant, hostile world was a far cry from the comfortable Germany I was getting to know in the west.

The GDR was the smaller, poorer part of Germany, lacking the industrial resources of the Ruhr. The huge battles which the Red Army had fought, dwarfing D-Day in the west, yielded the Soviet Union few returns. The Soviets bunkered down in their zone, which they made into a Cold War fortress. Their forces swelled to 380,000 soldiers, 4,000 tanks and 1,400 aircraft, spread over 777 barracks and 43 airfields, as well as medium-range nuclear missiles.[9] The number of Soviet and East German security personnel on East German territory eventually totaled 933,000, leading one observer to describe the German Democratic Republic as "a security service with a state."[cxxvi]

Until 1993, Soviet military accounted for half the population of my grandfather's town of origin, Neustrelitz. The magnificent Carolinum Gymnasium where my distant cousin Carl Roewer once went to school was turned into a Soviet military hospital.

In response to directives from Stalin, East Germany's Communist rulers in the early 1950s began terrorising their own citizens in order to consolidate the dictatorship. Thousands were imprisoned on imaginary charges of spying and sabotage. Victims later spoke of 12-hour interrogations, water torture, hunger, freezing cold, medical neglect, sleep deprivation, isolation, psychological terror and, as one put it, "this utter nothingness."[cxxvii]

East Germany remained mired in poverty, as the Communist command economy stumbled and failed. Many wartime ruins remained untouched for the next 40 years, as I could see for myself later when I came to live in East Berlin. Destruction in the eastern part of Europe had

---

9   A former member of the British Commanders-in-Chief Mission to the Soviet Forces in Germany, which had Allied rights to travel around East Germany, told me that the British military had comprehensive knowledge of all these Soviet deployments, down to the number plate of every Soviet vehicle. The Mission's advanced spying equipment and operational costs were paid by the West Berlin Senate.

everywhere been more severe than in the west. Marcel Reich-Ranicki, who lived in the post-war years in Warsaw, found East Berlin better off than devastated Poland. But he found West Berlin more prosperous than East Berlin, and East Germans were comparing with their German brethren in the west, not with Poland.[cxxviii]

By 1958, an estimated four million East Germans had fled to the West (2.3 million since the founding of the GDR).[cxxix] Cousin Carl crawled under a barrier into the West one New Year's Eve, evading the bullets of guards too drunk to shoot straight.[cxxx]

Berlin was a loophole. There were no physical barriers, since the division of Germany into East and West was not supposed to be permanent. Refugees could cross over into West Berlin unhindered, and then fly out to West Germany. Grete Roewer, the wife of cousin Carl, brought their four-year-old daughter out in this way. The Communist authorities wanted the girl to stay with her grandmother in Neustrelitz in the eastern zone. But Grete took the daughter to East Berlin, crossed into West Berlin, and from there they took a flight to Hamburg.

The Communist authorities had forcibly nationalised Carl Roewer's family grocery store in Neustrelitz in 1945 and placed compensation in East marks in a Neustrelitz bank. When Grete (a Hamburger) visited the remaining family, she was allowed to withdraw 15 East marks per day. To get it, she was summoned to the Director's office in the local bank, given the money and told to leave without talking to other customers. When she asked how much was on the account, the Director wrote it down on a piece of paper and silently showed it to her at a distance of six feet. She could not take the money out of East Germany, but she could spoil her Neustrelitz family with Hungarian salami and Bulgarian gherkins.

Many West Germans knew the East German state mainly through the hassle of maintaining relations with family members. The East German authorities harassed through border searches, travel hindrances and personal hostility. It was a means of exercising power over their strengthening western neighbour, and it corresponded with Communist dogma that life was a constant struggle between classes. Gradually, it became customary for West Germans to support relatives in the east with gifts and money. "With what we sent over the years, we could have built a house in Hamburg!" exclaimed Grete Roewer. But she did not begrudge it. It was a habit which would expand enormously over the years and serve West Germans well in the end.

In the meantime, East and West were growing apart. The two German populations separated by the Iron Curtain became alienated from each other. Marcel Reich-Ranicki found in 1958 that cultural journalists on the *Frankfurter Allgemeine Zeitung* did not know the name of the biggest publishing house in East Germany (*Aufbau-Verlag*)[cxxxi].

"We are not thinking of building a wall," declared Walter Ulbricht in August 1961 as East Germans fled in greater numbers to the west, bleeding his state of qualified specialists. A few days later he did just that. Or rather Erich Honecker did. Honecker, who was to rule the eastern part of Germany for 18 years, set up the post-war *Freie Deutsche Jugend* youth movement, which quickly grew to 400,000 strong. Members were taught Communist principles, and also to shoot and lead "an upright youth camp life."[cxxxii] The camps were much like the "Reich work camps" of the Nazis, except that they furthered the idea of an international working class rather than nation and race.

Honecker – few had heard of him in the west at that time – planned and implemented the building of the Berlin Wall, and brought it off without provoking a popular uprising among East Berliners or a military response from the West. The Western Allies scarcely reacted in the following days. As the Soviets had gambled, they did not want to engage in a major confrontation. Many on the Western side were quietly glad that the threat to East Germany's stability posed by the flight of its population was diminished. They reckoned the East German regime would feel more secure and be less prickly to deal with.

President Jack Kennedy told an advisor that the East German move was "not a very nice solution but... a hell of a lot better than a war." British Prime Minister Harold Macmillan wrote in his journal that "there is nothing illegal in the East Germans stopping the flow of refugees" and continued with his Scottish grouse shooting holiday. France's General de Gaulle did nothing. It was clearly unjust, but not worth upsetting East-West relations for.

Such *Realpolitik* cut no ice with me. I was only 17, but I was alert to the way Germans felt, and it seemed obvious that this was a deeply offensive act. West Berliners began deserting their city on the perception that the U.S. was weak and would not stand by them. Soviets and East Germans began multiplying provocations and obstructions around West Berlin.

Kennedy belatedly realised he was losing ground and sent General Lucius Clay back to West Berlin as his personal representative. Clay was privy to confidential security intelligence and knew the U.S. had clear military superiority over the Soviet Union. So when East German guards started checking American personnel at the Checkpoint Charlie border crossing, in contravention of agreements among the four occupying powers,[10] Clay ordered up American tanks to threaten them at pointblank range. He knew the Soviets would feel obliged to respond by bringing up their own tanks, but also knew they would never dare to escalate further. He was right. The sidelined East Germans ceased their checks. The Americans had retrieved the psychological advantage. We did not know

10   The Soviet Union, the United States, Britain and France

at the time, but the Soviets told Ulbricht to cool down, and the worst of this Berlin crisis was over.

Clay had again proved himself capable of thinking originally, accurately judging his opponents, acting decisively and keeping his nerve when his compatriots were losing theirs. Clay told Kennedy during the crisis: "I am not afraid of escalation." Kennedy's advisors continued to complain about him, as did Macmillan, but Kennedy backed Clay.[cxxxiii]

I myself watched fascinated from afar. I did not understand the subtle diplomacy behind the tank manoeuvring. I did not know that the Americans had military superiority over the Soviets, nor that General Clay was aware of this. But it was clear to me who had won.

In the following year, when Kennedy faced Khrushchev down over Soviet missiles sent to Cuba, my British schoolmates spoke fearfully of imminent nuclear war. Subsequent accounts showed the Americans did seriously consider launching nuclear strikes. On the British side, a retired Royal Air Force pilot told me 50 years later that as a 23-year-old he took to the air with fully-armed nuclear depth charges ready to destroy a Soviet nuclear-missile submarine which his squadron has been tracking for months through sonar buoys.

"We had to get it before it got Britain. We did not know whether we would have a country to return to, but we were young and did not quite appreciate what this meant," he said.

I myself sensed that the West had the upper hand and the crisis would pass. As others did in the past, I let instincts tell me. I was not alone in this judgment. In his memoirs, the British Ambassador in Moscow at the time, Frank Roberts, wrote that seen from Moscow the affair was less alarming and it was clear the Soviet leadership was not building up to a major crisis.[cxxxiv] Khrushchev later confirmed this in his memoirs.

One other personality besides Clay acted with the same gut feeling in the Berlin Wall crisis. That was the mayor of West Berlin, Willy Brandt. He publicly protested at the inhumanity of the Wall and called on the Western powers to act. He expressed the indignation and apprehension felt by millions of West Berliners and West Germans. The crisis established him as a leader, in the eyes of Germans and the world. Like Clay, he was to influence the course of German history by breaking the conventions.

Willy Brandt was a member of the Social Democrat (SPD) party, which had never held power in post-war Germany. He was no war hero, having spent the war in exile in Norway and Sweden. He was a different kind of German, in tune with the young people of the 1960s who wanted to transform everything.

I first visited Berlin in 1965 after the crisis passed its peak. I had finished a month's summer work in the Deutsche Shell offices in Hamburg, working alongside suave German executives with tans from their holidays in Italy. At that time, I cared little about what the British air force had done to Hamburg during the war, and it seemed a normal, well-run modern city.

There I became aware of the supreme quality of German theatre – every bit as good as in England or Russia, and I appreciated the priority Germans give to excellence in classical music and opera. I queued with my cousins and friends for cheap seats in the "gods" at the top of the house, peering down on to performances of unequalled quality. Beethoven, Schubert, Mozart, Bruckner and Mahler may have come from Austria, but in cultural terms at the time, this counted as Germany. At 18, I spent hours with a German student listening to different recordings of Beethoven's symphonies, arguing whether the best renderings were by Furtwängler, Karajan or Kleiber. I indulged in the best of a culture I did not know from England.

I told the German aunt I was staying with that I was going to visit Berlin, including the eastern side of the city. She was horrified. Why on earth did I need to go to those appalling Communists? I was 21, it was the 1960s, and I was having none of it. I wanted to see for myself. She insisted I check with the British Consulate in Hamburg, where a Vice-Consul gravely warned me that if I got into trouble in East Berlin, the British could not come in and get me out.

That too I dismissed as fuddy-duddy. I did not need the British to help me deal with Germany. So the next day I was on the train to Berlin. After 20 miles, there was a long wait at the crossing into East Germany, with endless checks and hanging around. Then onwards over a wobbly track, pulled by a steam engine at 30 miles an hour. In Hamburg I had been gliding to work on the efficient electric *S-Bahn*. This was a different world, and even by British rail standards it was backward. But nobody incommoded me, so what was the problem?

Then over from East Germany into West Berlin, through barbed wire and armed guards in jackboots who lent an air of dangerous adventure. This, I thought, was how it must have been for the spy who came in from the cold. I spent next day in the East of the city. The drabness, the ruins, the greyness and the penury moved me. This was my first acquaintance with the Communism which had figured so much in the news bulletins, that dangerous beast which reminded me of my own mother's threatened past. Here I found people who faced real challenges, who confronted issues of life and death.

Nevertheless, on this first visit West Berlin thrilled me most. Revived from the drama and fears of the recent crisis, the western half of the city throbbed with defiant confidence. I sensed that I was among people who chose freedom, against the odds. Every night I went to a theatre, a concert or an opera. I could feel the desire of West Berliners to demonstrate their vitality by mounting top quality performances in brand-new performance centres. I saw exhibitions of German Expressionist painters, such as Ernst Ludwig Kirchner, Franz Marc, August Macke, Emil Nolde and Karl Schmidt-Rottluff, with brash colours, disturbing forms and stark energies such as I had never seen before. Banned under Hitler, they were resurrected by Germans who now welcomed avant-garde and wanted to rediscover their cultural heritage after the shameful book burnings. I was in a city at the leading edge.

And its mayor was Willy Brandt. When I returned to Berlin later as a journalist, he was in Bonn, changing the course of German history. Already he and his associates were starting to sketch out a new way forward.

As the closest of those associates, Egon Bahr mostly operated in the shadows. In the speech he gave in 1963 in the Bavarian town of Tutzing however, he was Brandt's front man. On relations with Communist East Germany, he spoke of *Wandel durch Annäherung* (change through rapprochement) and *Politik der kleinen Schritte* (policy of small steps). He proposed a radical break with Bonn's policy of confrontation. West Germans had been brought up to consider the East German state as the evil enemy, an aberration to be done away with. Now Bahr spoke of growing closer.

Annäherung? With Ulbricht? That seemed improbable, and even less likely was the prospect that it would result in any *Wandel*. Communists considered their path was scientifically proven to be right, so why should they depart from it? As for *kleine Schritte,* West Germany's American protectors might interpret these as dangerous wavering.

However Brandt and Bahr had calculated right. The East Germans were interested in ending the diplomatic isolation the West Germans had engineered. The Soviets saw possibilities of wooing West Germany back their way. The Americans, on the other hand, trusted Brandt because he had defied the Communists over Berlin.

Brandt and Bahr knew that they must show firm support for the West and NATO if they were to carry the changes through. They could not afford to be exploited by the Communist side. The prize was eventual reconciliation with all Germany's wartime enemies in the East. It would end Germans' pariah status and open the way for Germany to free itself from the occupying powers and achieve real independence.

Those were the calculations, but it was a gesture that won over the world. On December 7th, 1970, Brandt knelt at the memorial to the Warsaw Jewish Ghetto, destroyed by the Germans in 1944. To see a German leader on his knees, in silent apology, was for me an electrifying moment. I could imagine no better way of acknowledging wrong. No explanations, no excuses, just an uncompromising act of humility at a place commemorating one of Germany's greatest crimes. Brandt said afterwards that he acted on the spur of the moment.

Here was a man who was changing the world. Brandt's domestic political reforms have long been forgotten, but his *Ostpolitik* had permanent effects. No subsequent German leader diverged from it. It was a dramatic breakthrough and as such appealed to my generation, the children who had grown up in the post-war deadlock and were now young adults.

Our generation felt empowered to push aside the old. At 26, I was beginning to be given significant responsibilities in my professional life. Brandt's conciliatory *Ostpolitik* represented a chance for far-reaching change, and was infinitely more attractive than the cold-hearted killings of the Baader-Meinhof group. *Ostpolitik* was a rallying call, to which I would soon have the chance to respond.

Chapter 12

BEHIND THE WALL

I strongly advise you not to go to bed tonight – anonymous caller, 13th August 1961

It was somehow inevitable that I would end up working for Reuters. It was a British household name. Between the wars, its Managing Director toured the British Empire like a viceroy. Yet it was founded by a German – who had changed his name from Israel Beer Josaphat to Paul Julius Reuter – an assimilated Jew who wanted to be a man of the world, free of restraints. He grew up in Kassel and started business in Aachen before moving to London.

So Reuters had a foot in both camps, or rather in many camps. After the war, it shed much of its pro-British slant, partly because its editors were Canadians, Australians and Scots, who felt little allegiance to the English establishment. Reuters editors who received "D-notices" from the British government asking media to suppress certain news began throwing them into the wastepaper basket. Reuters developed objectivity and impartiality into a quasi-religion. No one opinion or angle should predominate, whatever the reason. On every question, a correspondent was expected to look at both sides. That suited my upbringing and natural tendency.

As was only likely with a background such as mine, I had studied Modern Languages at university, including German. This familiarised me with Goethe, Schiller, *Sturm und Drang* (Storm and Stress), Lessing, Kleist, Herder, Grillparzer, Novalis, Mörike, Uhland, Fontane, Storm, C.F. Meyer, Stifter, Heine, Hölderlin, von Hofmannsthal,

Kafka, Hauptmann and Brecht, not to mention the epics of Middle High German. My fellow-students at university told me that still gave me no chance of winning a place on Reuters' trainee programme. Remembering Erhard and Clay however, I decided to ignore the voices of lily-livered doubt. As it happened, Reuters was indeed looking for German-speakers, since Germany was the key issue of the Cold War. Its General Manager was a Yorkshireman who had helped set up German media after the war and had later reported from Bonn. The Editor-in-Chief was a New Zealander who had worked in both Bonn and East Berlin.

East Berlin? No other western media had a bureau there. They covered the Communist part of Germany from West Berlin. Reuters set up a bureau on the eastern side in 1959 because it needed to spend money. The funds had been held by Reuters in Berlin before the war, were seized by the Nazis and then sequestered again by the East Germans. However the money belonged to Reuters, and could be spent in East Germany.

Opening the East Berlin bureau was an inspired decision which suited both parties. The East German Communists could not conceive that Reuters was independent of the British Government, and so considered it tacit recognition. For Reuters, it meant establishing a foothold in a place where one of the most important events of the 20th century was about to happen.

Correspondent Adam Kellett-Long, 26, sniffed that something was up in the early days of August 1961. Nobody was supposed to know, but one or two people in the East German Communist apparatus had a soft spot for the western journalist who had come to live amongst them. Horst Sindermann, the head of propaganda and a former newspaperman, told him on Friday the 11th: "If I were you, and I had plans to spend this weekend away from Berlin, I wouldn't."

Kellett-Long filed a dispatch predicting a major event in the offing. By the Saturday, nothing had happened and his editors in London suggested he was too far out on a limb and should file another dispatch backing down. He did not. By 2.a.m. on Sunday the 13th, all was still quiet. Then an anonymous caller came on to his telephone in East Berlin and said: "I strongly advise you not to go to bed tonight."

Thus did this particularly unpleasant German regime give the agency founded by a German Jew one of its greatest scoops. Kellett-Long never found out who it was, but he immediately drove down to the Brandenburg Gate and saw East German militia setting up a barbed-wire barrier between the two halves of the city. *Die Grenze ist geschlossen* "The frontier is closed," said a guard waving a red torch to stop him. He was first to tell the world.[cxxxv]

Disembarking from an overnight train in West Berlin in 1971, I felt on familiar territory. The cobbles, the guttural language, the slight air of menace in the air, I knew this from an early age. Four years after joining Reuters, this is what I had been prepared for. I was one of Adam Kellett-Long's successors as correspondent in East Berlin. The fantasies about war which I felt in Germany soon became reality. As I pulled up outside my future office and home in the Schönhauser Allee, I saw that the façade was riddled with bullet holes – Red Army bullets from 1945, shot in the last few days before Hitler committed suicide.

I was told that the water tower rising a few streets away on the Prenzlauerberg used to be a Gestapo torture centre. Down the road was a Jewish cemetery, with tombs still smashed up, and a plaque on a tree marking where deserters were hanged in 1944 after the Gestapo found them hiding in a hole. Not far away in the Oranienburg Strasse, was the flattened site of what was once Europe's largest synagogue. Desecrated in the Crystal Night pogrom of 1938 and bombed by the Allies in 1943, it was set alight by Berliners in 1944 and demolished by the Communist regime in 1950. At weekends, the remains of a concentration camp outside Berlin beckoned. It made for an interesting outing.

Atmosphere, I thought! I felt as if World War II ended only three weeks ago. If this is what happened in the past, I should be in for a stimulating assignment. East Berlin was a sought-after posting in Reuters. There was status in being the only western correspondent living behind the Wall. A number of German colleagues in West Berlin and Bonn let it be subtly known that they could have done the job better than me. How could a fresh young Briton have a clue what was going on? At this point, I remembered how I had dealt with condescending Germans as I grew up. I was not prepared to take any nonsense. I was one of them, but also British, which in my eyes gave me the edge.

Nevertheless I did have my hands full. A few days before I arrived, Erich Honecker had replaced Walter Ulbricht as the East German Party leader. As we learned 20 years later, Honecker went to Ulbricht's house with a dozen guards armed with machine guns and told him he was deposed. The nasty German had lost out to one just as nasty.

Honecker's role as builder of the Berlin Wall had brought him to the attention of the Soviets, who did not like Ulbricht's stubborn independence. The Soviets wanted to control everything in East Germany and frequently reminded the local comrades that "without the Soviet Union, there is no German Democratic Republic."

However East German Communists learned that they could play one Soviet leader off against another. Ulbricht was Stalin's man, but did not get on with Nikita Khrushchev. He tried to rally Khrushchev's domestic enemies to his side, including Leonid Brezhnev, who ousted Khrushchev in a palace coup in 1964. But Brezhnev had *his* eye on Honecker as the man who secured the borders of socialism with the Wall. When Brezhnev removed Khrushchev, he tipped off Honecker, but not Ulbricht. Honecker was thereafter Brezhnev's favoured East German, accompanying him on hunting trips.

"The Russians had Ulbricht deposed. They are responsible for everything that happens here," said Adam Kellett-Long, visiting in 1971 for a couple of days. As he had meanwhile covered the 1968 Soviet invasion of Czechoslovakia from Moscow, I felt he knew what he was talking about.

Ulbricht still had the ceremonial post of head of state and should have been present at the Party Congress about to get underway. He was not there. Ill, they told us. "Nonsense, the Russians don't want him there. If they did, they'd have stuffed him full of injections and propped him up in his seat," said Kellett-Long. I was learning Soviet practices quickly – a putsch and now a blatant cover-up.

The Soviet *Konkordski* supersonic airliner flew low over the Congress hall to give brotherly support. But what everybody was picking up were the hints dropped at the Congress that the way was free for a four-power agreement settling the conflict over Berlin. With Ulbricht out of the way, the East Germans would stop obstructing and things could start moving.

The hefty young Party minder who accompanied me into the Congress – I got in because I was accredited to the East German government – told me brightly that the quality of delegates was better than at the last Congress. As they were rising and applauding and chanting in unison, I wondered what on earth he meant. The delegates hardly needed superior qualities to confirm what was going to happen in any case.

Only some time later did it become apparent what he was obliquely talking about. Honecker wanted to open up to East Germany's intellectuals and make the regime more palatable. That did not go far before it petered out, but the claim that the delegates were more intelligent probably signaled readiness to engage in freer political discourse. A policy change... perhaps.

One person who was not opening up however was the head of the East German Government Press Office, Kurt Blecha. My editors in London had primed me about his Nazi past, and when I went to introduce myself, he was rude and bossy in the old German style. He told me I should not look down on East Germans as socially inept. "We too use fish-knives when we eat fish," he admonished (not knowing I had recently abandoned this practice). So... after the putsch and the cover-up, now a verbal roughing up.

I inspected my quarters. The entrance was on the first floor, on the right, with an adjoining door into another flat on the left. Inside was a long corridor with a dirty, worn carpet and a view over an overgrown bomb site at the back. My new home boasted brown coal heating stoves, a wobbling lavatory, furred-up water pipes, dingy paintwork, broken light bulbs and the accumulated rubbish of several bachelor predecessors. The brown coal left an acrid smell in the air and deposited an orange-brown dust inside and out. But the ceramic stoves were cosy, as was the whole atmosphere.

The plumber sent my wife Ursula to buy a lavatory lock in West Berlin – East Germany was out of them. Landing in East Berlin was certainly a culture shock for her. A few weeks earlier she had been leading a chic life working for a Geneva fine arts auctioneer. Proposing marriage, announcing the move to East Berlin and getting wed had followed rapidly one on the other.

Socialism however was a familiar concept to her. Her Swiss father had lived through the Depression and worked for 40 years as a watch maker, being paid piecework wages rather than a regular salary, with hardly any holidays. Socialism in her family represented a grass-roots political movement seeking decent working conditions for the poor.

In East Berlin, she found this concept was turned upside down. Here socialism was a rigid system imposed from the top on workers who were estranged from it. She soon adapted however. After a few weeks, she surprised everyone by returning with two East Berlin building workers pushing a barrowful of bricks she had purchased illicitly from a state building site for West German marks. She was learning the ways of east bloc socialism – improvise, help each other out and get around the system. To the bricks were added planks of wood, and soon we had a new bookshelf.

Inside the entrance of the flat was a one-room office where I was to work as a journalist. It was piled with copies of *Neues Deutschland* – the Party newspaper, and heaps of East German documents roughly printed on brownish paper. One corner was taken up by piles of Western newspapers. The latter were brought in by special delivery – they were forbidden to East Germans. The Reuters people could read them, but we were not allowed to throw them into dustbins, because East Germans would fish them out and read them too. The special truck which was supposed to fetch them had broken down.

Women of various kinds bustled around. Erdmute Behrendt, an East Berliner, had been the office assistant since the bureau opened in 1959. Frau Birk, the housekeeper, made coffee, cooked breakfast, lit the fires and cleaned. Under the circumstances, one would have expected the housekeeper to be a spy. She may well have had to report on us, but Frau Birk was a simple, kindly soul, with a long history of personal suffering but admirable humility and a perky Berlin feistiness. She was one of those Germans who never came out on top, distrusted lofty promises of a better life, and had the proletarian's witty scorn for the people higher up. After my wife and

I left Berlin, she knitted me a pullover and came to stay with us in Prague.

In and out of the office/flat drifted various beautiful girls of vague origin, looking for the bachelors. And a good-looking man too, kissing the hand of my wife and presenting her flowers with phallic blooms. Social life flourished, in a way. Later Erdmute told me that Reuters' biggest impact in East Berlin was that it lifted the social level. So my predecessor and I had to arrange parties in West and East Berlin for the handover. The ones in the East really rocked. A bevy of Slav journalists and East German officials flocked into the office. My young minder from the Party Congress got hopelessly drunk. The journalists tossed back our alcohol and treated us like the closest of colleagues. That was on our ground. When my wife and I went later to a "Press Ball," nobody came up to speak or offered to dance. They would have been sticking their necks out too far.

Moujik, a ginger cat we brought from Geneva, considered the overgrown bomb site at the back a paradise. He prowled around it for hours and proudly returned to the flat from time to time to deposit a headless bird on the corridor carpet. One day he came back heavily the worse for wear. He had clearly been beaten by an occupant of the block. East Berlin was dog territory. Cats were deemed the evil torturers of poor little birds, not without reason, I must admit.

As winter drew in, Moujik fell ill. I coaxed him into his cat basket and went round to a vet for the evening surgery. I sat in a circle of East German men, each with a huge Alsatian dog. The dogs were immediately overcome by irresistible urges to tear Moujik to pieces. They broke out in frenzied barking and lunged towards his cage. The owners strained at the leashes and frowned at me as a provocateur. Moujik hissed to keep the dogs on edge. Finally the vet appeared and released the Alsatians from their torment by inviting Moujik and me in first. That annoyed the men, who had been waiting longer, but peace returned to the waiting room and Moujik got his medicine.

So I gradually got used to East Berlin. When I was not giving parties or caring for Moujik's ailments, I was covering one of the top news stories of the year, week in, week out. The four occupying powers of Berlin were pushing ahead with negotiations to settle Berlin's status and end a conflict that had been at the heart of the Cold War for decades. This sounds grand, but much of the time I was in journalistic terms a foot soldier manning the trenches. I had to wait for hours at meeting venues, finally to receive a statement, each of which outdid the last in vacuity.

The four powers – the Soviet Union, the United States, Britain and France – were still formally responsible for Berlin, but the West Germans were making much of the running. With their *Ostpolitik,* they were signing treaties with the Soviet Union, Poland and Czechoslovakia acknowledging war guilt and paving the way for reconciliation. Germany was changing from being a problem to a solution.

I frequently met Egon Bahr in East Berlin. The two German states were negotiating a treaty too and he was in charge as Willy Brandt's right-hand man. "Met" perhaps goes too far. I many times stood in front of him while he declined to say anything besides the same few curt phrases he emitted after the last meeting. He did not give me background briefings. I was a British correspondent, and the purpose of his *Ostpolitik* was to gain power and influence for Germany. The occupying powers should be involved only insofar as they helped that cause.

West German journalists however clearly did have an inside line. They would come over for the day to East Berlin – they were not allowed to stay longer – and bustle around importantly as if they were part of the West German delegation. There seemed little separation between the two – I detected nothing of the Anglo-Saxon concept of the press as an independent "fourth estate" checking executive power. The German journalists were in their 50s and wore suits with waistcoats. They seemed strait-laced and conventional. I was half their age, and felt it.

It was clear from the car Bahr used that the West Germans would eventually come out on top. He arrived in a black Mercedes – modern, practical and sober. His counterpart, Michael Kohl, drove up (he could have walked the short distance) in a huge, elaborately-decorated Zil saloon made in the Soviet Union. Frilly white curtains obscured his presence in the back. This pathetic attempt at grandeur was not to be taken seriously. It was clearly a loser's vehicle.

This may seem a frivolous judgment, but I had long been reading all sorts of signs that the West was on top in the Cold War. Never during my time in East Berlin did I think otherwise. Subconsciously perhaps, the values of an earlier age coming down from a patrician Belgian grandmother influenced me to assume this superiority.

U.S. National Security head Henry Kissinger, born a German Jew, found Bahr "a slippery fellow" and worried that the West Germans would be sucked into making concessions to the East and weaken their commitment to West European unity.[cxxxvi] The U.S., Britain and France were interested in reducing tensions over Berlin, but were tacitly content to see the two German states remain apart. Reunification raised fears from the past and rapprochement seemed risky.

The Germans were more ambitious because they had more at stake. When I saw the two German delegations scurrying to and from lengthy meetings, I wondered if the four powers really knew what they were up to. From what we all found out afterwards, I was right to have such doubts.

As negotiations between the two German states got under way, the East German Foreign Ministry let it be known that only two journalists would be allowed access to the delegations – one from the East German *ADN* agency and one from the West German *dpa*. I was not having that. I was the only accredited western correspondent in East Berlin, and now I was to be excluded from one of the biggest stories? My professional reputation was at stake, all the more since the presence of a correspondent in East Berlin was the main selling point of a new German news service Reuters had started.

I marched round to the East German Foreign Ministry and went to see the head of its press service, an uptight, nervy man with balding head and pebble glasses. I told him I was appalled that the East German state should give preference to a West German agency rather than the agency accredited in the capital of the German Democratic Republic. If that was to be so, I could see no reason for keeping the Reuters bureau open in East Berlin. I was out on a limb, since my superiors had not authorised me to make such a threat. However communications were such in those days that correspondents could often plead inability to consult.

The press service chief looked me up and down and I thought I caught the glimmer of a smile on his hatchet face. The next day I had access. When agreement between the two German states was finally announced at the East German Council of State building, I promptly telephoned the Reuters East Berlin office and dictated the news. An assistant prepared a teleprinter tape, pressed a button which rang a bell at the East German *ADN* agency, and the technicians there linked us up with London. It was belts and braces, but faster than anybody else. The *ADN* technicians always jumped to it. I appreciated their German efficiency.

The *dpa* journalist was meanwhile left shouting down the phone demanding "an echo call." This was a privilege for top East German officials giving priority access to the very few telephone lines to the West. The *dpa* journalist had been offered this facility, but it did not get him a line when he needed it. Ten minutes after Reuters published the news, he was still fuming in front of a silent telephone.

Reuters had one more perk. Its offices in East and West Berlin were connected by a permanent telephone line. I wound a handle on a camp telephone to make a ringing sound at the other end. I smugly speculated it must have been the most listened to telephone line in Berlin – tapped by the Soviets, the East Germans, the West Germans, the British and the Americans. At that time, East Germans were waiting 25 years for a telephone.[cxxxvii]

I had been warned about tapped telephones and bugs implanted in the walls of the East Berlin office and flat, including no doubt my bedroom. I did not let it bother me much. On balance, I felt pleased that someone always wanted to listen to me.

After the fall of the Berlin Wall in 1989, the then correspondent in East Berlin heard a ring at the door and found two young men standing outside. They politely introduced themselves as *Stasi* secret police who had been recording and typing transmissions from the bugs in the adjoining flat. So that was where the next door on the landing led to. They showed him the tape recorders and other equipment they had been using. They thought he should know about it now that things had changed.

They had some interesting visitors to listen to over the years. One was Herman von Berg, a cultivated, liberal-minded official who had the go-ahead to maintain contacts with Westerners, including me. We had engaging conversations about the nature of socialism. I was not impressed with the East German version, and nor patently was he. But when he said the crucial question was whether one favoured state ownership of a country's assets, I was not against. I was the 1960s generation. I had personally benefited from the British welfare state – all my school, university and health care costs had been paid from public funds.

One day, before any of the agreements were concluded, von Berg asked me if I would ask Günter Struve, a young speech-writer for Willy Brandt (and later programme director of the *ARD Das Erste* television station), to call him when I was next in West Berlin. I passed the message on, and never knew what it was about. I was nevertheless pleased to do my bit of cloak-and-dagger work to further détente.

Another occasion came when I visited the dissident East German writer Stefan Heym in the East German suburb of Grünau. He was a German Jew who emigrated to the United States when Hitler came to power and returned to Germany as a U.S. Army soldier. He chose to live in East Berlin because he believed in socialism. He then fell out with the regime, which banned him from publishing. However West German publishers continued to bring his books out.

One day at his home, Heym asked me to carry his latest political novel, "The King David Report" over to West Berlin and mail it to his West German publisher. At the same time, he said, he was sending another copy of the manuscript through the East German postal service. He knew it would never get through, but he did not want to be accused of acting in an underhand way.

I agreed. The next two times I passed through Checkpoint Charlie, I did not take it with me. I wanted to see if they would search me and my car. Reuters would not have been amused if I had been expelled for smuggling somebody else's book, but I felt that as a correspondent behind the Iron Curtain I should not shirk this task. It was a question of principle. The guards gave my car the usual cursory check to ensure I was not smuggling people – opening the boot and pushing mirrors on wheels under the chassis – but otherwise waved me through. The third time, I took the book and there was still no search.

The East German secret police must have known what I was doing. They certainly had Stefan Heym's home bugged and so overheard the conversation in which I agreed to take the book. In this cat-and-mouse game, they must have let me do it deliberately. Subsequently I understood this resulted from the new Party policy of giving frustrated intellectuals a bit of leeway. Later in 1971 Heym was allowed to publish again in East Germany.

I got on well enough with the guards at Checkpoint Charlie, where American and Soviet tanks faced each other across the concrete blocks 10 years earlier. I felt it better to remain serenely above whatever chicanery they had in store. I acted as if the whole checkpoint business was normal and treated them as if they were doing a job like any other. I chatted about East German soccer scores. They got to know me.

I had a *Grenzempfehlung* (a frontier recommendation) issued by the East German Foreign Ministry asking for the Interior Ministry guards to treat me, well, OK. I still had to fill out visa forms in triplicate every time I passed through. The *Grenzempfehlung* enabled all this to be processed within about half an hour. However I considered that if I treated them like normal human beings, they could at least give me prompt service. So as the wait stretched out when I had one of my British bosses accompanying me, I told them this would not do. "Gosh, Marcus, you gave them a talking too," he said admiringly. Thereafter he nicknamed me "rusty nails Ferrar."

The straightforward approach paid off when I was passing through with my wife to catch a plane from West Berlin to go skiing in Switzerland. I told the checkpoint guards armed with machine pistols that we were going skiing in Switzerland and risked missing our plane as we had left late. So could they please hurry up? It was a ridiculous request, but they did, and we caught the plane. Thank you.

When I was preparing to take up a new posting Prague, I took out a set of Meissen china in the boot of my East German Wartburg car. I was not supposed to have it as I had arranged for my housekeeper Frau Birk to buy it in a shop reserved for East Germans, where the prices were very low. A jack-booted officer in his dull, grey-green uniform opened the boot at Checkpoint Charlie, saw the china stacked up inside, and remarked with a smile: "So, you're having a party in West Berlin!" I could almost hear him saying to himself: "Don't mess with the Reuters people. They are the ones who came to live with us." Thank you again.

The *Grenzempfehlung* exempted me from most customs restrictions. So when my wife went shopping for food in West Berlin, she left it in a luggage locker at the Zoo railway station. As I opened the door and removed the bag, blood dripped out of a bag from an unfrozen chicken. The shadowy characters lurking in the station gave me suspicious looks, but I walked away with aplomb. In Berlin, it was not out of place to look sinister.

My best moment at Checkpoint Charlie came when ceremonies to mark an East-West treaty were being held on either side of the Wall on the same day. I drove up to the barrier and the guards immediately raised it and sent me sailing through with scarcely a glance at my papers. It was as if the Wall for a moment did not exist. Fleetingly, I had the sensation of Berlin as a single city, not two different worlds.

Reuters bought a new East German Wartburg car every year from the funds outstanding from the Hitler time. It was the larger of the two models East Germany produced (the other being the Trabant). However within two months of purchase, mine was already overheating on a trip to Warsaw. It smelled of the primitive plastic which

East Germany made out of brown coal. It had a two-stroke engine emitting clouds of sweet-smelling blue smoke.

On the Leipzig-Berlin motorway I almost met my death in this contraption. As I was overtaking a long West German truck, I rounded a bend and caught sight of a hay wagon parked in the fast lane. Workers were cutting the grass in the central reservation. I jammed the brakes on and nothing much happened. The Wartburg had only drum brakes, no discs. After an eternity, I swerved just behind the truck. East Germans waited 16 years to purchase this beauty. As with many other consumer goods, demand far outstripped supply.

Gradually I began to feel more at home in East Berlin than in West Berlin. It had an old-fashioned, authentic feeling which racy West Berlin now lacked. West Berlin had shops, hotels and the Zoo railway station situated in a sleazy district. It had become bohemian and radical – a place where young men came to avoid military service (West Berliners were excused). East Berlin felt like the core of the old Berlin, as indeed it was – most of the centre was in the eastern zone. Its theatre and opera were as good as anywhere else in Germany. The public flocked eagerly to the performances, and even as an accredited correspondent I sometimes had difficulty obtaining tickets. Bookshops sold phenomenal numbers of the limited range of world classics allowed by the regime.

In the East, people focused more on simple human pleasures, since the material ones lacked. In the words of actress Katharine Thalbach, who left for the West when she was 22, "in the East we had better jokes, better sex and more to laugh about – there were simply no diversions."

On warm evenings, I strolled up the nearby Oderberg Strasse. Children played on the street and grown-ups leaned out of windows to chat and enjoy the evening sun. At the end of the street, we came up against the Berlin Wall. On a watchtower on the western side, I saw people standing and looking over into the East. They pointed at me and my newly-wed wife. I am convinced they were remarking how shabbily dressed we were.

East Germans spoke a rather archaic, long-winded German. The American vocabulary and slick rhythms which were modifying German spoken in the West were absent. Chancellor Angela Merkel, who grew up in East Germany, spoke of buying things in a *Kaufhalle* (shopping hall) for 15 years after the Communist regime collapsed. Only around 2005 did she start talking of a *Supermarkt.*[cxxxviii]

In 1971 I struggled to grasp the lengthy words and ponderous phrasing of the East Germans I dealt with. The bureaucracy spewed out German which sounded as heavy and pompous as that used by the Nazis. Study course material defined underground political activity thus:

"Inspired by the use of concentrated application of political-ideological diversion, and organised by imperialistic centres, organisation and forces, it is the search, collection and bringing together of hostile, negative forces in order to create a personal basis inside the GDR, which, through execution of hostile, political-ideological platforms using conspiratorial means and methods orientated in the long term against the GDR, battle to create positions hostile to socialism in socialist society, to stir up citizens of the GDR against socialism [and] to carry out hostile actions, with the aim thereby of triggering the process of counter-revolutionary changes for the final elimination of the workers' and peasants' power."[cxxxix]

Useless word massed upon useless word to bludgeon home the point. I felt sorry for the many East Germans who were obliged to study Marxism-Leninism, and had to pass exams based on their understanding of sentences such as these.

I was not the only British journalist in East Berlin.

The other was John Peet, a former Guards officer with twirled moustaches. In 1950, when he was Reuters correspondent in Berlin, he crossed into the eastern sector and announced he could "no longer serve the Anglo-American warmongers," by which he meant his employer. He followed this up with a lengthy dispatch to Reuters which strayed far from the agency's principles of objectivity. Thereafter he stayed in East Berlin and published an English-language news-letter about the German Democratic Republic. It was slanted in favour of the regime, but he had been trained by Reuters to be concise and clear. It read like normal news and was the only coherent review of East German affairs non-German-speakers could understand. As such, it carried some weight in the West.

For the sake of old times, John Peet regularly invited the Reuters correspondent in East Berlin round to his flat in the Karl-Marx-Allee, where privileged Communists had their residences. In private he was under no illusions about the shortfalls of the regime, so conversation over dinner flowed easily and British humour flourished in Berlin as if we were sitting in Somerset. His wife had a darker side which prevented the laughter from getting out of hand. She was a Bulgarian, with the tattoo of the Ravensbrück concentration camp on her forearm and deep sadness in her eyes.

Then came the invitation from Mr Li. China was opening up to the world, and this was happening in Berlin too. The first opening for renewal of relations between China and the United States is commonly believed to have been a visit by a U.S. table tennis team to China in April 1971. Some of us believe otherwise. Mr Li was the East Berlin correspondent of the New China News Agency. He took to visiting the Reuters office in West Berlin, where the journalists cleared the papers from the desks and invited him to play ping-pong, which he did. Only after that did the American team visit China.

Thereafter relations only became warmer and it is thus that my wife and I were invited to dine at Mr Li's residence one vile November night on the outskirts of East Berlin. We found ourselves in Karlshorst, where the Soviet military had their headquarters. It was not a neighbourhood where Mr Li could feel at home any more, the two countries having come to the verge of war a few years previously. It was not the sort of area where one would normally go to have a meal either. As we parked our Wartburg on the deserted street outside Mr Li's abode, a shadow moved on the other side of the street. A sentry peered out and shifted from one foot to the other. We were not alone.

I laughed as I came inside Mr Li's flat. In the middle of the floor was a brand-new electric heater, which he sheepishly admitted he had just bought in West Berlin. During Mao's Cultural Revolution, which forced intellectuals to perform menial tasks, he had been obliged to fire his own brown-coal stove, an activity which this cultivated and intelligent man clearly did not relish. His new heater was one more sign that the Revolution was over.

He regaled us with lurid stories of the inhuman treatment to which he was allegedly subjected in transit across the Soviet Union on the Trans-Siberia Express. This was followed by even fiercer denunciation of the East German practice of socialism, and Germans as a whole. It was amazing to hear such anti-Communist, anti-German invective in the heart of the enemy's lair, so to speak, even though I found it a bit overdone and not entirely sincere. The Party line, the new Chinese version, was clearly guiding him, and his remarks had an unpleasantly violent undertone.

I sympathised, but felt I should be a little more diplomatic in expressing my own opinion, which was no doubt carefully noted to be passed higher up. Meanwhile, servants from the Chinese Embassy crossed the dark street through the encroaching sleet with delicately perfumed Chinese dishes. It was a stimulating evening, and I was pleased to have done my bit to further China's return to the world.

As the winter days grew shorter, East Berlin became extraordinarily grey and dreary. A few hundred feet overhead slid American airliners on their approach into Tempelhof airport in the western part of the city. Just out of reach above our heads were people from another world, of freedom and plenty. An hour earlier they had been in Hamburg or Hanover.

My head office asked me to gather comments on the street when the two German states announced agreement to establish diplomatic relations. I walked to a crossroads and asked East Berliners what they thought. Most were scared to talk to me as a westerner and gave non-committal replies. One however stopped, looked me in the face, said: "The treaty is useless – men can fly to the moon, but I still can't even go to West Berlin," and disappeared into the night.

He had hit the nail on the head. For all the new détente, East Berliners were still walled in.When I spoke to her in 2008, East Berliner Liselotte Kubitza picked out the Berlin Wall as the one act which really set her against the regime. She came from an old Communist working class family and otherwise got along well enough with her rulers. Berlin was always a socialist city, which made the Nazis feel uncomfortable there, and she remembers as a child hearing endless wartime jokes about Goebbels and Goering in her family. The Russians did not trouble them much when they arrived, and by 1949 the new Communist regime was giving her a professional education.

She realised that in the East they were worse off than in the West, but for her that was because the Russians were less able to help than the Americans, having been devastated by the wartime German invasion. Her standard of living was in any case better than ever before, and in 1955 the family could move into a better home.

She pursued "an honourable profession" as a senior administrator of a social insurance institute. She dealt with complaints. In the German Democratic Republic, this may sound a hopeless task. However somebody had to help the population deal with their lot and at least try to be fair. "There was full employment, free education, social assistance, music and sport, and women could work," she said. In the summers, she sunbathed on nudist beaches on the Baltic.

The Wall however she denounces as a crime. Her husband came from West Berlin, and from one day to the next he was cut off from his relatives, unable even to visit his mother's grave. He said he was going to swim over the River Spree into the West, but she objected: "What about me and the children? We're not coming with you!" Between the two of them they had 23 relatives in West Berlin. The Wall spoiled a life which she generally found "bearable." It was an unnatural act disturbing her value system, which was otherwise not so out of line with the regime.

The husband became resentful and in the school where he taught sports he made his opinions known in his classes. When President Kennedy was assassinated in 1963, he told the children: "Kennedy was OK. We'll have one minute's silence." The school blocked his promotion as a punishment, but went no further. The regime did not want to make too many enemies. "My husband never stopped complaining about the Wall. Maybe that's why he got cancer and died in 1978. I did not," said Frau Kubitza.

She was a sympathiser but did not join the [Communist] *Sozialistische Einheitspartei Deutschlands (SED)*. Following the rapes of 1945, the Party never attracted significant numbers of women into its ranks. She never lost the scepticism of a working-class Berliner: "If we didn't want to march on 1st May, they asked us if we were for peace. If we didn't go, they said we were in the resistance. We knew what we couldn't say to the SED. The GDR was half a dictatorship."

Other East Germans found satisfaction in their work like Frau Kubitza did. Klaus Wenzel was manager of the Grand Hotel in Warnemünde on the Baltic, which attracted ferry-loads of partying Swedes and already, in 1971, had a swimming pool with artificial waves. "I was convinced I was working for a reasonable system, for which it was worth making an effort. I had fun, it was my life, for my colleagues too," he said. Markus Wolf was gratified to be respected on both sides of the ideological divide for running an effective East German spying operation. Likewise, architect Ronald Korn expressed pride long after the fall of the regime for the Council of State building he conceived in 1962.[cxl]

During my year in the German Democratic Republic, I saw people going to work normally and trying to make the best out of the only life they had been allotted. It is small wonder that many took a quiet satisfaction in achieving what was within their reach.

Nobody was starving. I remember reporting a statistic that the fat of overweight East Germans would have filled several thousand railway wagons. My wife found plenty of sausages, one sort of mediocre cheese, eggs, grey-brown rye bread with a satisfyingly sour taste, Bulgarian pickles, occasional tomatoes and once or twice in the summer fresh strawberries and cherries. It was nevertheless a hardship diet. Long queues formed from one minute to another when a rare provision came on sale. She learned to join any queue she saw and then ask what it was for.

When I was in East Germany in 1971-1972, many things fell into short supply – furniture, shoes, stockings, women's sanitary articles, butter, textiles, meat, citrus fruit and coffee. Although I did not know it then, there had been 63 strikes in the six months before I arrived. For East Berliners, the shortages were all the more galling since they knew the best of everything was available a mile or so away in West Berlin.

Lack of homes was causing particular dissatisfaction among young workers whom the regime could ill afford to antagonise. Many East German dwellings then still had no inside sanitation, and overcrowding was chronic. Young couples were forced to live indefinitely with their parents. When I lived in East Berlin, only 10% of East German homes had central heating. Most people lived in pre-war accommodation, which was almost impossible to renovate for lack of boilers, tiles, pipes, taps, lavatory bowls and cookers. Not all women appreciated having to work and look after children and a home. Many were overworked and exhausted.

One reason why Honecker was able to summon support to get rid of Ulbricht was that the latter had wastefully ploughed scarce resources into developing an East German computer industry. It failed because the East German economy was too isolated from world trends. The people were forced to pay for his mistake.

I constantly felt during this year that the system could not last. Its ideal of social justice had clearly lost its drawing power, since there was no wealth to redistribute. Every evening the population could see on West German television how Germans lived far better under the opposite political system. I had little confidence that Honecker would make any difference. He seemed the same type of bossy, rigid dictator as his predecessor. Perhaps drier in character, but that fitted with the pseudo-scientific foundation of the Communist ideology. If the Communist way was scientifically-proven, as the leaders believed, there was no need for anything except coldly clinical execution. Popularity was not a factor of success.

I could see with my own eyes how reality flew in the face of such dogma. Everything was dictated from above, leaving no scope for individuals to contribute with their own initiatives. Original impulses were repressed as threats to the "science," leaving people excluded and frustrated. Like the Nazis, the Communists refused to acknowledge that ordinary Germans could decide about life on their own. They tried to keep them in childlike submission, at the service of an ideology which had long lost its credibility. The paternalism harked back to the 19th century.

East Germans had employment, but were aware that too often the outcome of their hard work was of limited use. Except for the other poverty-stricken countries of the Soviet bloc, their state was largely isolated from the world, hermetically pursuing an experiment that failed to work.

As a Westerner, I stood out in all respects as alien. Although I tended to the left then myself, I was treated mostly as the enemy, to be tolerated but kept at arm's length. My upbringing as a Briton with a German family had taught me to take people as they were. I was ready to engage with the bureaucrats, but not they with me. I was dealing with a Leninist regime which considered secrecy a virtue. Nearly everybody in authority meticulously refrained from telling me anything newsworthy. Only a few people, mostly ordinary citizens, were prepared to risk retribution by talking frankly.

Like other journalists reporting on Communist Eastern Europe, I developed an intense sensitivity to the little pieces of genuine information which filtered through cracks in the monolith. Sometimes they were apparently innocuous sentences hidden in the text of a four-hour speech. Or hints dropped by diplomats and journalists of Communist countries which did not toe the Soviet line, such as Yugoslavia and Romania. Or chance remarks by people I came across in daily life, who did not quite realise the significance of what they were telling me.

Then of course there was the black book of "sources" passed on from one Reuters correspondent to another. These were the names and telephone numbers of people who for one reason or another had contact with us. Each correspondent added new sources and crossed out old ones. Doubtless the regime's spies knew what was going on, but they had their own motives for allowing certain information to reach the outside world through carefully-watched channels.

How could I know whether the sources were telling me the truth? Sometimes I would check one with another. Otherwise, with an untested source, I would not immediately use information offered. I would wait to see if events showed it was true. By that time it was often too late to use, but I could gradually draw up a track record of reliability. After a source had proved accurate several times, I knew it was safe to use the information in a news story.

Gathering information of course was the underlying reason for the contacts with Herman von Berg, Stefan Heym, John Peet and Mr Li... not to mention the senior British diplomat who invited me one night to dinner in his sumptuous residence in West Berlin. As the port circled the dinner table, he and other invited diplomats picked my brains about East Germany, and I probed for snippets about the four-power negotiations.

Together we scratched at this none-too-fertile ground, while my wife Ursula listened upstairs to the diplomats' wives talking about giving birth. Then we got in our Wartburg car, started up its engine emitting the usual clouds of blue smoke, and drove back towards Checkpoint Charlie. Waiting there, I wondered whether the remark I had just heard about the Soviet ambassador was significant. Before I could come to a conclusion however, I was fast asleep in our home in the East.

Again, I relied on my instincts, and in 1971-72 they

told me correctly that the peace-making I was witnessing in Berlin would eventually bring down Communism, which for its survival needed an environment of perpetual conflict that increasingly lost its purpose. I continued to believe this in the next decade, even when the Soviet Union expanded its influence into Africa, built a large high seas fleet and set up nuclear missiles in its satellite countries pointed at Western Europe.

In 1983, I felt vindicated when the Soviet Union quit medium-range missile talks in Geneva, leaving the U.S. free to respond with its own missiles sited in Europe just a few minutes flying time from Moscow and other major Soviet cities. I was among the journalists standing in the corridor when Soviet negotiator Yuli Kvitsinsky walked out of the talks, ceding the upper hand to the Americans. When I flew low over the Berlin Wall four years later to attend a congress in West Berlin, it came as a slight shock to see it was still there.

However I had no idea when the system would come to an end, and even less how this would happen. I assumed that Western ways would gradually infiltrate East Germany and draw it into the West. That did not happen, and it never remotely occurred to me that the Soviet brother instead would turn out to be the weak link.

My year in East Berlin was totally fascinating. I was covering a top world story and what I lived through could hardly be more interesting. But gradually the dismal side took the upper hand. The prevailing dirt, decrepitude and low, grey winter clouds took their toll. So too did the German spirit of old, still alive in East Berlin. The bureaucrats behaved in the aggressive manner I associated with the Nazis of my boyhood war books. The Prussian manner made itself felt in overbearing attitudes that even other Germans could not stand. I sensed an unreconstructed German love of things military. Guards slammed jackboots violently into cobble-stones as they marched. Voices were constantly raised and the whole language was militarised.

Politics was a class struggle. West Germans were "opponents" or "the enemy" and foreign policy was a struggle against Fascism and revanchism. The 1st of May was a "day of struggle and celebration." The Party was the "conscious and organised vanguard of the working class". Military brass bands paraded through the streets at dawn on election day to rouse voters for the required 99% turnout. Children had to do pre-military exercises at school, and girls were taught to shoot. The new historical hero was the 18th century warrior king of Prussia, Frederick the Great, and in the year I spent in East Berlin four people were shot dead trying to cross the Wall.

These were warlike habits which West European countries had largely put behind them. The regime was intent on keeping its subjects in a state of agitation and bellicosity. It made no pretence at being pleasant and cared little about internal esteem, nor of the opinion of foreigners. It was a regime of Germans who had scarcely moved on since the war.

After a year, my wife and I climbed into our own little car and set off to a new assignment. We had used up practically all the confiscated Reuters funds remaining from 1939. Spring was blooming, the air was soft, and as we crossed over the frontier into Czechoslovakia, we breathed a sigh of relief. East Germany with its reminders of a sinister German past was behind us.

Czechs could hardly have been worse off. It was only four years since the Soviet invasion of 1968, and repression there was at its worst. But the moment we arrived in Prague, the Czechs took us in hand to show us how we could live as humans despite the system. We had arrived in the land of the Good Soldier Švejk, where sly evasion and dumb insolence comforted the spirits, and life could be fun again.

Chapter 13

STASI IN THE MIDST

"Suspected of political-ideological diversion" – the Stasi's assessment of the author

Elderly couples edge cautiously into a reception room of a large building in Dresden which used to house a packaging company. They look nervous. The staff are expecting that and speak to them gently in hushed tones as they settle down. These people have come to look at their *Stasi*[11] secret police files. It is some 20 years since the Communists were removed from power. Thousands of East German citizens are only just summoning the courage to look at the records the old regime's *Stasi* kept on them. They have been averaging about 100,000 per year and do not slack off – in 2009 applications were up 11 % on 2008.[cxli] Ahead of such visitors is a confrontation with deceit, treachery and terror. They sit down and prepare for an ordeal. They will see how a dictatorship peered into their private lives in order to blackmail and threaten them into submission if the need arose. They will probably see how close friends, even family members, betrayed them to save their own skins. They may discover adultery by their spouse. They may even have to acknowledge shameful compromises into which they themselves entered.

Inside the huge old building are miles of malignant archives, a registry of Hell. The *Stasi* was the special hallmark of the East German regime, operating under the direction of the Party. The *Stasi* spied on citizens by following them, listening to them through bugs, stealing people's clothes

11   Ministerium für Staatssicherheit – the East German secret police.

to obtain "smell samples", and even irradiating them. It coerced tens of thousands of informants, opened 90,000 letters a day, and tapped 20,000 telephones in East Berlin alone. Those whom it classified as "enemies" it persecuted with torture and imprisonment, which it was able to do outside the normal court system. If the *Stasi* sentenced somebody to years in prison, relatives were left in the dark. The person just disappeared indefinitely.

The more the regime got into difficulties, the more it oppressed its citizens through the *Stasi*. All East European countries had similar security apparatuses in the Cold War, but not on the scale or ferocity of East Germany. Its emblem represented the "shield and sword of the Party." Its official hero was Felix Dzerzhinsky, founder of the Bolshevist Cheka secret police, which conducted state terror in Russia in the early days of Lenin. This was German thoroughness put to the service of intimidation, in a way all too redolent of bad old times.

At its height just before the Berlin Wall fell, the *Stasi* employed 91,000 full-time employees and 173,000 unpaid informers *Informelle Mitarbeiter (IM)* – in a country of 17 million inhabitants. The Nazis by comparison had some 7,000 Gestapo to cover the whole of Germany, while West Germany employed around 15,000 secret police in the Cold War years.

The East German regime was so unpopular that it felt obliged to double the numbers of *Stasi* on average every 10 years. The cost to the economy was eventually four billion GDR marks (about one billion DM) per year, sucking away resources which could be ill afforded. On the other hand, the *Stasi's* political prisoners were also a commodity to trade: West Germany paid 2.5 billion DM to free 35,000 detainees from the mid-1960s on.[cxlii]

Their presence was all-invasive. When dissident writer Stefan Heym saw his *Stasi* files after 1990, he commented: "We lived as if under glass, like impaled beetles, and every wriggle of the little feet was observed with interest and commented on at length."[cxliii]

In 1971-72, I wondered to what extent my movements around the country were being tracked. I detected nothing. Once I went to visit Hermann von Berg in an East Berlin suburb and thought a car was a long time behind me. I drove half-way back again and the car had disappeared. Perhaps the *Stasi's* skills were such that I could not spot them. But one of my successors in the 1980s saw when he looked at his files that the *Stasi* took months to notice that he was frequenting a certain East Berlin pub and had become friends with the regulars.[cxliv] 20 years earlier, correspondent Frederick Forsyth (later an author of spy thrillers) drove for days around East Germany looking for a crashed U.S. plane without being detected.[cxlv]

I too applied to see my *Stasi* files, and received... practically nothing. I wondered why there was so little. Were my files so hot that the *Stasi* selected them for shredding after the fall of the Berlin Wall? Or worse, did they just not find me that important?

The documents showed that one East German woman reported to the *Stasi* that my wife had provided her with all the books published in West Germany by the dissident East German singer Wolf Biermann. That was doubtless true: we had listened to Biermann performing to a circle of friends in her home. That was it, for my whole year as a western journalist in East Germany.

Then in 1976, four years after I left the country, the files showed a colonel of the *Stasi* sent an identical letter to his counterparts in Poland, Hungary, Czechoslovakia and Bulgaria asking whether I had been "operatively noticed" and were there indications of connections to "enemy centres and secret services?" The order coming from a Major-General heading Department X stated that I had come to notice "in the direction of political-ideological diversion."

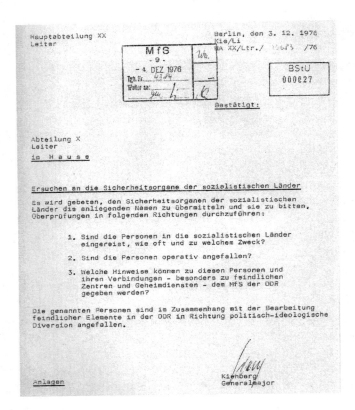

Hauptabteilung XX
Leiter

Berlin, den 3. 12. 1976
Kie/Li
HA XX/Ltr./ 1663 /76

MfS
- 9 -
- 4. DEZ 1976
Tgb.Nr. 4314
Weiter an:

BStU
000027

Bestätigt:

Abteilung X
Leiter
im H a u s e

Ersuchen an die Sicherheitsorgane der sozialistischen Länder

Es wird gebeten, den Sicherheitsorganen der sozialistischen
Länder die anliegenden Namen zu übermitteln und sie zu bitten,
Überprüfungen in folgenden Richtungen durchzuführen:

1. Sind die Personen in die sozialistischen Länder
   eingereist, wie oft und zu welchem Zweck?

2. Sind die Personen operativ angefallen?

3. Welche Hinweise können zu diesen Personen und
   ihren Verbindungen - besonders zu feindlichen
   Zentren und Geheimdiensten - dem MfS der DDR
   gegeben werden?

Die genannten Personen sind im Zusammenhang mit der Bearbeitung
feindlicher Elemente in der DDR in Richtung politisch-ideologische
Diversion angefallen.

Kienberg
Generalmajor

Anlagen

The Stasi ask for checks on the author four years after he left East Germany.

The Czechoslovak secret service came up with trumps.
They replied that they had negative knowledge about
me since 1974, that I was indeed suspected of obtaining
information "in the direction of political-ideological
diversion" and that I had commented on it tendentiously
in a way which damaged the interests of the Czechoslovak
Socialist Republic.

All of which implied I was a provocateur in the pay of
a Western secret service. But in essence it just described
my work as a journalist for Reuters. It was strange that the

Czechoslovak secret service supposedly spotted this only in 1974. By that time I had been a resident correspondent in Czechoslovakia writing about dissident trials for two years. Even stranger was that the *Stasi* launched this absurd paper chase four years after I last set foot in East Germany. The whole operation smacked of sloppiness. There were mistakes in the date and place of my birth. Some of my records were still being re-catalogued in 1988. The fearsome *Stasi* also had its useless pen-pushers.

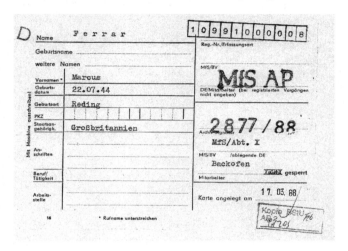

My Stasi file, including mistakes, still being reordered in 1988, 16 years after I left East Germany.

In 2008 I asked my former East Berlin assistant Erdmute Behrendt whether the *Stasi* had ever sought her help. She replied indignantly no, and said she would have quit her work if they had tried. One of my successors as correspondent who had seen his own files noticed that none of the information could have come from her, and apologised to her for assuming she had been informing. Possibly the *Stasi* thought they were picking up quite enough from the bugs in the office and living quarters. Or perhaps they did not want to create trouble which could prompt Reuters to pull out.

Erdmute did however find a thick file about herself. Most were endless records of trips she and her husband took into the countryside to a cottage. As they passed from village to village, always on the same route, the local *Stasi* man telephoned through to his counterpart along the road announcing that they were coming. She also found that the obstetrician who helped her give birth to her son was a *Stasi* officer. She shuddered at the intimacy of this intrusion.

The most likely reason why scarcely any files of mine were found is that the *Stasi* decided they were not worth keeping and threw them away. Or they were caught up in the indiscriminate shredding when the regime fell.Half the people who apply to see their files are told nothing can be found. The *Stasi* were mainly interested in keeping files on people they could threaten or blackmail. They intimidated their citizens into avoiding contact with any western journalist, and I was thus to some extent insulated – or so they thought.

The *Stasi* felt no obligation to preserve documents for the historical record. Ilona Rau, head of the archives in Dresden, says that many of the files were damaged by having been stuffed in garages, damp cellars or behind hot pipes.[cxlvi] Others were torn up by hand or shredded. After the population occupied *Stasi* buildings in late 1989 and early 1990, the scraps of paper they gathered filled over 15,000 sacks. Eighteen years after reunification, only 400 bags had been sorted through and the files reconstructed. Calculating that the task would take 700 years at this rate, the archivists embarked on a project to speed up reconstruction by computerised matching of the scraps.

The *Stasi* files are thus an immense challenge to professional archivists. After 1990, they had to secure the files against further destruction or theft, establish order among the jumbled documents, and then extract any incriminating evidence for prosecutions against *Stasi* agents, for which the cut-off point was 1995. In the end only one *Stasi* agent was convicted. Since then, the emphasis has been on making files available for inspection by concerned individuals and for historical research. With 112 kilometres (70 miles) of files to administer, many in poor condition, it is a massive task.

Some individual files run to 400 or more documents, going back four decades as far as 1950. If a person applied to go abroad on a trip, the *Stasi* would snoop into the person's marriage to assess the probabilities of return. By drawing in unpaid *Informelle Mitarbeiter* informers, the *Stasi* not only broadened their knowledge about the lives of East German citizens, but also increased the number of people morally compromised by their collaboration. That exposed them in turn to blackmail.

The *Stasi* attracted some informers by threats. They also looked for loners who might feel important by being asked to help. Typically, the candidate was summoned to meet in a "conspirative dwelling," a residential flat reserved for *Stasi* secret meetings. All important was the initial reaction to the request to collaborate. Many were tempted to make non-committal replies, hoping to play for time so that the *Stasi* would lose interest. That did not work. The *Stasi* sensed the vacillation, and summoned them back time and again. Only if the candidate refused at the outset did they possibly relent.

Some of the *Informelle Mitarbeiter* were extraordinarily industrious: one filled 20 folders over 12 years. Others mistakenly believed they were handing over harmless information. After all, if a colleague went on holiday, the whole office knew. But the *Stasi* did not know, and if they were tipped off, they could break into the absent person's home to place bugs.

Ilona Rau shows a few files from the archive containing only one or two papers. These are of people who refused straightaway to cooperate. They are marked "unsuitable." As with the Nazis, there were some Germans who knew immediately they were being asked to do wrong, refused and got away with it. These slim, dingy folders testify to the strength of human spirit, also among East Germans.

I look into the folders she has brought out for me and shudder. They seem harmless today, much as medieval instruments of torture do in a modern museum. But in their day these writings were weapons of terror. They were the reason why so many people I accosted in my year in East Berlin shrank and turned away.

German Chancellor Angela Merkel was one of those approached to collaborate by the *Stasi*. From the age of three, when her parents emigrated to East Germany from Hamburg, she grew up in East Germany, and for the first part of her adult life made a career there much like any other East German. When she was applying for a job as a physicist at the Ilmenau University, she was summoned to a room where she thought her travel costs would be reimbursed. Instead there was a *Stasi* officer who asked her to become an *Informelle Mitarbeiter*.

"I very quickly said that that was nothing for me, because I could not keep my mouth shut and always told such things to my friends. And that broke it, since keeping quiet was the basic pre-condition for being suitable," she said.[cxlvii]

Merkel did not get the job she was applying for.

Nowadays the methods and scope of the *Stasi* operations start to look old-fashioned and even quaint. Modern states have more advanced technology at their disposal enabling them to peer into their citizens' lives. In Europe, Britain has the largest number of closed-circuit TV cameras (CCTV) in public places – some four million in about 500 towns and cities. Germany has CCTV in

Chapter 14
ENDGAME 1989

Wir sind das Volk – We are the people

At the beginning of the 1970s, in my mid-twenties, I still espoused many of the tenets of socialism, if not as practised in East Germany. By the end of the decade, having also lived through the left-wing revolution which brought Portugal to its knees, I had had my fill of socialism. I was back in Britain under a Labour government which had lost control of the country's finances and had to call in the International Monetary Fund to bail the country out. Inflation in the late seventies ran at over 20%. Economic growth stagnated, and the British salary I earned scarcely lasted to the end of each month. In that "winter of discontent," strikers stopped work en masse and even blocked medical supplies from reaching cancer hospitals.

Under Margaret Thatcher, elected in 1979, the tide of political opinion turned irrevocably against socialism. Private enterprise rather than the state became the main driving force in the economy, and not just in Britain. By the middle of the 1980s, socialism had retreated all over Western Europe, never to recover its old prevalence. Social safety nets continued, but free markets otherwise predominated. In Britain, the number of days work lost through strikes fell from 29 million in 1979 to 460,000 in 2009.[cl]

It was as if Europe, like me, was growing up and taking its responsibilities rather than looking to a paternalistic state for direction. No doubt my mother's visceral aversion to state power which she learned in Hitler's Germany fed through to me. Also, I was 35 and for the previous 10 years I had been to all intents and purposes disenfranchised. I could not vote in Britain because I lived in another country. In those countries I could not vote either because I was not a citizen. Under the circumstances, I counted on my own resources to get on. However my inborn tendency to see both sides of a question made me reject the divisiveness of the neo-liberal ideology. As the son of my mother, I was sceptical of any ideology at all.

In the western part of Germany, the lives of my German relatives came increasingly to resemble those of the rest of us in Western Europe. Citizens enjoyed civic rights, freedom of speech, freedom of travel and growing prosperity based on market economies. We went to university, applied for jobs, took out mortgages and went on holiday in much the same way. The national differences between Germans and other peoples gradually dissipated.

Eastern Europe carried on however regardless of this sea change in the West. On the other side of the Iron Curtain, 17 million Germans lived quite differently and under constant duress. In western Germany, there were still some regional divergences between, say, Hamburgers, Rhinelanders and Bavarians. But the differences were trivial compared with the huge gulf which separated Germans in west and east. Rather than the western Germany of my cousins, it was the Germans in the east I felt most concerned by, amongst whom I had lived for a year. That was where the friction and tension was located which made Germany still a source of instability in Europe.

The man most responsible was the dour, colourless Erich Honecker, whose aim was to make socialism better for the inhabitants than what Ulbricht had been able to achieve. In the year I lived in East Germany, Honecker promised "a raise in the material and cultural living standard of the people."

In countries such as Yugoslavia and Hungary, Communist regimes were also seeking to improve the lot of their citizens. But they did this by easing the state's iron grasp over the economy. Honecker on the other hand believed that *more* socialism, not less, was the key. He set about constructing a socialist society from the top down. Whilst I was there, he eliminated the small private firms which employed 15% of the working population and accounted for 11% of gross domestic product, including 40% of clothing and 30% of leather.

The minimum wage and pensions were increased, mothers had to work less, a premium was paid for births, young people received cheap credits and prices and rents were frozen. Thousands of new flats were built, basic in comforts, but appealing because they were not damp, the walls were straight and they had central heating. They were all the same, reflecting the idea of one standard for all.

This vision of better living standards, a truly equal society and a more enlightened attitude to intellectual thinking was attractive as a concept. Honecker was making one last attempt to make state socialism work. But from my own experience, it was obvious that the Communist system would never be able to produce enough wealth to accomplish it. Elimination of the private economy made it harder to deliver on his pledge of a better material life. The building programme faltered after a few years: at the end of the 1980s, 72% of dwellings in Leipzig were still in urgent need of renovation.[cli]

With his reputation riding on the promise of a better life, he shied away from imposing austerity measures to bring public finances back in order. All the generous social perks remained in place. To Honecker's mind, socialism must be seen to be improving the people's lot. He refused to countenance that maybe it never would.

Honecker and his Soviet overseers wanted to glean the benefits of recognition by West Germany but prevent

Western ideas from permeating East Germany. This meant tightening political restrictions, not easing them. So I found myself reporting on Honecker's new policy of *Abgrenzung* (demarcation) from West Germany, imposed by force in the true spirit of Lenin. From then up to 1980, he increased the number of *Stasi* from 40,000 to 80,000. In my year, he ordered fragmentation mines to be placed along the Wall and the border with West Germany, and thereafter maps of East Germany showed a large white space where West Berlin was – no streets, no names, no landmarks, just a blank.[clii]

The experiment of allowing intellectuals more freedom led nowhere. Some wanted to use their latitude to criticize the regime. In a dictatorship, this could not be tolerated, as it might release pent-up opposition among the population. In 1976, the East German government expelled one of its most talented artists, the singer Wolf Biermann, and deprived him of his citizenship. A few years earlier, I could sit in a private East Berlin home and listen to his protest songs. Now even these twilight performances were too much. For the artists who had been waiting to see, his expulsion was the final straw, and eventually others were driven out or followed voluntarily into exile. Stefan Heym signed a petition of protest and was again banned from publishing.

By 1977 Honecker was in a cul-de-sac, only six years after coming to power. He was struggling to meet the material expectations he had raised, intellectuals were disaffected and the population was living under stricter political constraints than before. He had to borrow heavily abroad. As the costs of servicing this debt rose, East Germany in the 1980s was exporting eggs, butter, meat, cement, furniture, household gadgets, gas cookers, high-quality porcelain, bicycles, industrial machines and weapons to earn foreign exchange.[cliii] Nearly all these goods were sorely needed by the domestic economy.

The assumption had always been that the Soviets would stand by their East German brothers. But the Soviet Union was sagging economically too, and not only provided no help but even reduced its oil exports to East Germany. Meanwhile, strikes began shaking the Communist regime in Poland, and Hungary began liberalising its economy.

The only brother prepared to help out was the West German brother. Bonn extended billions of DM of credit to East Germany, which became increasingly dependent on the partner from whom it wished to "demarcate" itself. West Germany exacted easier travel between the two states, more family contacts and removal of the fragmentation mines in return. Its belief was that help would gradually mellow the East German regime, which would feel more secure. That did not happen. There were still umpteen ways of getting killed at the border. East Germans began to resent the cosiness of West German politicians with a regime they detested. They considered the West Germans were tacitly accepting the status quo, and felt let down.

Despite this, the West German détente policy, pursued without let-up from 1970 to 1989, stands out for me as another great milestone in Europe's changing values. This state at the heart of Europe was offering conciliation as well as large-scale financial assistance. The underlying conflict was not set aside, but the West Germans tried to resolve it by peaceful, generous means. Americans and West Europeans had their doubts, but the West Germans proved right in the end. After a first half century setting new records of horror and cruelty, Germans – at least in the West – were demonstrating the power of generosity.

The Communist part of Germany slowly fell into disarray. The failure of Honecker's policy led to recriminations within his own Politburo (as is now known). Hardliners such as Prime Minister Willi Stoph and *Stasi* chief Ernst Mielke complained about the dependence on West Germany and wanted closer relations with the Soviet

Union in the hope that the latter would take over the debts. The Soviets blew hot and cold. They liked West German détente for their own interests, and Soviet leader Leonid Brezhnev had good personal relations with West German Chancellor Helmut Schmidt. But they were suspicious of any East German rapprochement with Bonn, and insisted Honecker keep up the *Abgrenzung*.

It was a hopeless situation. Many in the West continued to seriously overestimate East Germany's capabilities, half believing the regime's own boast of being the world's 10th strongest industrial power. But my own experience told me this could not be true. After the cuts in Soviet oil supplies, East German industry had to reconvert to its indigenous brown coal, which was inefficient, polluting and onerous to extract. The plant processing it was decrepit and breaking down. In the winter of 1978-79, ice rain brought production to a halt, resulting in power cuts.[cliv]

An attempt to turn East Germany into a producer of micro-electronics foundered because it was years behind the rest of the world and uncompetitive on costs. In strategic industries such as the Carl Zeiss Jena optics plant, the Party was ignored. The chemicals industry became increasingly dangerous due to ageing plant.[clv] A land that was supposed to become a workers' paradise instead slipped further and further into working class poverty.

For the ordinary people, mostly doing their best to make things work, these dire conditions were deeply discouraging. Social tensions rose as workers noticed their living standards were falling far behind those of privileged bureaucrats and people with access to foreign currency. The government built a grandiose hunting lodge reminiscent of the Austro-Hungarian Empire. The Politburo lived in villas fitted out with Western household equipment. Honecker collected valuable paintings including a Picasso.

The working class was supposed to be in the vanguard of the ruling Party, but those in power had been professional politicians and administrators for years, and their way of life was anything but proletarian. To compensate, the regime designated officials, military personnel and workers' children as working class. Nobody except the inner circle was fooled.

East German author Reinhard Firgl wrote later of East Germany as "a land and its earth, sunken in like old graves." He felt "an unrelenting, crippling, seemingly all encompassing vexation, satiety, loathing and disgust."[tlvi] His tortured twisting of the German language conveyed an unsettling *Angst* that harked back to Germans of an earlier age.

Honecker could not win. The Communist economic system could produce neither wealth nor social justice. In its last year, its foreign debt reached 40 billion valuta marks, and a top official (Gerhard Schürer) wrote a report predicting state bankruptcy within one year. Honecker was tied to a Soviet friend who neither let him off the leash nor helped out materially. Soviets and East Germans were locked in a mindset which failed their own citizens and maintained a generalised hostility that no longer had a place in Europe. For somebody like myself, used to moving easily among nations, such antagonisms were primitive and archaic.

As I had observed these Communist leaders talking endlessly about doctrine, it came as a surprise after the collapse of the regime to perceive how driven they were by personal rivalries. As tongues of former comrades loosened, it became apparent that Honecker had turned against Ulbricht mainly to further his own ambition. Once in power, Honecker sidelined the other Politburo members, keeping them quiet with threats and privileges. They too clung to power, keeping out younger rivals. Security chief Erich Mielke protected his interests by locking away files about Honecker's Nazi imprisonment, during which the latter is rumoured to have betrayed comrades under torture. It was personal and sordid.

The outcome was a stalemate in which Communism stood still in a rapidly changing world. The only living idea was to preserve what already existed, at all costs. That eroded any incentive to change leaders. Brezhnev carried on long after he was incapacitated, as did Hungary's János Kádár. The Communist leaders I knew from the early 1970s, such as Czechoslovakia's Gustáv Husák, Romania's Nicolae Ceauşescu and Bulgaria's Todor Zhivkov were all still holding on at the end of the 1980s. They grew old in what was supposed to be a dynamic form of government, becoming more stubborn, but losing energy and increasingly incapable of new thinking. When he was finally deposed in late 1989, Erich Honecker was seriously ill with a gall bladder affliction and he could speak only in a quavering voice. Five years later he died of cancer at age 81.

These leaders counted on the steadfastness of the Soviet Union for their survival, and to the surprise of everyone this was no longer sure. A younger leader, Mikhail Gorbachev, came to power. His family had direct experience of the Gulag prison camp regime, he was morally disenchanted with the system he headed, and he could see that its economy was tottering.

Gorbachev set about liberalising the Soviet economy in the hope of galvanising it. To stimulate a new way of thinking, he encouraged transparency and freedom of speech. Normal though this may have been in the West, it was an astonishing departure from Communist practice.

The failings of the Soviet system had been evident for a long time, and there was no particular reason why he should not have tried to plod on along the same path as his predecessors. But Gorbachev was another exceptional individual who dared to swim against the tide. He concluded that any hope of reviving his people's fortunes excluded a costly arms race with the United States or propping up unpopular regimes in Eastern Europe. He acted accordingly, and the outcome was an end to tyranny, an opening up to the world and removal of a major threat to peace. Hundreds of millions of people have had better lives because of Gorbachev, who seems to have been driven more by humane instincts than any master plan.

Honecker bet that Soviet hardliners would eventually remove Gorbachev, as they did with the previous reformer, Khrushchev. But that did not happen, and the peoples of Eastern Europe gradually sensed that the leaders were marionettes whose strings nobody was holding any more. Everything changed, almost from one moment to another. The legions of Soviet tanks, aircraft and armies in East Germany lost their menace. The police who had cracked down on dissidents at the behest of the Soviets were now acting on their own. The Berlin Wall served as *Abgrenzung* against a West Germany to which nobody was hostile any more.

Honecker's last success was not a victory over West Germany, but an official visit there in 1987. He was finally admitted to a world of state dignities from which he had been largely excluded. Satisfying personal vanity was the last throw of a man who had failed in his life's work. When Gorbachev arrived in East Berlin for the 40th anniversary of the German Democratic Republic in October 1989, everybody understood that his ritual embrace of Honecker was a Judas kiss. He berated the East German leadership for failing to move with the times. Like Willy Brandt kneeling before the Warsaw ghetto memorial in 1970, the image of Gorbachev's spurious kiss became engraved in the world's psyche.

The subsequent demonstrations and confrontations with riot police culminated in a popular uprising which set new standards of courage and civil responsibility reaching far beyond East Germany. The East Germans, better than anyone in the West, sensed that without Gorbachev's support, their dictatorship was crumbling. And without a dictatorship, power was there for the people to seize.

Wir sind das Volk, "We are the people," they chanted to the threatening *Volkspolizei*, sensing the historical moment. They wrested ownership of the word *Volk* from the Communist state. The protesters had to endure beatings and arrests as the police savagely fought to keep control over the streets. As in Prague and Warsaw however, the demonstrators proclaimed their non-violent intentions.

When police threatened a bloody attack in Leipzig, Kurt Masur, *Kapellmeister* of the Leipzig Gewandhaus orchestra, mediated with local Party officials, the Soviet commander and the police to allow 70,000 demonstrators to march peacefully through the city centre singing hymns. The moment of danger passed. The police ceded control of the streets. Thereafter the people pushed on a half-open door.

These uprisings set a notable moral benchmark in 20th century history. The German people successfully resisted tyranny, but unlike the British after Munich they did not resort to force of arms to do so. They were weak but morally strong; peaceful not warlike. It was a victory for "soft" values. And in the person of Kurt Masur, a German intellectual had risen to an honourable political challenge and triumphed. Their victory consummated a turnaround in German values.

With Honecker deposed by his own Politburo, the new Communist leaders desperately back-pedaled to try to gain favour with the people. It was too little, too late. The regime foundered in a mess of decisions taken on the spur of the moment. They decided to allow free travel, and Politburo member Günter Schabowski was so disorientated that he blurted it out at a press conference on 9th November 1989 before the border guards could prepare.

The people went to the Berlin Wall and gathered as guards milled around in demoralised confusion. Then the barricades which nobody had the will to keep shut any more swung open, and the people walked through, laughing, weeping and shouting for joy. This too was a symbolical act – East Germans passed a historical threshold. It was the deed not of one inspired person, but of a whole people, the sons and daughters of the Berliners who had been too frightened to talk to me in the early 1970s. With those steps, the people of East Germany walked back into the world.

I watched it all happen on television from afar. The moment I saw the first breach in the Wall, I knew it was all over and Europe would never be the same again. I was no longer a journalist. I felt no temptation to join in the euphoric street parties. I had already been there, and I sensed it would turn out like this, one day.

The future German Chancellor, Angela Merkel, then an East German physicist, did not quite grasp the implications.When she went on a working visit to Poland a few days later, her Polish friends told her: "Next time we meet in Berlin, your country will be one." She laughed in disbelief.[clvii]

Chapter 15

AFTER THE PARTY

There will still be two Germanys 50 years from now
— British scholar 1989

When I gave a talk in Berlin in 2008 to the *Zeitzeugenbörse* – the "witness to history" group – most of those taking part raised questions about the Nazi era. In the testimony the *Zeitzeugen* give in schools and the media, the time of the Nazis is the key period of interest, almost as a matter of course. However, two women came up to me afterwards and said they had long come to terms with German guilt for the war. What Germans had not digested, they said, was the Communist past of East Germany.

I agree. The collapse of Communism in 1989, leading to reunification of Germany a year later, is no less important a historical milestone than 1945. It caught not only Angela Merkel by surprise, but also Gorbachev, who said 20 years later he never expected the Wall to give way so soon. Even after the opening of the Berlin Wall, the East German state did not collapse immediately. The Communist regime governed, albeit to little effect, the *Stasi* remained in their offices all over the country, and the world outside was not sure if it really wanted change to go much further.

Former wartime enemies of Germany were confronted with a prospect they feared – of a Germany reinvigorated and flexing its muscles over the rest of Europe. But people were breaking free and claiming a new future not just in Berlin, but in Poland, Czechoslovakia, Hungary, Romania, Bulgaria and Yugoslavia. The Czech Václav

Havel was proclaiming from balconies a vision of truth, non-violence and humane values, while his Warsaw contemporaries sat at a round table persuading a resentful Polish dictatorship to share power, and Hungarian Viktor Orbán told a quarter of a million people on a Budapest square: "We must see to it that the ruling party can never again use force against us."

This was the rising of the people the West had always dreamed of for Eastern Europe, but when it came it disturbed a status quo which suited many. For those, a separate East German state remained preferable.

The principal worriers were Britain's Margaret Thatcher and France's François Mitterrand. Recently released Foreign Office records of a meeting between the two in January 1990 show that the prospect of reunification brought old fears of Germany swelling back to the surface.

Mitterrand maintained that the effect on Germans had been "to turn them once again into the 'bad' Germans they used to be." He detected "a certain brutality" and complained that the Germans were upsetting the political realities of Europe. He predicted that reunited Germany would seek to regain lost territories in the East and "might make even more ground than Hitler." It would dominate Czechoslovakia, Poland and Hungary, the Russians would persuade Britain and France to ally against Germany "and then we would all be back in 1913." He urged that France and Britain should not allow the Germans "to throw their weight around."

Thatcher expressed sympathy for people who rose up against Communist oppressors, but insisted that Germans were not yet ready for reunification, adding "at the moment they are getting away with too much." She and Mitterrand should do all they could to slow the process down and even block certain decisions, enlisting Soviet help in doing so. "We must not let it become a decade of fear," she told her host gloomily.[clviii]

Thatcher then summoned British historians to her country home in Chequers to assess the character of Germans. The minutes drafted by one of her aides spoke of *Angst*, aggressiveness, assertiveness, bullying, egotism, an inferiority complex, sentimentality, and a tendency to excess and kicking over the traces.

Thatcher herself declared: "I do not believe in collective guilt, but I do believe in national character... Since Bismarck, Germans have veered unpredictably between aggression and self-doubt." She said it would be at least another 40 years before the British could trust Germans again.

Professor D. Cameron, a scholar at the London School of Economics, wrote in early 1989: "There will still be two Germanys 50 years from now."[clix] This echoed the forecast made in 1961 by Oxford historian A.J.P. Taylor, who wrote:"Only a divided Germany could be free. A united Germany would cease to be free: either it would become a militaristic state in order to resume the march towards European domination, or its power would be compulsorily reduced by foreign interference, if the former allies had the sense to come together again in time." The allies he had in mind were Britain and the Soviet Union.[clx]

Beatrice von Mach experienced this entrenched hostility to Germans on a personal level in 1989 when she took up a post as a financial trader in the City of London. Aged 30 then, she was the daughter of a German diplomat who served on the European Commission and told his children when he went to work: "I'm going to fight for Europe" (the little girl wondered if he kept a spear in his office). Her grandfather had helped negotiate West Germany's peace treaty with the Soviet Union in 1970. She was brought up in Brussels, spent a year at Oxford University and had studied and worked in the United States. But as soon as the British traders heard her name and grasped that she was German, they paraded up and down in front of her desk shouting "Heil Hitler!" and giving Fascist salutes.

"I didn't consider myself completely German any more, but they didn't care a shit how German I felt. They saw my Prussian-looking name, I was a woman and I spoke several languages. I was the sort of person they loved to hate," she said.

"I had a hard time from the British already during the year I studied at Oxford. When I went to university in New York in 1980, a Jewish professor once asked me whether I felt guilty about the war. I felt he had a right to ask and get an answer. Otherwise nobody in America made any comment on my being German. They noticed rather that I was blonde."[clxi]

Around the same time, my German cousin, Marie-Luise, sent her children to language schools in England, and says young Britons they came across also taunted them as Nazis.

This was the zero-sum philosophy. If Germany through reunifying does better, we will do worse. It assumed that mutual hostility was a permanent given, and ignored the decades of post-war reconciliation at the heart of the European Union.

Having become accustomed to the Cold War, in which the Soviet Union was the enemy, I found it hard to believe that such experienced political leaders as Mitterrand and Thatcher could be tied to the fears of a preceding era. It flew in the face of my own experience of Germans.

Some prominent Germans were just as pessimistic at the time of reunification. The writer Günter Grass, who had prodded Germans to acknowledge their wartime guilt since the 1960s, complained that reunification had brought back the old class society. As late as 2002, he published a novel, *Im Krebsgang* (Crab Walking), about neo-Nazis gnawing away at the fabric of German democracy.[clxii] Stefan Heym, who emerged as an East German éminence grise after the Communist collapse, worried that reunification would eradicate social achievements and leave Germany just as unstable as before.[clxiii]

Mitterrand had to abandon his opposition after criticism in France for being insensitive to German feelings, while American President George H. Bush was sympathetic from the start. Britain became isolated and irrelevant, but the big question remained: how would the Soviet Union take the loss of its stronghold in East Germany? Gorbachev had indicated readiness to move, but only so far. He did not appreciate what he had unleashed through opening his country up to free thinking and removing the Soviet military threat. He told Mitterrand in December 1989:

"In the case of German reunification, there will be a two-line announcement that a Soviet marshal has taken my place."[clxiv]

The one who caught on quickest was Helmut Kohl, West German Chancellor at the time. In November 2009, on the 20th anniversary of the fall of the Berlin Wall, the *Frankfurter Allgemeine Zeitung* urged that Kohl be awarded the Nobel Peace Prize, because "when the possibility for reunification offered itself, he seized it without hesitation – while most politicians, historians and also philosophers both in Germany and abroad timidly wavered, warned against unity or even tried to hinder it."[clxv]

Kohl was an unlikely man of the moment. Burly and rough-mannered, he seemed a provincial politician not up to great concepts. But he proved doubters wrong. He prepared the ground already before the Berlin Wall fell by continuing to subsidise the East German state. He was a member of the conservative Christian Democratic Union (CDU), but he did not hesitate to continue a policy pioneered by the Social Democrats (SPD). He also continued providing loans to the Soviet Union.

This much needed aid deterred Soviet hardliners from blocking West German ambitions.

Kohl believed from the start that the opening of the Berlin Wall would eventually lead to reunification. He rushed back from a visit to Poland to address a rally the next day in West Berlin, at which Willy Brandt stood alongside him and said: "What belongs together is now growing together."

At first, even Kohl believed the East German state would continue for some time, with a reformer such as Hans Modrow carrying out deep changes in the meantime. He understood otherwise on 19 December 1989, when he appealed to an East German crowd to show patience, and they responded with rousing calls for unity. His experienced political antennae picked up that East Germans had no confidence in any reforms initiated by the old regime.

The Soviet Union, Britain and France were all hoping that Modrow would deliver, but Kohl realised that time was on his side, and reunification would happen by itself unless there were a major upset. As is now known, some of the Soviet military were pushing for just that: they wanted the Red Army to close the East German borders again through the armed intervention of one million Soviet soldiers. But it was far too late for that and Gorbachev demurred.

The forces of history were running against the fears, worries and antagonisms of the old guard all over Europe. They were out of step with their times. It was Kohl, the heavy, provincial German politician, who proved nimblest on his feet. He took over the driving seat and never got out. The more time passed, the less possible was it for the Soviet Union to retrieve a steadily deteriorating situation in East Germany. The less Kohl pushed, the more Gorbachev gained confidence that a reunited Germany could be a friend.

Kohl agreed to pay for the bases the Red Army was leaving in East Germany, as well as for retraining, rehousing and schooling of troops repatriated to the Soviet Union. West Germany's aid to the Soviet Union reached 60 billion Deutschmarks over the years. Britain and France fell in behind an outcome that was increasingly inevitable. The act of reunification in Berlin on 3rd October 1990 celebrated a process which had already largely taken place.

Kohl thus completed a policy, begun by Brandt, of showing Russians, Poles and others that Germans could be trusted. He achieved a reunified Germany that was democratic, not authoritarian as in the past. The new Germany, integrated as it was in NATO and the European Union, was surrounded by friends, not enemies as before. Germany took its place at the centre of a new European order better than any other in the 20th century.[clxvi] As for myself, I shared Willy Brandt's judgment that the coming together was a natural process. I rejoiced, not because German unity was virtuous as such, but because the downtrodden East Germans were at last free. I was not surprised that a lumbering, ordinary German such as Kohl had come up with trumps. I had learned since early days not to underestimate such characters, who had created the German economic miracle.

Now that it has become clear that a re-unified Germany endangers nobody, the divide between British and Germans in my family no longer seems as awkward as it once was. Having a foot in both camps has turned out to be helpful, not a hindrance.

On the way to unity, the West Germans took two decisions which caused problems of a different nature. Firstly, they incorporated East Germany into West Germany itself, taking advantage of an article of the West German constitution providing for this possibility. This meant the East German state ceased to exist, and gave the impression of a takeover rather than a merger. The other option was to draw up a new constitution for the combined states, but this could have taken years. It was a quick solution, but left East Germans with a sense of lost independence: West Germans would henceforth decide their fate.

Secondly, the West German government decided to change East marks into Deutschmarks at a generous rate of one for two, and even one for one for limited amounts. This was much better than the black market rates, which reflected real economic conditions. The decision gave East Germans the impression they could enjoy western levels of prosperity without moving en masse to the West, but it condemned much of their economy to bankruptcy, since at a stroke their costs became uncompetitive on world markets.

When I visited Berlin in 1991, it seemed every dwelling in the East had a new Volkswagen parked outside. The population was already benefiting from handouts from the West German government. But in the meantime, the factories where the people worked were being closed down at a dramatic pace. I could for the first time travel freely around Berlin and noticed that like London it stretches in a long line from east to west. But East and West were still different worlds.

The East Germans were rid of an oppressive, suspicious regime and could freely vote for whatever government they liked. However they were no longer protected from free markets, where efficiency and competition determine advantage, not social justice or a controlling state. The result, as in all of ex-Communist Eastern Europe, was an economic catastrophe which caused immense distress for millions.

The break-up of the state-controlled system had to come sooner or later, and free markets promised a way eventually to attain much greater levels of prosperity.

But Westerners accustomed to long years of relative affluence underestimate the pain the populations of ex-Communist states went through in transitioning to the market economy. People had their livelihoods destroyed, and were made to feel that all they had done in the past was for naught. By the time the economy picked up, it was too late for those whose best days were past.

East Germany's international trade fell apart overnight. The system of controlled exchanges among Communist countries could no longer be insulated from the pressures of free markets. East Germany was in credit with most of its East European partners, but got nothing back. It could no longer export to the West, as the new currency exchange rate made its costs too high.

Most East Germans owned practically nothing personally when Communism collapsed. All their wealth was tied up in the state, and in order to adapt to free market conditions, that wealth had to be privatised. West Germans assumed that their greater experience in running a free market economy qualified them to undertake the privatisation themselves. As a result, East Germany was overrun by West German entrepreneurs and experts. They did indeed understand better how to do it, but exclusion of East Germans from the process left the impression of colonisation. Whatever value the East Germans had created was perceived as passing into the hands of West German profiteers.

East Germany's worn-out, dirty industry producing outdated goods that nobody wanted was bound to disappear. However, even a successful enterprise such as the Wittenberger Mühlenwerke, which as a GDR company had 13% of the world market for cereal processing machinery, was swept away in a wave of liquidations. [clxvii] One third of the population of Wittenberg, where Martin Luther once launched the Protestant Reformation, subsequently left for the West.

Within a year of the currency exchange, the number of East German employed had fallen from nine to seven million. One third of those laid off never found another job in their lives. Three-quarters of the professors at East Berlin's Humboldt University, including scientists, were forced out of their jobs.[clxviii] By 1991, East German industrial production was only 31 % of what it had been in 1989. Other East European countries suffered big declines too, but they were at least enjoying independence after freeing themselves from Soviet domination. They held their fates in their own hands. East Germans felt they were passing from dependency on the Soviet Union to a new dependency on West Germany.

Twenty years after reunification, it was estimated that 87% of the former East Germany economy was in the hands of West Germans, and only six per cent belonged to former GDR citizens.[clxix] None of the 30 leading German companies quoted on the DAX stock market listing was headed by an Easterner.

Those East Germans who had served the *Stasi* or the frontier troops were excluded from any significant positions in the reunited Germany. When dealing with ex-Nazis, the occupying powers hesitated to act against them because they wanted to deploy them against each other in the Cold War. This was not a factor this time. Nobody wanted to recycle the Communists' henchmen. When the armed forces of the two German states were merged, most of the senior East German officers were left out because they had links with the *Stasi*. Twenty years after reunification, only one of the German Army's 200 generals came from the East.

But thousands of East Germans who collaborated with the Communist dictatorship on a lesser level went unpunished. I remember such people from my time in East Germany. They were neither innocent nor pleasant. They have been allowed to evade personal responsibility for acts that harmed others, in a way which West Germans learned they could not do concerning Nazi deeds. Little has been done to rehabilitate and compensate the victims of Communism.[clxx] A moral doubt still hangs over millions of these older East Germans. Many live in the private knowledge that they once acted deceitfully.

The East Germans were ill-equipped to face the challenges of the modern world into which the West had already moved. Since 1933, their state had not required – or even allowed – them to take personal responsibility for their lives. First the Nazis, and then the Communists, insisted that the only salvation lay in loyalty to the collective. Individual initiative was frozen out, and the entrepreneurial middle-class that powered the post-war West German revival was lacking.

After 1989, few East Germans had the expertise or even inclination to set up on their own and take the calculated risks involved in creating wealth. Many saw the notion of personal property as exploitation, the rule of law as arbitrary and free markets as gangsterism. They were unprepared to compete in a globalised economy in which West Germans were already moving with ease. If West Germans had not moved in to take over, the eastern part of the country may well have struggled for much longer to reform itself.

What the East Germans remain skilled in is helping each other out when the state system fails. Beneath the surface today persists this socialist way of informally working with each other to make things happen without money changing hands. As one Englishman remembers from visiting friends in East Berlin, in a single street one person would have a car, one a washing machine and another a bath. They shared these belongings around on the basis of personal relations, rather as peasants did in earlier times, going from farm to farm to help each other with harvesting. If a problem arose, people resorted to improvisation rather than the fixed rules of modern institutions. I have observed this grassroots socialism enduring, not just in East Germany, but also in Hungary, former Yugoslavia, Romania, Bulgaria and other ex-Communist countries.

Germans voted with their feet in judging the effects of reunification. Since 1989, 2.7 million West Germans went to live in former East Germany, while 4.3 million of East Germany's 17 million citizens moved to West Germany. The West Germans saw fertile pickings in the East, while the Easterners perceived nothing left for them any more. The drain to the West was as bad as it had ever been under Communism. It reminded me of the five million Germans who emigrated to America in the 19th century, just before my grandfather's generation began to see opportunities to move ahead in Germany itself.

Many of the East Germans leaving were young and female. Whole villages were emptied and fell into ruin. Instead of the "blooming landscape" which Kohl had rashly forecast, parts of East Germany turned into a desert.

The government of reunified Germany poured West German money into the East in an attempt to revive the economy and assuage East German discontent. Over the first two decades after reunification, the sums transferred totaled €1.6 trillion. Traveling around East Germany today, I cannot miss the new motorways, railways, stations, airports, redecorated dwellings and restored historical monuments which this funded. As I ride on the overhead railway along the Schönhauser Allee in East Berlin, the facades gleam attractively with bright new colours. Gone are the bullet-holes of my time in 1971-72. Indeed it looks smarter than what one sees from London's suburban trains. Subsidies for all types of economic activity continue to pour in.

I am impressed by the continuing generosity of West Germans. They are using the same recipe as with the

Communist regimes of old: trying to buy a better future with financial aid. Forgotten however is the fact that all that aid did not stop the Communist economies from disintegrating. As in other underdeveloped countries, official aid does not always finance projects helping indigenous economic development. West Germany chose to help in this way rather than stimulating a system of capitalism in which the locals had a stake. The practice, unlike Erhard's liberalisation measures in 1948, encourages dependency rather than initiative. One economist calculated in 2009 that a large part of East Germany's economic activity would disappear if subsidies were withdrawn. Half of the East German population then was receiving state support.

Twenty years after reunification, polls showed two-thirds of East Germans considered themselves as second-class citizens in reunited Germany, and three-quarters believed they were disadvantaged compared with West Germans. East Germans tend to have the same corrosive pessimism and cynicism as citizens of other former Communist countries in Central & Eastern Europe. They all feel the new deal is better than the old dictatorship, but sadly assume that they are condemned to inferiority compared with the richer West. Confidence in their potential as individuals, never high in the past, remains at a low ebb.

Time will no doubt solve many of these issues. Large majorities of both West and East Germans continue to believe reunification was the right course, and Gross Domestic Product per person in the east rose from 40% of West German levels in 1991 to 70% in 2010.[clxxi] But people only have one life, and if a cataclysm strikes at a key moment of their development, they may never wholly recover. For these East Germans, the reunification so long yearned for by their compatriots in the West brought grief not happiness.

Chapter 16

A DIFFERENT PEOPLE

For what and for whom this chase after life...?
— inscription at the Berlin Holocaust Museum

A few miles down the road going east from Ratzeburg, I cross over a stream and I am there, in former East Germany. There is no signpost: after all, this is a reunified country. But I feel the difference. The façades of the villages tell of an older Germany, less touched by change. When I stop over to see a historic castle, the staff is surlier than where I have just come from, as if the entrance money I pay does not justify friendly service. In the West, a heritage site is marketed as a branded product designed to attract as many customers as possible. In the East, opening it to visitors is a cultural obligation dictated from above.

This lack of commercial intent can also be charming. Bowling along an empty Mecklenburg road lined by towering lime trees, as in the old days, is satisfying in itself. The series of lakes near Neustrelitz, the home of my German grandfather, are as beautiful as they have ever been.

But everywhere there is ambivalence. Alongside the eternally beautiful lakes are resorts developed for the new rich of Berlin. They smack of crude western commercialism. On the Baltic coast near Wismar, a gaggle of brassy beachside amusement kiosks set up with West German money has replaced a gaunt trade union colony. Between run-down villages on the way up to the coast is a gaudy new amusement park, set down in the middle of nowhere.

I drive past an empty airfield with bumps covering underground bunkers designed to withstand NATO nuclear attack – one of the 43 airfields the Soviets maintained to keep up the Cold War. Some housed military aircraft, others nuclear missiles trained on West European cities. A Chinese millionaire has bought one of these airfields to develop as a dropping off point for Chinese goods entering the European Union.[clxxii] Normalisation is having some weird outcomes.

I arrive in Neustrelitz and park alongside a curb, anywhere I choose. The town was laid out by a forward-looking duke in the early 19th century, and still feels spacious. Traffic is thin.

I walk past the Carolinum, where my late cousin Carl went to school. The military lazaret the Red Army set up inside has gone, and the building has been magnificently restored. It is once more dedicated to "the moral and educational upbringing of youth" prescribed by the enlightened Grand Duke Charles of Mecklenburg on its foundation in 1795. The nearby houses have been restored, but a few in the row stand out in ruins. These are the ones where legal ownership is still disputed (2.3 million claims for the return of expropriated property were made after the East German state collapsed).[clxxiii] They remain in limbo, waiting for the rule of law finally to settle down.

I spend the night in a hotel adapted from a former factory constructing tiled stoves. It is adequate but a little forlorn in its brown-orange-grey industrial setting. The horses for guests to ride stand miserably in large puddles as the rain pours down. Nearby are vegetable allotments surrounded by high fences. They are well protected because the inhabitants in Communist times grew fresh food that was unavailable from state shops. The leeks and cabbages inside were among the few forms of private ownership permitted and had considerable value.

In the heyday of Neustrelitz in the early 19th century, the resident Duchess of Mecklenburg was important enough to negotiate personally with Napoleon. The Red Army burned down her palace in 1945 as an act of revenge and class warfare. In the grounds are the tombstones of Soviet soldiers killed in the two days of local fighting before the German surrender. An inscription reads: "We do not envy you, our comrade. For three years you were a Soviet man. In heart and soul, you were a Soviet man." A picture of a tank is engraved into the stone, but the red stars are starting to peel off in post-imperial decay. Nearby are three birch trees planted in 1993 as a gesture of conciliation when the Soviet armoured Guards garrison left for good.

I drop in at the Roewer fine grocery store, which was expropriated from my cousin in 1945. It was run as a state shop under the Communists, and now has new owners. They have nothing to do with my family, but for the sake of the old Roewer name under which they trade, I make off with a few bottles of Roewer Sekt.

At midday on Saturday the shops shut and the place gradually falls asleep. It is time to go. 150 years after my grandfather grew up here, I feel as he did: this is not a place to stay in.

Some members of his family however took great pleasure in going back to Neustrelitz. During its Communist period, it was for Carl's three daughters in West Germany the happiest of holiday destinations. It was the place they went as children to be spoiled by relatives.

"I loved going swimming and playing in the back courtyard and the gardens round about. There were plenty of children of the same age to play with. I still like going back every now and then. It's so old-fashioned!" says Elke.

"I remember queuing for oranges and bed-clothes, just because they were there. But we had plenty to eat from the garden – all sorts of redcurrants, gooseberries and other fruits," adds her sister Gertrud.

The third sister, Emmi, appreciated that her aunt had plenty of time for her when she was on holiday there. She was told to keep away from Soviet soldiers, whom she could see in the barracks behind barbed wire on the other side of the lake where she swam. She was taken aback by the large numbers of soldiers in uniforms she saw walking around Neustrelitz. On the streets of post-war Hamburg where she grew up, she never saw any military uniforms.

I remembered my mother describing how she enjoyed growing up in Germany in the hardest of times in World War I. Now I met people for whom grim Communist East Germany was likewise a childhood paradise. My distant nieces, Elke, Gertrud and Emmi, savoured the spirit of mutual kindness and the simple pleasures of playing, swimming and letting the red juices of ripe fruit trickle down their throats.

Arriving in Berlin, I take rooms in *Mitte,* right in the middle of the city. They are clean and practical, but the coarse concrete of the construction tells me which side of the Wall this once was. These are Communist building standards and materials, the product of industrial workers who were the backbone of the regime. Their rough and ready craftsmanship is a hallmark of the half-city that was once my home. Outside, bullet marks scar the neighbouring buildings – the last remaining traces of conquering foreign troops who have departed.

A nearby restaurant is serving *Königsberger Klöpse*(Königsberg meat balls), as if Königsberg were just down the road, not 600 kilometres away. Once the main city of East Prussia, it became Soviet Kaliningrad after World War II. Only a few years ago it was isolated behind the Iron Curtain. Now Königsberg gives local flavour to a menu in Berlin, as the capital renews its links with its distant hinterland to the East.

As for German Chancellor Angela Merkel, 20 years after reunification she confessed to preferring the typical East European fare of Turkish coffee, solyanka (sour soup) and shashlik (grilled meat on a skewer).[clxxiv] These are Slavic tastes which East Germans picked up because they were on that side of the Iron Curtain.

In the Schönhauser Allee, the first-floor flat where I lived has been joined up with the little apartment alongside reserved for the *Stasi*. The Oderberg Strasse has become a trendy neighbourhood for the radical chic, combining style with a social conscience. A little restaurant which was not there in 1971 charges me a socially-correct €4.30 for an ecological meal, with one euro off for seniors. The 100-year-old terraced houses of what seemed like the grimiest of streets now sparkle with new paint – very much the dignified residences they were conceived as.

In the Friedrich Strasse, where West Germans visiting relatives used to queue to pass through checkpoints, the passing cars are gleaming and new, but still relatively scarce. Move down the street a little further, and the traffic peters out as one approaches the old Checkpoint Charlie, almost as if it were still impossible to proceed further. Friedrich Strasse is right in the middle of the city, but at the curbside I find plenty of parking spaces. A few discreet lines along gutters of side-streets trace where Honecker's men put up their barrier on 13th August 1961.

Since Berlin has become the capital of reunified Germany, new buildings have been springing up all over the centre, creating whole new neighbourhoods over the piece of arid central land once blighted by the intruding Wall. As I wander easily around in the area of the *Reichstag* parliament, it is hard to remember that I could not walk those few yards 20 years ago. At the Pariserplatz, a striking agglomeration of skyscrapers has replaced the no-man's land where in my time the Wall snaked around the buried ruins of Hitler's bunker. A slogan on a building site alongside reads: "Central Berlin is getting a new heart, just here."

Berliners keep up with the rash of new building by attributing cheeky nicknames. The curved, flattish House of Culture is "the pregnant oyster" and Chancellor Merkel's new Chancellery is "the washing machine." When not in her washing machine, Merkel lives on the Eastern side opposite the old central Museums, which are having *their* last bullet-holes patched up too.

The reunited German capital is above all determined to commemorate the nasty parts of German history. London's statues remember the great acts of British heroes going far back in time. Berlin remembers torture and genocide committed by ordinary Germans in living memory. London's memorials are uplifting; Berlin's, harrowing.

The worst collective German crime to commemorate is the extermination of the Jews. How can Germans appropriately honour Jews whom they themselves massacred? What can a museum show if there is nobody left any more? It is a demanding act of contrition and there was much agonising before the authorities decided what to do.

The Holocaust memorial which finally took shape is located on a prime site close to the Brandenburg Gate. On what used to be the mined death strip of the Wall extends a large field of tall, rectangular slabs of stone, standing slightly crooked like a medieval Jewish cemetery. Underneath are the families torn apart by the German genocide – or rather pictures of the families as they once were, displayed in an information centre. Normal fathers, mothers, children and aunts, celebrating normal birthdays and Sunday lunches, picked up from all over Europe and slaughtered just because of their race.

I shudder. They look much like the old photos of my own family, in Germany and in Britain. In a few last written words, the condemned convey their sentiments as they prepared to die:

"We left the camp singing, father and mother calm, Mischa as well. We will be traveling for three days" – Dutch girl Ette Hillesum, murdered in Auschwitz.

"For what and for whom this chase after life, putting up with everything, always holding out? For what?" – Herman Kruks, died in a concentration camp.

"If something like this was possible, what is there any more? Why war any more? Why hunger any more? Why the world any more? – Oskar Rosenfeld, Austria, murdered in Auschwitz.

"I say good-bye to you before I die. Good-bye forever. I kiss you tenderly," – Judit Wischatskaja, Belarus, killed in a death camp.

Just south of Checkpoint Charlie, Berlin commemorates how its Jewish community once was, before Germans murdered nearly all of them. The city has built a large new Jewish Museum for the 172,000 Jews who used to be its citizens. The message is that Jews contributed notably to German society, in particular in science and industry at the time when my German grandfather was active.

"Crooked nose, crooked stick/eye is black and soul is grey," reads an anti-Semitic doggerel from the popular 19th century German poet Wilhelm Busch. Nearby is a quotation from one of the leading rabbis, Nehemiah Anton Nobel, who wrote that he was happy to have roots in the Jewish world, but needed Goethe to help him think. It is a lavish memorial to a harmony that once was and still could have been. If only, I think.

My next stop is a monument to those killed in the 1953 workers' uprising against the Communist East German regime. It is alongside the building that used to be the East German Prime Minister's office and before that Goering's Air Ministry. The plaque is already deemed inadequate, since it is etched into the pavement and hard to notice. A campaign for something bigger and better is under way. No act of persecution should escape notice.

Nearby is a building which should remind me of home – the new British Embassy in Wilhelm Strasse. But it looks anything but homely. It strikes a jarring note. The façade is a long slab of stone interrupted by square, black windows, with an outsize Union Jack flying above. A glass watch-tower sits over the main entrance, which is a hole in the wall. I cannot help thinking of a concentration camp. The stretch of the Wilhelm Strasse where the embassy is located is barricaded off to prevent terrorist attacks. War, one feels, is not far away from this British patch of new Berlin.

I walk on up to the Museum of the GDR, located in the Karl-Liebknecht Strasse, named after the Spartacus leader murdered in the 1919 Communist uprising. This is the place where *Ossis* – the former East Germans – evoke with discreet dignity the lives they once led. In a city full of monuments to a grim past, it is surprising to note that this one has existed only since 2006.

This museum is quite positive in tone, though the guides are frank about the nasty sides of the GDR. They tell how long it took to wait for a flat and the furniture to go into it. They demonstrate how the *Stasi* inserted listening bugs into people's homes. They describe how GDR sportspeople suffered agonies of sweating because their track suits were made of artificial material derived from crude chemicals.

But I overhear one guide telling visiting schoolchildren from the West that East Germans were not lazy, and that all women had a right to work in the GDR. A few teenage girls nod thoughtfully. The guides speak of the West's hostile attempts to undermine their state during the Cold War.

Guide Gregor Schabitzsky, who has just finished showing round a group of schoolchildren from Hamburg, is the son of a woman who fled to the West. The *Stasi* tracked him thereafter, always knowing where he was, even on holiday. He did not like that, but nor did he like East Germany being simply incorporated into West Germany, nor that West Germans look down on *Ossis*. West German children arrive at the museum with a sense of superiority, he says, but mostly know next to nothing about how the GDR actually was.

A 45-year-old dentist I met shortly afterwards in Bavaria admitted this ignorance. He said nobody in West Germany before 1989 took any interest in what went on in the GDR. The only "knowledge" he had was that East Germans had jobs but did little real work. Only when I asked him how he knew this did it occur to him that he was perhaps unfair.

As I tour the Berlin museum, I remember how in 1972 the editors of the new Reuters German news service asked me to go out into East Germany and write about any aspect of life I chose. I felt this was a vague goal at the time. But they were right. As the only Western journalist accredited behind the Wall, the greatest service I could render was to fill the yawning gap in West Germans' knowledge about their compatriots in the East. The GDR Museum has the same mission. It remembers how 17 million Germans once lived, and tacitly asks visitors for a minimum of respect.

On the train from Berlin's Schönefeld airport, once serving just the Communist sector, another *Ossi* guide is sitting with a group of foreign visitors with bicycles. He has just taken them on a tour of the empty areas around Berlin where East German industry has been razed to the ground. The guide, who was born in the year I spent in East Berlin, says the old industries had to go, as they did in the 1980s in Margaret Thatcher's Britain. But he thinks people should see what is left of once-busy workplaces, and understand what their disappearance meant for those who lived from them. The tourists nod in agreement. They clearly thought their day out in the post-industrial desert was well spent.

In the evening, I go to the Berliner Ensemble theatre to see Bertolt Brecht's *Mutter Courage* (Mother Courage). Brecht's plays had anti-capitalist themes, and his Berliner Ensemble used to be a cultural showcase for Communist East Germany. His language is original and compelling, but also edgy and combative, not that of a "nice" German. He sought deliberately to "alienate" audiences so they would concentrate on the polemical message rather than lose themselves in emotional identification.

I wondered how relevant his best-known play would seem to today's young Berliners. Very much so is the answer. The theatre is packed out, and the audience emerges gleaming with, well, emotional identification. What appeals still is the anti-war message of *Mutter Courage*, which is set in Germany's 30 Years War. He need not have worried about being out of place. Today's Berlin youth find he still speaks powerfully to their hearts.

Last stop is Alexanderplatz to pick up cakes with Liselotte Kubitza, 74 years old, daughter of a poor Communist family and an East Berliner from head to toe. I feel back at home. Shopping for a few humble bits and pieces in the Alex helped make life in the GDR bearable, even homely.

We head off on the underground railway to her home near the Ostkreuz station, which 20 years after the fall of the Berlin Wall is still a scruffy neighbourhood. We get off and cross a temporary walkway alongside the old bridge, which is on the verge of collapse. The station looks as if it has not been renovated since 1945. It is a busy junction, and trains clatter noisily across the points.

As we walk past the empty spaces where bombed houses once stood, brass plaques are set into the pavement recording the names of Jews who once lived there and were murdered in the camps. The plaques were placed after the end of the Communist regime, which refused to recognise any responsibility for the Holocaust. For 40 years, the Communists told East Germans the Nazis were a bourgeois, capitalist class enemy, and portrayed wartime German crimes against Jews, Slavs and Roma as part of a class struggle rather than racist genocide. As socialist citizens, East Germans were said to be class victims and not perpetrators. They were only too ready to swallow this convenient alibi. Only after the fall of the Berlin Wall, did the East German Parliament pass a resolution acknowledging the responsibility also of East Germans in Nazi atrocities.

Frau Kubitza's flat is spacious, freshly decorated and elegant in the *Jugendstil* style of the beginning of the 20th century. She is appreciative of the improvements, but cannot refrain from pointing out that Marx foresaw the global financial crisis which was unfolding as we spoke. She has a sense of history and a natural balance. She combines acceptance of the inevitable with the defiant pride of an authentic proletarian unimpressed by Western values she finds a little seamy.

There is little money in this city, flats are cheap, and young people starting out in life set the tone. They give it an energy which is special. They are unencumbered by the past, but ensure every horror committed by Germans is engraved in the stones of their new capital.

Berlin is a living example how long the after-effects of Communism last. The population votes as if the Wall were still there – red to the East and black to the West. It remains two different worlds, populated by people with different mindsets. But it is one of the most vibrant cities of Europe, inhabited by people who have been forced to confront the past and break with it.

Chapter 17

COMING TO TERMS

All too many of us claimed to have known nothing or only suspected – West German President Richard von Weizsäcker

Berlin teenager Peter Lorenz fundamentally changed his attitude to life over just a few weeks when the war ended in 1945. Before then, his school and the Nazi youth movements had corralled his ideas. He knew nothing of what his parents thought – there had been no discussions at home. The church held no sway over young people any more, since the Nazis had more or less eliminated it from public life.

"Within a few weeks I changed my mind completely. I felt anger and disappointment that we allowed ourselves to go along with the Nazis. I felt betrayed, pretended to, lied to. I had no sense of loss for the old Nazi values. I laid them aside like old coal. Instead of the community spirit, individual feelings awoke. I questioned everything. I felt self-assertive and had to stand by my decisions," he told me.

Peter knew deep down that something was dreadfully wrong already in 1943, when he was sent at 14 to a sports school in Łódź in Poland, and saw dying children as he passed in the tram through the Jewish ghetto, as my cousins Fritz and Hilde once did.

"Until then, I thought Jews were being sent to re-education camps to make them better. There was a break when I saw these Jewish children dying in Łódź, but I couldn't ask anyone about it," he said. He noticed that the propaganda of the Hitler Youth camps became increasingly negative – "Victory or Bolshevist chaos". He felt they were no longer offering a way of life.

When the Soviet tanks entered Berlin, Peter remembers people embracing each other with relief, but he could not work out whether they were being occupied, conquered or liberated. This disorientation lingers on today:

"For 20 years after the war one was not free to talk about the Jews. Even now, Germans still think of themselves as victims. As for me, it is clear: we are guilty. We started it. I was quickly disenchanted with the Nazi philosophy, but there was nothing to take its place. Now I have an inferiority complex as a German. I have lost any national feelings, except at football matches."

Down in Bayrisch Gmain in Bavaria, on the border with Austria, I meet people who feel less directly concerned by the Nazi past. Britta Danzl is annoyed that foreigners do not accept that Germans have atoned enough for acts by Nazis for whom she feels no personal responsibility:

"National pride only comes up with football. At first I found the German flag in the stadium strange. I was not used to national pride. I thought: am I allowed this? I hope it will not continue like that for our children."

In this quiet corner, families are mostly rooted in the traditions of the Catholic Church, which was ambivalent towards the Nazis. It appreciated the Nazis as a bulwark against Communism but it did not like their neo-paganism or competition for hearts and minds. For people like Britta, passing ideological fads weigh less than the eternal truths of a church two millennia old.

The Nazis could not get near to these people's hearts. Britta considers Nazism to have been "a marginal phenomenon" and feels no particular need to acknowledge personal responsibility. There is no great pressure to either. This beautiful spot amid lush green meadows at the foot of the Bavarian Alps was little touched by the war. Few foreigners pass by to ask questions about collective guilt.

In the mountains on the horizon however is a sinister spot which bring memories of the Nazis right back. It too is strikingly beautiful, affording stunning views over green alpine pastures and neighbouring peaks. But it reeks of tyranny: this was Hitler's Berghof mountain retreat. My British hostess, who lives nearby, says all the guests she takes there come away with their flesh creeping.

At Berghof, Hitler played the role of a man in harmony with nature rising above human mediocrity. He claimed he did all his most important thinking there, though it is likely he came also to escape the grind of hard work in Berlin. He could surround himself with his closest Nazi subordinates and plot and imagine together, untrammeled by the constraints of the world beyond. He made foreign guests such as Neville Chamberlain travel long distances to visit him there, waiting at the top of a flight of stone steps as the visitors climbed up to reach his level and clasp his hand. The photos show one after another making the effort, smiling at the dictator's hospitality.

I too felt the evil of the place seeping into my fibres. The burrow of concrete tunnels and bunkers dug beneath the mountain evokes apocalypse – the "Twilight of the Gods" of the Nazi regime. An inscription records the distress expressed by the wife of Martin Bormann, Hitler's right-hand man, as she realised she and her family had no future except squatting in cold, damp tunnels, a fate which in 1945 she still blamed on the Jews, indulging in a last fantasy to avoid the pain of personal responsibility.

It is a strange place, and only tenuously exists. Besides the tunnels, there is little to see except a visitors' centre containing documentation dutifully recording the evils of Nazism. Hitler's Berghof villa was bombed out at the end of the war, and the remains are some way away, with precious little signage to help find them. One is not supposed to. Today's German authorities do not wish the Berghof to become a neo-Nazi shrine. The most obvious building on the mountain top nowadays is a large hotel belonging to an international chain. It offers fresh air, glorious views and healthy walks, but no trips back to dark nostalgia. The global branding of the hotel chain wraps over the evil subsoil, insulating modern pursuits from unwanted history.

Back in the house where I am staying, my host's husband Dankwart Rost does not shirk the difficult questions of the past. He tells of his joy at belonging to the Hitler *Jungvolk* movement and his painful eye-opening when he realised in his last wartime weeks that it was all wrong. His conclusion is:

"The Germans have to acknowledge that they can never rid themselves of the guilt for what they did to the Jews. This will never go away. They must live with it forever and get used to that."

This is the pragmatic judgment of a man who is 100% German but knows how others think, having worked for a German company operating around the world. He does not feel guilt as a rush of sentiment. He is making a sober assessment of the moral environment in which Germans now live. He is retired now. He goes out to clear up leaves which have fallen on the lawn overnight. There is a whiff of autumn in the air.

In Berlin-Spandau, Hans Werk, the former SS-man, has gone through a complete change of heart. He volunteered for military service at age 16, having been thrilled by lectures he was given at school by *Luftwaffe* pilots. His main fear at that time (1944) was that the war would finish too early.

"I was afraid that I would not get to take part. That's what I got from propaganda. It's unimaginable nowadays," he said. He hoped for the *Luftwaffe* but was content also when he was allotted to the *Waffen-SS*, an elite unit engaged in the most difficult battles and equipped with the best weapons. Werk said he never actually shot at anyone in his six months of service, carried out mainly in logistics and communications. I wonder whether he is downplaying his military record to evade blame. He comes across as a "Good Soldier Švejk" figure, blundering good-naturedly around to little effect, risking hanging as a deserter by driving around without military orders in the last days of the war.

But Werk frankly acknowledges that as an individual he must share the guilt for what all Germans did:

"I'm ashamed. One can't shrug off the blame. I hold myself responsible."

Werk has been preaching this message ever since he accepted how wrong he had been. He ardently supported Willy Brandt and the "building of democracy" undertaken by the Social Democrat SPD Party in the 1950s. He traveled to Budapest and Prague to talk to Communists on behalf of the SPD at the time West Germany was negotiating its treaties of reconciliation with East European states.

When he went with a tour group of Germans to Prague, the others did not want to enter a tavern because it was full of Czechs. Werk could feel the old anti-Slav feeling again, as if the Czechs inside were the enemy. He told the Germans they had to go in, adding: "You can't stop here. You have the task that something like that cannot happen again. You must realise what your fathers and grandfathers did in the German name." They went in.

Now Werk gives talks on the subject to German schoolchildren and visitors from abroad. Afterwards his wife invites me to join them for supper in their modest Spandau flat. As I swallow his German Pilsner, I shiver a little that I am breaking bread with a former SS-man. Werk looks at me with a slightly forlorn look. He senses what I am feeling. But he is doing what he can. What more can I expect? I take another piece of smoked ham, spread it over the rye bread and silently give him credit.

Others were less sincere in admitting guilt. One high-ranking Nazi, Albert Speer, acknowledged responsibility at the Nuremburg trials of 1945, and was cold-shouldered by his fellow defendants for doing so. He was sentenced to 20 years in prison, and clearly hoped his admission would help rehabilitate him as an architect on release. By that time however, the German conscience was stirring, and as a leading Nazi he no longer stood any chance of resuming a career (except as a macabre media celebrity).

When Gitta Sereny, a Jewish-Austrian journalist working for the *Sunday Times*, interviewed him, she found his confessions were qualified with reservations. He was still proud of his achievements as head of war production and his closeness to the *Führer*. She concluded his assumption of responsibility was "an elegant ploy; behind it lay a nightmare of unavowed knowledge, a minefield of unalleviated guilt."[clxxv]

Sereny tried to bring guilt to the surface, as psychoanalysts do. She interviewed prominent Nazis at length, including also Franz Stangl, commandant of the Sobibor and Treblinka extermination camps. She was after the apocalyptic confession, the moment when a person agonising under a burden of guilt breaks and allows their true feelings to surge forth in a moment of truth. She persuaded them to talk freely in a way they may never have done with anyone else, and thereby produced a unique historical record. She tried to get as close as she could without betraying her own principles. She stayed in the home of Speer and his wife, and when Speer came knocking on her bedroom door late one evening, she allowed him to continue his explanations to her in her dressing gown. To Stangl, she brought his favourite soup in prison.

But she never achieved the psychological breakthrough. Her counterparts weaved and ducked, spoke frankly and evasively, never quite coming to terms with what they had done. Stangl died of a heart attack in the course of her interrogations, and Speer kept up his guard and moved on to an aimless life in limbo between good and evil.[clxxvi]

Some hold that German guilt has not gone nearly far enough. Ruth Kitschler, a half-Jew designated as "half-caste, first grade" under the Third Reich, thinks no differently than she did during the war. She has neither forgotten nor forgiven. Her father was a Jew but her mother was an Aryan German. The mother's provenance saved Ruth from being classified as a Jew herself and sent to an extermination camp, but the whole family was exposed to constant harassment.

"Worse than the anti-Jew laws was the hatred of the population. They looked at us with hate. It was persecution, a constant feeling of fear. We felt like criminals. I was blind with fear on the street. It still affects me today".

Kitschler said the Gestapo repeatedly searched their flat and her father was taken away for questioning several times. He was full of lice when he came back, and when the bombs came, as a Jew he was not allowed into the public shelters. Her brother was caught trying to escape into Switzerland and sent to Auschwitz. Later he was moved to another camp to build V2 rockets underground, and he was almost dead when liberated.

"My brother is completely without hatred. My own hatred keeps growing. I cannot be mild. I cannot give pardon. They had no pardon for us. They still protect the Nazis. Anti-Semitism is still there. The slogan goes that it is time to put an end to this. I say: it is not yet ended, it can happen again. It is a sign of guilt that they do not want to talk about it any more. All of them are guilty. I so much hoped that humans would change, but I have given up that hope. I am not reconciled. There will be a revenge for this."

Equally unforgiving was the American Jewish historian Daniel Jonah Goldhagen. In a book published in 1996,

Hitler's Willing Executioners, he argued that Germans as a whole participated in Hitler's war crimes. Drawing on extensive research, he showed that ordinary Germans who had nothing to do with the Nazis committed some of the worst atrocities. He implied that no Germans were innocent.

His argument was directed against Germans who had comfortably believed that the crimes could be blamed on Hitler and the clique of gangsters around him. Coming 40 years after the end of the war, it reminded the new generation that outsiders did not necessarily believe they were honestly confronting their ugly past. The book was a best-seller in Germany, and the point went home: Germans as a whole were responsible for the atrocities.

But it hardly came across as objective. It was an angry book, shot through with Jewish pain and desire for revenge. It held out no hope of repentance, redemption or reconciliation.

Ten years earlier, West German historian Ernst Nolte had taken the opposite tack. He asserted that Hitler and the Nazis were a reaction to the much greater crimes committed by Stalin and the Soviet Communists. By then it was known that Stalin had more people murdered than Hitler did. Nolte was backed by conservatives who felt left-liberals were fixated on guilt. But not everybody agreed there was a causal link between the Soviets, who were waging a class war, and the Nazis, who were obsessed by race. His thesis looked suspiciously like another attempt to evade German responsibility. After animated arguments among German historians, it lost traction.

American writer Ron Rosenbaum thought he could find resolution by tracking all the various theories explaining Hitler as a phenomenon. But he found the process risked making implicit excuses for what the Germans had done collectively. He was fiercely taken to task for trying to "explain" Hitler by Claude Lanzmann, celebrated creator of a nine-hour *Shoah* documentary about the death camps. Through "the misleading exculpatory corollaries of explanation" Rosenbaum feared he was giving Hitler exactly the exaggerated attention the dictator craved.[clxxvii]

Some Germans *benefited* from guilt. My *Tante Anneliese* in Bergedorf profited because the post-war West German state tried to make up for the Nazis having sent so many millions of young Germans to their deaths. This reflected guilt for what Germans did to their own kith and kin rather than to other peoples. For over 60 years – she died at 92 in 2008 – she received a war widow's pension, calculated according to the salary her first husband would have received if he had reached his potential rank in his profession. He had been a jurist and it was assumed he would have become a judge if he had not been killed in the war. So she was paid as the widow of a judge. Later she presumably also received a pension as the widow of my uncle, Walter, the elder brother of my mother, whom she married in the 1950s. In the latter part of her life, she lived comfortably and took holidays around the world.

She had been a kind and helpful aunt to me, and we conversed warmly when I visited her just before her death, but I wondered about the merits of such largesse. Was it right to compensate Germans for a war they started? That did not quite square with the concept of collective responsibility. However the German "economic miracle," which made the money available, made little distinction between the deserving and the lucky.

When considering individuals, the question of guilt is decidedly tricky. Take for example my *Onkel Johannes*, the one who was banned from his profession for a year after the war for serving in the Nazi SA. I notice that his children, who are clear about the wrongs of the Nazis, remember him with great affection. His younger daughter, Marie-Luise, helped him in his X-ray practice in Nuremberg and admired how he sensitively comforted cancer patients confronted with bad news. Marie-Luise's sister Hilde described her father as a loner who often fell out with his bosses, but also a generous man who never lost his sense of humour.

His son Fritz, who emigrated to America and became a successful kidney specialist, remembers discussing ethical issues with his father. Johannes argued that euthanasia may be justified if there was war and starvation. Fritz disagreed. The father considered that when snipers were protected by locals, it may be justified for the military to make reprisals which result in innocent deaths. Fritz again disagreed. But on one point, he was adamant:

"I never considered my father as a Nazi. He was a pacifist. I learned my own pacifism from him."

Fritz's wife Evelyn, American-born but of German extraction, says she loved her father-in-law:

"I spent time with Johannes after Luz went to bed. We would talk of his X-ray work on frescoes in the *Lorenzkirche* St. Lawrence Church in Nuremberg. I appreciated his humanitarian side and how just he was in not being judgmental. I felt he knew what was right and wrong. I became very close to him."

Fritz, who in the American context is a liberal, remembers how in the 1980s, a cousin of his received a phone call from a woman who asked: "Are you related to Johannes Port?" When he replied he was, the woman said: "I want you to know your uncle saved my life."

She was a German half-Jew, whom Johannes and Luz had taken on as a nanny. The family had taken her with them to Łódź in Poland, which exposed them to possible punishment by the Nazi authorities. Luz wrote in her diaries of her worry at the risk the family ran in employing a half-Jew, though she preferred her to the Poles. According to the woman who telephoned, Johannes sent her to southern Bavaria after people in Łódź started asking questions. He arranged travel papers which enabled her to escape Germany and she ended up in America, from where she was calling.

At the end of the war, many Germans involved with the Nazis came up with stories of helping the Jews, and the Allies treated them sceptically. After all, the Jews had been largely wiped out. But some of these stories have been shown to be true. Many others are impossible to prove one way or the other. Suffice it to say that this woman took the trouble to track down a Port and told him Johannes saved her life. There seems no particular reason for her to make it up.

My British father had been no great friend of his brother-in-law. In a letter to my mother from Burma in 1945 when she told him her German family had survived, he wrote: "I refrain from undue gratitude for the deliverance of Herr Dr. Port."

When a British government set an annual £50 allowance for foreign travel, my father was annoyed at having to rely on relatives such as Johannes for financial support on visits to Germany. When Johannes took him for a walk in 1982 on the outskirts of Nuremberg however, both men took distance from the past. After a time, they came upon the overgrown ruins of the stadium built by the Nazis for Hitler's rallies. Johannes stopped and said to my father:

"I wish I'd never got mixed up in all that."

My father found him a sad figure and felt sorry for him. He felt obliged at that moment to reconsider how he had been judging men like Johannes, who had been moving in the grey areas of Nazi allegiance:

"I had always thought: Luz good, Johannes bad. Now it no longer appeared to be quite so clear. It was quite an awakening to me."

My father felt the same when he was interrogating surrendered Japanese generals at the end of the war. He was frustrated by their obduracy and angry that they had been doing their best to kill him and his fellow-soldiers only a few weeks before. Then he decided his bitterness was not worthwhile. He allowed his anger to seep away.

"I have learned not to get angry about things that don't really matter," he wrote to my mother in 1945.[clxxviii]

On that walk with Johannes my father let go any lingering resentment about his brother-in-law's Nazi past too. It was his final verdict. The next morning, Johannes came to my parents' pension and fell dead in front of them with a heart attack.

I took Onkel Johannes as he was: smoking his cigars at age 21.

My cousin Fritz became ambivalent about his German origins. He found his family connections with Britain gave him prestige among fellow-Germans. It was "a feather in my cap" that he could visit our family in England as a teenager in the 1950s. He did things he had never done before, like queuing, going shopping on a bicycle and having picnics. "I also realised I didn't need to be afraid of the British bobbies, unlike the German policemen at home."

He qualified as a doctor in Germany, but was tempted by the wider world. On a camping trip across the United States, he came close to the Mayo Clinic. He had packed a suit in his rucksack, just in case. He pulled it out from the back of his tent, smoothed out the creases and applied for a job at one of America's most prestigious clinics.

He got the job, and found the next challenge was to fit in to his new environment as a German. The war had finished less than 20 years before, and on a boat journey across the Atlantic, he was the object of bitter complaints by a Briton about Germany's industrial revival. One of his new bosses in America was a Jew and said:

"You know, Fritz, I hate Germans."

"I was too young," Fritz replied.

"When were you born?"

"1938."

"OK, you were too young."

Such was the delicate path a young post-war German had to tread in America. His wife Evelyn, also of German ancestry, found it easier to mix with Jews because she was American-born:

"My family had Jewish friends, and as a child I learned Yiddish from a friend. I am comfortable with Jews, and some think I'm Jewish myself, even though I'm not. I laugh at Jewish jokes. Fritz doesn't. He doesn't get them."

Fritz remembers going to a Scotch whisky tasting in 1980 in the university town of Ann Arbor where he lives. It turned out that most of the other guests were Jews, and he overheard one say: "Why was Port invited?" He stayed. When he went with a group of Americans to Cracow in Poland, some went on to visit nearby Auschwitz, but Fritz said: "I couldn't. It was too painful."

After the daughter of one of his step-children visited the Holocaust museum in Washington, she told her grand-mother, Evelyn: "I would rather you didn't speak German with Fritz."

Fritz and Evelyn live among the woods in an American clapboard house with a wooden porch running around it. Inside, it is not quite so American. Fritz has the same vintage of inherited German furniture as came down to me. On his walls hang paintings by the German Alf Bachmann. The artist was a favourite of Hitler – and of Queen Elizabeth II and Churchill, he diplomatically adds.

Fritz and Evelyn tried returning to live in Germany, but Fritz was annoyed when a German teacher humiliated one of his step-sons at school as a dumb American. He was revolted by listening to a German relative complaining about Jews taking power again and the Holocaust being exaggerated. He found the medical establishment in Germany was more rigid than in America. He feared that if he stayed, he might be a foreigner in his own land. He had changed. So he opted for America and returned there for good.

Evelyn however *likes* the German connections she has made through Fritz. As an American, they enable her to make contact with her ancestral roots. She and Fritz frequently visit Germany to allow her to feel a culture which Fritz no longer entirely embraces.

Peter Plesch, who grew up in England after his Jewish father emigrated from Germany to escape Hitler, remained intimately linked with German culture, quoting long passages of Goethe's *Faust* in German at the age of 90. After he started an academic career at Keele University in England, Heidelberg University tried to woo him back to Germany with a more highly-paid job. After going to meet his potential employers, he and his Viennese Jewish wife Traudi looked at each other and shook their heads. The weight of the past was too strong. They decided they could not live in Germany and returned to England forever.

Judgments about Germans and their past swung to and fro for many years after World War II ended. It seemed as if there would never be any satisfying consensus. Eventually one man pronounced a verdict to which both Germans and foreigners could lastingly subscribe. He was Richard von Weizsäcker. Like two other notable Germans, Ernst Reuter and Willy Brandt, he had been mayor of West Berlin.

When he addressed the moral implications of Germans' wartime record in 1985, he was speaking as West Germany's President. As the descendant of a distinguished line of diplomats, he had stature. He had taken part in the German invasion of the Soviet Union, so he could talk to Germans who had fought in the war. He also had democratic credentials through links with plotters against Hitler.

In his speech on the 40th anniversary of the German defeat, von Weizsäcker talked of the catastrophe the Germans had brought on other nations, but also of the Germans' own suffering and their achievements in post-war Europe. Most significantly, he told Germans that they could not pretend they did not know of the genocide against the Jews:

"Every German could witness what Jewish fellow-citizens had to suffer, from cold indifference through hidden intolerance to open hatred. Who could remain unsuspecting after the burning of the synagogues, the stigmatisation with the Jewish star, the withdrawal of legal rights, the endless desecration of human dignity?

"Whoever opened their ears and eyes, whoever wanted to inform themselves, these could not fail to see that deportation trains were leaving ... A crime was committed even in the attempt of all too many, including those of my generation who were young and did not take part in the planning and execution of the events, to ignore what was happening.

"There were many ways of allowing one's conscience to be diverted, to be not responsible, to look away, to keep silence. Then when the whole unspeakable truth of the Holocaust came out at the end of the war, all too many of us claimed to have known nothing or only suspected."

Von Weizsäcker said the younger generations of Germans born since the end of the war did not have to bear personal responsibility, but added: "All of us, whether guilty or not, whether old or young, must accept the past. All of us are affected by its consequences and are made liable for it."

This was tough talk by a man whose position was largely ceremonial. But the speech went down well, both in Germany and abroad. It was warmly accepted in Israel, and since then German leaders have kept to the balanced line he took.

Thus, on the 60th anniversary of the liberation of Auschwitz in 2005, Chancellor Gerhard Schröder said ordinary Germans had supported Hitler: "The evil of Nazi ideology did not come from nowhere... Nazi ideology was wanted by humans and made by humans."

Three years later, his successor, Angela Merkel, told the Israeli Knesset: "The Shoah fills us Germans with shame."

Von Weizsäcker brought the guilt out into the open in a way that Germans could acknowledge without being demeaned. He struck a balance which was honest, dignified and humble. Few foreigners thereafter questioned German contrition, and Germans felt little need to analyse further. Von Weizäcker pronounced the historical record, and it has stood the test of time.

Chapter 18

WAR AND PEACE

A peace is of the nature of a conquest
— William Shakespeare

I sit in the front hall and feel nothing in particular. The couch is threadbare, the windows and walls are dirty, and the front door creaks when I walk in. I am back in north Germany, in the management building of the former *Nobel Dynamitenfabrik AG* – the name can just be made out on the façade – trying to conjure up the past.

My mother had told me that Krümmel "no longer exists." Yet I am sitting in the same hall through which she skipped as a child on the way upstairs to sit in the office of her father, the Director. As I walk up to the building nearly a century later, I behold the same bricks and mortar as she saw in those years just after World War I.

I close my eyes and try to imagine the little girl coming through the entrance, joyfully anticipating sitting with her father as he wound up his business for the day. The images she had evoked so warmly float through my mind. Then there is a clatter of feet, and as I open my eyes, two stout young German men clump past holding a crate of beer between them, talking loudly as they head up the stairs.

The bricks and mortar have moved on to another life. Although the air raid at the end of World War II did not completely destroy the plant, it left the management building much the worse for wear and the approach road strewn with rubble. The bodies of the dead Ukrainian forced labourers were stacked in wooden dynamite crates and wheeled away over rail tracks. Then the British hauled off the remains of the damaged plant as war booty to relieve their weakened economy. Nobody ever managed anything again from the management building. It was converted into flats for people who need cheap lodgings and enjoy a crate of good beer.

Likewise with the former Director's home nearby. I walk up the path my mother ran along as a little girl and come upon the same house as in her childhood pictures. However the prestigious residence of yesteryear has been divided up for a number of families to live in. Instead of flower and vegetable gardens, there are washing lines and plastic toys. It has become anonymous and unkempt. I look for the glorious landscapes through which my mother roved as a girl. Trees have grown over the river bank on which it was built, obstructing the views. I see nothing special.

In its heyday: the Nobel Director's house on the Elbe where my mother grew up.

Krümmel, as my mother said, is not there any more. Not the place that she knew, at any rate. But one thing *does* exist in Krümmel today. A huge white presence looms over the River Elbe and its tree-clad slopes. After two World Wars, nobody wanted Germany to make dynamite any more. But Krümmel remained an ideal site for activities best kept away from humans. So a nuclear power station was built there. It rises long and high and silent over the place where my mother grew up. Silent because, somehow appropriately, in this place which my mother said did not exist anymore, it has broken down. No dynamite, no business, no Director and his family, no glorious nature – and no electric power generation either.

What remain for me today are the inspirations my mother drew from her childhood in these surroundings. By passing the memories on, she influenced the children she brought up, as well as her grandchildren, who listened curiously to her stories, imagining what that world had been.

When I sit later with the museum director at the nearby town of Geesthacht, he frowns slightly as I tell how my mother described her German father as an admirable human being.

"Yes, but your grandfather shares responsibility for the ecological mess which was left at the site after it was used for making dynamite," he says.

"He must be a Green!" hisses my cousin in my ear. I accept the implied rebuke however. My grandfather must have had his faults too. At the museum they are patiently gathering material to create a balanced picture of local history to guide future generations. The museum director's assistant is an American of German descent, specialised in Gotthold Ephraim Lessing, the playwright of the 18th century German Enlightenment.

They are still fighting against any possible resurgence of Nazi sympathies, and their attitude reassures me. I appreciate that they mistrust the extent to which Germans have changed, and that they look askance at a foreigner claiming that *his* German ancestor was good. They have heard that alibi for the sins of the majority too often. I would not want them to let up.

However I still honour the memory of a German grandfather who inspired my mother and future generations to be humane and enterprising. It is a subjective judgment, but guides me in my life all the same. On the negative side, his girth showed he clearly ate too much, and yes, no doubt he polluted.

As for my Belgian grandmother, whom I saw just once at the age of three when she visited England, I draw the lesson that tyranny was not a monopoly of Germans. Yet for all her rigid discipline, she also passed down high standards, elegance and courage. If my mother stood up to the Nazis out of principle, it was her Belgian mother who showed her the way.

So individuals set examples which diverged from the norm. But in the Nazi period, Germans acted en masse rather than as individuals. For reasons which I still find hard to fathom, the large majority chose to turn away from human decency and follow the hateful ravings of a vulgar demagogue. They acted collectively in brutally asserting selfish German interests, making war on behalf of the German state. Even when many soldiers realised the crimes of Hitler in the last months of war, they continued with great ingenuity to obstruct the Allies who were trying to vanquish Nazism. These were the crimes of a whole nation, not just of criminal leaders.

World War I defeat, the humiliation of Versailles, hyperinflation, social unrest and economic depression offer Germans no excuse for war, invasion, stealing, slavery and genocide. Guardians of German memory such as the museum curators in Geesthacht continue confronting their fellow-citizens with this inconvenient truth.

With the passing of time, outsiders have acknowledged that following generations of Germans could not be held responsible for sins of their fathers and mothers. This has tended to take the pressure off. However another phenomenon works against the trend to forgiveness: the past is increasingly judged according to the norms of today's peace, not yesterday's war.

Two World Wars hardened people in all countries to accepting killing and cruelty as usual. Many had been involved in it themselves, and the Cold War prolonged the habit of thinking of life as conflict. However, post-war generations have known many years of peace, in particular since the collapse of Communism.

Expectations of human behaviour have thus risen. Today, I and many others judge by the criteria of peace. This is the reason why large numbers of people remain reluctant to let the Germans off the hook. What seemed perhaps understandable at the time is perceived as unforgivable today.

For example, the polite questioning of Albert Speer by a British television interviewer in the 1960s came across as obsequious when retransmitted 50 years later. The interviewer seemed to accept too readily that he was a reformed human being. The Discovery Channel which rebroadcast it in 2010 concluded there must have been a conspiracy to treat Speer leniently.

This of course means the same acts are being judged by changing standards, which makes things harder for the Germans. That may be, but my generation and those which followed should have no regrets that we have raised the bar of expectations for human behaviour. These rising standards balance the opposite trend to forgive and forget.

The Germans have no need to take this badly. Acknowledging guilt and making good by acts of repentance and generosity have enhanced their reputation as a nation. Admitting a fault is a virtue not a sin, an act of strength not weakness. It deserves to be admired rather than scorned.

No other nation in the world has gone so far in admitting their wrongs and reforming. Germans have learned to behave with restraint and humanity, when before they trampled others underfoot. The contrasting leadership styles of Adolf Hitler and Angela Merkel bear this out. The one radiated nervous hysteria, hatred and domination. The other is dumpy, low key and down to earth, and readily acknowledges her slightly dubious past in the Communist *Freie Deutsche Jugend* youth movement.

Germans have converted to democracy, reconciled with France, joined in European solidarity, and concentrated on hard work and wealth creation rather than disruptive ideology. Having won the confidence of former enemies, they are now acknowledged as Europe's natural leader in times of emergency. When crises arose in the European Union over the indebtedness of Greece, Portugal and Spain in 2010-2012, the rest of Europe looked to Germany for solutions and financial help, as it did before with East Germany and the Soviet Union. Having rebounded vigorously from the recession of 2008-2009, Germany was uniquely placed to do so. As a consequence, its values of thrift and sober economic management will surely carry greater weight throughout the Union. A Germany which is wealthy, hard-working and generous can only benefit the rest of Europe, including Britain.

My German grandfather already 100 years ago set an example through his humanity and preference for science and business over militarism. The post-war German "economic miracle" I observed at close quarters is a continuation of a long German tradition of hard work and efficient organisation, tempered by a "social market economy" system which helps the less well-off. Living for a year in Communist East Germany, by contrast, taught me how humiliating the misery can be if wealth creation is prevented.

Having brought war to the world through following Hitler, Germans have in the meantime become the "peace party" in Europe. Germans do their bit in some NATO military operations, but keep to secondary roles. During the Cold War, their army recruits grew their hair long in silent protest, and it was tolerated. Germans refused to take part in George W. Bush's Iraq war and subsequently also in the West's military actions in Libya. In Afghanistan, their 3,500 soldiers have been drinking some 1.6 million pints of beer each year and 40 per cent of them are overweight.[clxxix] They are a far cry from the hardened German warriors of the Eastern Front in World War II.

The rest of the world is better off for their pacifism. Nobody wishes to see them take the lead again in making war. If they had, I could perhaps have been drawn into another world war, as my British grandfather and father were. Millions of people have benefited that the economic powerhouse of Europe is so inclined.

Through these "soft" values, Germany has helped dispel the pessimism which pervaded European opinion-makers for several decades after the war. Joachim Fest concluded his Hitler biography in 1973 by asserting that Europe's civilisation was gone for good. A.J.P. Taylor predicted that a reunited Germany would revert to militarism. Stefan Heym and Günter Grass thought it would destroy German democracy. Sebastian Haffner wondered sadly whether German patriotism could ever return.

All these dire prophecies have turned out to be false. Events such as the 2006 soccer World Cup and the 20th anniversary of the fall of the Berlin Wall showed that Germans can also lighten up and create a playful atmosphere. Even German patriotism has made a decent comeback. When a German singer won the Eurovision Song Contest in 2010, she wrapped a German flag around herself, but nobody batted an eyelid. It is what contestants do nowadays.

As for my British father, it took me some time to work out whether he was on the side of peace or war. For many years he spoke only badly of his wartime experience. As a teacher and a civilian, he had not intended to spend years drilling in boot camps, nor sloshing in mud behind mules through Burma's jungles, and certainly not exposing himself to Japanese bullets, grenades and bayonets.

Having been called up at the age of 25, he was growing a paunch and his hair was thinning by the time he was demobilised in 1946 at the age of 31. "I entered the army as a young man and came out middle-aged," was his gloomy appraisal. As a small boy, I was exposed to countless stories of war heroes in my readings, but had to note disappointedly that my own father did not seem to be among them.

Then in 1995, on the 50th anniversary of the end of the war, I came into his house in Oxford to find his war medals hanging on the wall of the front hall. At the age of 80, he was proud after all. Besides the campaign medals, there was a "Mention in Dispatches" notified to him "By Order of the King."

At 94, confined to a wheelchair in a nursing home, he gave a lecture on his war to his fellow inmates. Speaking for an hour without notes, he described the nature of fear and courage in a war which he had not sought:

"The first time I came into physical danger, I had to pull myself together with a great effort. After that, it came more easily. I was scared, but everybody else was too, so we were all in it together."

He feared his last moment had come as he came "under the most incredible hail of fire and grenades in all directions" from surrounding Japanese troops, who made "desperate bayonet charges right up to our lines."

His audience of extremely old people in the home seemed half asleep as he talked. But when he ended, one who was bent double with Parkinson's craned his head up sideways and asked a pertinent question about post-war Burma. A woman looked fondly at him and said she had heard stories like those about her brother – "unfortunately he was killed in Egypt."

I was sitting among a generation for whom the hardship of war was a familiar destiny. I was one of a dwindling number whose fathers were heroes, even if reluctant ones. They never wanted to make war, but when the call came, they did the best they could. In the peace which has brought us Europeans so many benefits, fewer and fewer children will know such fathers.

Yet my father ended his talk by saying there should be no more war. At the time, Britain had just finished one war in Iraq and was continuing another in Afghanistan. So my father, unlike the two main British political parties and much of the media, disapproved. He was for peace not war, even though he had fought himself. I understood why he discouraged me as a little boy in the 1950s from over-indulging in wartime pride.

Later I read the memoirs of Harry Patch, the last surviving veteran of Britain's trench fighting in World War I. After a reunion with a German veteran who had fought against him, he said: "War is organised murder and nothing else... No one deserved to go through that war."[clxxx]

So Patch too belonged to the "peace party." He and my father were proud to have served their country, but in the final analysis both came down against war.

This is not so of the rest of British society, which remains influenced by the shameful appeasement at Munich in 1938 followed by resistance and military victory over

Nazism. Britons are brought up to admire the Battle of Britain, the spirit of the London Blitz, the final victory in 1945 and more recently the sacrifices of its professional soldiers in Iraq and Afghanistan. The messages are: war redeemed the honour lost in appeasement, and the British character forcefully resists evil, even when others bow the head.

Since World War II, Britain has waged wars in Malaya, Kenya and Aden as rearguard actions to defend its Empire. It invaded Egypt in 1956 in a vain attempt to topple Gamal Abdel Nasser, whom British Prime Minister Anthony Eden compared with Hitler. It drove the Argentinians out of the Falkland Islands in 1982, and then sent troops to the war in Bosnia in the 1990s and again to Kosovo in 1999. Further military interventions followed in Afghanistan from 2001, in Iraq from 2003 and in Libya in 2011. British troops were still fighting in Afghanistan 12 years after they started.

In Switzerland, where I worked for a number of years, foreign policy discourse practically never touches on military matters, since the last foreign war Switzerland fought was in 1515 (it ended badly). Before that, Swiss fought as mercenaries, but since then they have not fought outside their country. As a member of the Royal Institute for Foreign Affairs (Chatham House) in Britain however, I notice that many of the lectures are about "security," or in other words, war.

Britain justifies its wars not by a desire for national aggrandisement, but because they are considered morally right, either in defeating dictators (Hitler, Nasser, Galtieri, Saddam Hussein, Milošević, Gaddafi), suppressing terrorism (Malaya, Kenya, Aden, Afghanistan) or peace-keeping (Bosnia).

British soldiers march with a calm, measured tread. They radiate dignity rather than aggression. Ceremonies to commemorate military actions convey sorrow over sacrifices rather than joy at victory. Bugles sound poignantly through cathedrals, and flower petals shower down from the roof of the Royal Albert Hall. Churchmen lead prayers.

It was not always like that. When I was a teenager in the early 1960s, Remembrance Day on the 11th of November consisted of a service in Worcester Cathedral, a brisk clatter past the war memorial in our cadet uniforms and hob-nailed boots, and it was all over by lunchtime. We perceived it as a necessary act of respect, but to be accomplished with dispatch.

In latter years however, Remembrance Day celebrations have extended over a 10-day period, with the Queen taking part on several occasions. When her grandson Prince William married in 2011, the bridegroom and best man wore military dress uniforms and were attended by over 1,000 armed forces personnel, many of whom had done combat service in Afghanistan. Three aircraft used to fight Germans in World War II flew overhead. Creative talents and multi-media technology lend magic to the occasions. Television has turned British pride at war sacrifices into highly-charged, colourful drama broadcast around the world.

New memorials to British wartime bravery are planned on ever-increasing scale. A £3.5 million monument to the 55,000 airmen of Bomber Command killed in World War II has been given planning permission in London's Green Park. My distant uncle Henry, who died trying to bomb the Ruhr, will thus have another memorial to go with his grave in Germany.

A 380-foot beacon higher than Big Ben is planned for the fighter pilots of the Battle of Britain. It will be located at the Royal Air Force Museum at Hendon on the outskirts of London, and will be visible from the city centre.

All of this may seem the excessive response of a nation unsure of its respect in the world, as if there were not enough admiration already for the courage of those who fought in the war.

Yet foreigners do respect Briton's readiness to stand up and fight for good. When I was a correspondent in Zurich in 1982, a senior Swiss banker who had otherwise scorned me as a representative of a financially dissolute nation, came up and pumped my hand, declaring: "I congratulate you on resisting the Argentinians over the Falklands! You British are the only ones to stand up to dictators." In 2005, foreign television channels highlighted Londoners' stolid fortitude when terrorists bombed London public transport. They broadcast the re-born spirit of the Blitz around the world.

Foreigners appreciate the civic decency and long-established values which pervade much of British life. My cousin Hilde likes to hear me speak German with an English accent "because it sounds noble." Britain has not been undermined by the wartime collaboration which infected societies of continental Europe with treachery, egoism and dishonesty. This is the greatest achievement of British wartime resistance, aided by the geographical luck of being an island.

Britons have a moral attitude to war, but it exacts a painful price in living standards. By 2012, Britain was once more undergoing economic stagnation, high unemployment, inflation, over-indebtedness and social service cuts. Over the preceding four years, the British pound had weakened by 25% against the euro.

The value of the belligerent way of life therefore has its limits. It certainly ignores the admonition of Saint Paul to the Romans, read by the civilian brother-in-law of Prince William at the 2011 royal wedding, which says: "If it is possible, so far as it depends on you, be at peace with all men."[clxxxi]

Germans fell into the trap of idly going along with Hitler's war "because it was the thing to do." But I have concluded from observing Germany since then that their subsequent humility, pacifism and thrift stand up well alongside Britain's pride, pugnacity and free spending.

My mother was all for the struggle when Britons decided to fight in 1939, but she also set the example that after war must come peace. That meant dealing with Germans who had gone along with the war and giving them a chance to redeem themselves. For me, it meant dealing with Nazi sympathisers who subsequently became good aunts or uncles. I had to make up my own mind about sensitive issues, but also put acrimony aside, as my father did with the Japanese generals and *Onkel Johannes*.

When it comes to resistance, I particularly respect the rebels who stood up for their own perceptions of good in the face of strong opinion running against them. They were often alone and at risk, but persisted all the same. People like West Berlin mayor Ernst Reuter, who dared to tell the Western Powers immediately after the war that they could not honourably abandon Berlin; General Lucius Clay, who faced down Stalin and Khrushchev when his own people were wavering, but also gave rein to Ludwig Erhard over economic reform others predicted would be disastrous; Willy Brandt, who broke the logjam of the Cold War by conciliating when others wanted to remain hard; Mikhail Gorbachev, who dared to democratise a despotic Soviet Union; Liselotte Kubitza, the working-class Berliner whose family opposed Hitler from the start; and my mother, who boycotted the Nazis even though she knew they would try to ruin her life.

No religion, doctrine or teaching showed these people which way to go. Rather they instinctively felt back to simple values in their inner consciences, as people have done throughout the ages. "Decency, manners, consideration," was how Joachim Fest's persecuted father put it.

The son wrote at the end of his 1973 biography that Hitler had destroyed old Europe.[clxxxii] But resistance to injustice, speaking out for right as a lone voice, acknowledgement of faults, hard work and an inclination towards peace – all these are values which go far back in time, and they have survived. When my mother was asked as a little girl what she wanted to be when she grew up, she answered, "a mother." And that is exactly what she did. She brought up a traditional family, as if Hitler had never happened. She perpetuated a way of life she had been born into before WWI.

Chapter 19

FIRE

Whoever has forgotten how to weep learns to do it again with the downfall of Dresden — German writer Gerhart Hauptmann

Finally I head for Dresden. At Berlin's state-of-the-art *Hauptbahnhof*, I expect a sleek high-speed train to whisk me there in 45 minutes or so. I am in for a shock. The smooth speedsters head for the West, whilst I am going deep into the East German hinterland.

Up rumbles a none-too-clean Czech train of elderly vintage: Dresden is on the line to Prague. The ticket-collector speaks only a few words of any language besides Czech. The coach is full of Western back-packers and *Ossis*. I can feel they are *Ossis* because there is something meek and resigned in the way they sit and chat. This is not a train for high-flyers.

After half an hour, it slows and trundles along a long stretch of track at 40 miles an hour. I am back in another age, when East bloc trains slowly rocked and swayed over dicey rails, and the only Westerners who felt the adventure worth it were the back-packers – or foreign correspondents such as myself looking for the Cold War. The only significant difference from my last journey on this line in 1972 was that the train is no longer pulled by a steam engine.

I first came to Dresden in 1972 as a guest of the East German Foreign Ministry. Dresden and Meissen were places they liked to show off as examples of old German culture the Communist state was nurturing. Meissen continued to turn out the fine porcelain which it pioneered in Europe under a Saxon Duke in the early 18th century. As for Dresden, the East German government wanted to show the progress it had made in rebuilding the city after its destruction by the British Royal Air Force on 13th and 14th February 1945.

The Zwinger museum had been put back together and restocked with the Duke's fabulous paintings and treasures. Restoration of the majestic Semper opera house was about to start. We had been brought there to appreciate the regime's commitment to cultural renewal and respect for the past.

The city still had vast empty spaces however. As I stood among the ruins then, I remember looking across the River Elbe and wondering how the British bombers had apparently missed the black frame of the central railway station, surely a prime strategic target. It was blackened but still standing amid the flattened wilderness around it. Only years later did it occur to me that its modern metal structure was harder to destroy than the tightly-packed older houses. At the time, I found this a mere curiosity and soon put it out of my mind.

For many years, to my British-educated mind Dresden was one more destructive air raid among countless others. That was how it seemed to the British public at the time. The war had less than two months to run, but the Germans were still fighting for all their worth. Progress was slow and new German weapons such as the V1 flying bombs and V2 rockets were razing parts of London.

Dresden had been spared, but not because it was full of great cultural treasures. The British command was so hardened by the immensity of the military challenge that this scarcely came into consideration. Rather, it was the furthest big German city from the British bomber bases and had no direct military importance. However the British were running out of cities to lay waste with firestorms.

A Royal Air Force memorandum of January 1945 read: "Dresden, the seventh largest city in Germany and not much smaller than Manchester, is also far the largest unbombed built-up the enemy has got. In the midst of winter with refugees pouring westwards and troops to be rested, roofs are at a premium. The intentions of the attack are to hit the enemy where he will feel it most, behind an already partially collapsed front, to prevent the use of the city in the way of further advance, and incidentally to show the Russians when they arrive what Bomber Command can do."clxxxiii

The thrust of the argument was clear: Dresden offered itself as another opportunity to break German morale by the methods of total destruction the British now mastered. Moreover, by that time, practically everything Germans did was orientated to supporting the military effort. If the human consequences would be devastating, the planners clearly believed the Germans had brought it upon themselves.

So Bomber Command targeted Dresden. The raid, aimed to pass directly through the historic centre of inflammable old houses, was a spectacular success, creating a firestorm as fierce as Hamburg, with the same devastating effects on the population. 1,300 bombers reduced 13 square miles of the city to rubble and blackened stumps. The death toll was possibly as much as 25,000. Most were killed by collapsing houses or suffocated in cellars, but many were burned alive by the fire.

It was appalling, but when peace came, interest subsided. For many years, I and others saw it as just a particular nasty event in a dreadful war, now thankfully over.

However the British knew immediately afterwards that they had done something quite out of the ordinary. They had ruined one of Europe's finest cultural jewels with enormous loss of life. Churchill drafted a note regretting it as an act of terror, but was persuaded to withdraw it when his Air Force chief reminded him that he, Churchill, had approved the raid beforehand.

The East German government guide who addressed my group of foreign correspondents in 1972 disapproved too, but took a different tack. He told us the British raid was not only cruel but pointless. Cruel? This was rich coming from a regime that had its own history of atrocities.

Pointless? In that, he was taking his cue from the Soviets, who may well have been impressed by the capacity of Bomber Command to wreak havoc, but were certainly not prepared to give credit afterwards. To minds which considered all judgments must serve an ideological purpose, it was convenient to belittle the military importance of the Dresden attack and decry its morality. According to their warped class doctrine, the sole credit for victory over Fascism should go to the Soviet Union. Britons were the class enemy and deserved only blame.

I was offended. Britain had been fighting the same Nazi enemy as the Soviet Red Army, which had put the East German Communist regime in place. I bristled all the more since this was coming from a German. I heard the distant voice of my Belgian grandmother telling me Germans were barbarians. I wondered whether I should interrupt with objections, but thought better of it. I assumed a tight-lipped aloofness.

The eyes of the other foreign correspondents were on me, the sole Briton in the party. They were Russians, Poles, Ukrainians and Yugoslavs – Communists, but all victims of Nazi barbarity. A wave of silent sympathy flowed over to me, in tacit approval that the British had brought such devastation to a people none of them liked. I could feel their contempt for the distortions of the German lecturing to us. I felt comforted. I was not alone.

Like Auschwitz, Dresden would not go away as a moral issue, and everybody had a word to say. It became a touchstone of right and wrong. Most British historians argued that the destruction was justified on military grounds in order to finish off the war. But the doubts persisted. The man who ordered the raid, Air Chief Marshal "Bomber" Harris was never fêted after the war, and retired in dudgeon to South Africa. When a statue of him was finally erected in London in 1992, protestors vandalised it with red paint.

Having largely assumed their war guilt, Germans began to feel free to think of Dresden as a raid too many. In his book "The Fire," Jörg Friedrich felt confident enough about his nation's reformed credentials in 2004 to condemn the British bombing as a "war of extermination." His book was translated into English and received widespread interest. I and other Britons were readier than before to hear a critical view, even from a German. But Friedrich's single-minded focus on the bombing, and his angry indignation, made me wonder whether he was, deep down, still questioning German guilt.

Neo-Nazis, who persist in Germany as small, embittered groups, were all too ready to exploit anger over Dresden to do precisely that. They picked on the exceptional nature of the event to argue that Germans were victims of the war rather than the perpetrators. It was a way of diverting attention from Nazi crimes such as Auschwitz. They spread vastly greater estimates of the death toll, some going as far as 500,000, claiming that many bodies were reduced to nothing by the heat of the blaze.

A German Dresden Historians' Commission in 2010 laid to rest the dispute over numbers. After five years of investigations, it came to the conclusion that the death toll was "at least 20,000 and no more than 25,000."[clxxxiv] This was lower than the consensus estimate of around 35,000 circulating until then, though it hardly diminishes the horror of the event.

When I returned to Dresden in 2008, the issue of right or wrong was still alive, and I therefore felt obliged to ask where I stood myself. Did I think the dead Germans deserved a fate they had brought upon themselves? Or did I consider the whole raid was wrong? And if I thought that, was I comfortable in agreeing on this with Neo-Nazis?

I could no longer see the main railway station from across the river, since the flat bombed-out spaces in between had been filled in with new buildings.But instead of indignation at the accusations of the East German Communist in 1972, I felt an immense sadness for this still wounded city. Sixty-three years after the raid, there were still old bomb sites overgrown with weeds in the centre.

Half a century of Communist government had given the city little chance to arise from the ashes as West German cities had. Walking around the old city centre at night, I saw few cars passing by. The empty, dimly-lit cobbled streets reminded me of the Prague I knew in Cold War years. In the Neumarkt central square, a concrete cultural centre of the Communist period offended against the graceful harmony of the restored ducal buildings around it.

Amid this sadness however, there was a shining beacon. The *Frauenkirche* "Church of our Lady" had been rebuilt. Before it collapsed in the shock and heat of the raid, it had been one of Europe's finest Baroque churches. Its beauty was quite exceptional. Covering a relatively small space of ground, it soared towards the heavens in a long, elegant cupola.

When I was last there in 1972, it lay as a heap of charred rubble in the Neumarkt square. I scarcely even noticed it. The East Germans were ready to restore secular culture, but declined to rebuild a church, even though it had been the pride of Europe. Only after the collapse of Communism – the "turn" as the Germans euphemistically call it – did the Protestant church and local authorities get together to pursue what was henceforth their prime vocation – to rebuild the *Frauenkirche*. The whole population rallied to this act of renewal breathing life into the lamed city. A few British pilots who took part in the raid sent money to the building fund. A son of one of the airmen helped craft a gold cross and orb placed at its top.

I walked into the rebuilt *Frauenkirche* in 2008 and felt I was in heaven. Not the heaven which Catholic churches evoke, far above in the skies, but heaven on earth, gloriously shining in the here and now. The interior was ablaze with golden light reflecting off pastel stuccoes. I was not alone. At any time of the day the church is packed with fascinated visitors – eight to nine million people visit Dresden each year. A pastor came to a table in front of the throng and spoke for a few minutes of the spiritual significance of the restored building. There was a brief pause in the bustle and chatter as the message slipped discreetly into their consciousnesses.

Fifteen minutes later I met the pastor at the top of the dome explaining the church to local schoolchildren. He told how Germans started a war which led to the destruction of the church and how the Communists refused to rebuild it because they did not approve of religion. Then he moved on to the present, asking the children to identify the surrounding buildings they saw, old and new. No morbid dwelling on the past, but no punches pulled either.

When I descended towards the exit, my personal moment of truth had come. The visitors' book invited inscriptions. Should I comment, or pass by, aloof again? If I wrote, should I remark on the building's extraordinary architectural merit? Should I express pleasure that it was standing again?

All of this missed the point: that my own people had destroyed this deeply moving place of the spirit. People like my own uncle Henry, shot down while trying to blast another German city. Should I regret that he and the other brave young men commemorated in the graveyard of Middleton Stoney in middle England summoned up their courage, did what they were ordered, and died? Should I observe the British custom that to Germans "we don't mention the war," because to do so would oblige us to point out that they were to blame?

None of this was adequate. I could not honestly walk out writing nothing, as if I did not care, or felt the victims deserved their fate. If I ever did feel like that, I no longer did. And if the Germans mentioned the war themselves, and acknowledged their responsibility, why should I shirk the issue? It all came down to one question: was I sorry the British did it, and was I prepared to say so?

When my turn came, I wrote in the book: "I am British. I am sorry my people destroyed this church. It should never have happened."

I walked out relieved. I had taken a stand. I had distanced myself from the excuse that the end justified the means, or that the British had inadvertently become infected with the brutality of the Germans. I felt no less proud of the wartime bravery of my father and uncle, and remained grateful that the British military saw the war through to the end.

But in Dresden, I acknowledged a wrong and offered sympathy to a people who had finally earned it. I made my own gesture of peace after war. My inscription meant that when the balance is finely tipped between the two, as it was in deciding to launch the Dresden raid, I choose peace rather than the British penchant for war.

When I talked to the German *Zeitzeugen* (witnesses to history) in Berlin about my view of Germany's past, a woman told me afterwards that my readiness to change my mind about Dresden was what impressed her most.

That evening, I came back to hear a Bach organ concert played beneath the dome – intellectual, down-to-earth music, played amid bright lights. I experienced harmony on earth, as have thousands of others who have felt the spirit of the new *Frauenkirche*.

I left Dresden early next morning, my task complete, a foot still in both camps, but knowing where I stood.

Epilogue
FULL CIRCLE

An unexamined life is not worth living - Socrates

Since starting this book, I have returned to live in England after 40 years living on the continent, in Germany, France, Czechoslovakia, Portugal and Switzerland. I have moved to the north Oxford house where my mother and father once lived. This is where I came as a child to spend holidays with my grandparents.

I am surprised how much I feel back at home, even though I never lived here before. I speak my own language, and for once I am not a foreigner. My yoga teacher used to give lessons also to my mother. An elderly ex-colonial official across the road tells how he conversed in the Nigerian Hausa language with my father.

I relish the intellectual life of Oxford. I go to functions in resplendent halls decorated with portraits of eminent forebears, and realise they are my ancestors too – examples to be respected, admired and followed as a fellow-Englishman. They represent the confident heritage of my people. I find no difficulty in identifying.

Yet I am embarrassed in 2011 when a British Prime Minister vetoes a treaty endorsed by the 26 other members of the European Union to achieve greater fiscal discipline. I cringe at the cocksure assumption that only the English can be right, and that harmony can be sacrificed for national self-interest. All this seems to ignore the lessons of the 20th century.

At such moments I realise how accustomed I have become to moving easily among peoples of different nationalities, languages and histories, finding common ground and common values. It was no great effort. It just grew on me. In the moves towards greater union in Europe I see only greater convenience. Not long ago I had to have four currencies in my pocket and show my identity document six times on a single day's journey from Switzerland to Slovenia, the home country of my present wife. Now I can drive through the frontiers without stopping and purchase all requirements with one currency.

If I speak several European languages, this is because for much of my working life abroad this was a requirement, not a luxury. Conversely, young professionals on the continent master English as a matter of course. In many larger enterprises, English is used exclusively for working documentation.

My English school already laid the foundation for this openness. By 16, I had a broad overview of ten centuries of British history, as well as Ancient Egypt, Greece and Rome, the Holy Roman Empire, the Habsburgs, Louis XIV, the French Revolution, the Italian Renaissance and the Spanish and Portuguese explorers. This in Worcester in the West Midlands, on the fringes of Europe. It is considerably more than I would learn in an English school today.

But it is growing up with a mother from Germany that has inspired my openness most. That it was natural to travel there from the earliest age just after the war affected my view of the world. Although the heritage of Nazism and Communism still appalls, Germany has influenced me also in more enlightened ways. It has taught me the value of honesty, reconciliation and hard work.

Not that this impresses my mother any more. Now that I have finished this book, she scarcely recognises me. As she retreats deeper into old age, she tosses her pony-tail and pulls her knee up on to her chair. In her English care home, she is once again the little girl of 1912.

My cousin Hilde tells me my mother was a model for her – more creative and easy-going than her own mother, Luz. My mother does not communicate with me anymore, but I do not hold it against her. Some things she never wanted to talk about anyway. She thrust on with her life regardless, as she does now in her 100th year.

I push her in a wheelchair through the snow to celebrate Christmas in her old home. Her woollen cap brings out the beauty of her heart-shaped face. She looks elegant with a neat scarf around her neck and blanket over her knees.

Snow lies thick on the ground. There are no buses, no mail services. When she was growing up, her winters must have been much like this. A hundred years have passed... and it seems like yesterday.

ACKNOWLEDGEMENTS

I am grateful to the many people I interviewed for the time, trust and thought they offered most generously. Some also gave access to private family documents. Of particular help in arranging contacts were Marie-Luise Plassmann (Friedrichsdorf), Grete Roewer (Ratzeburg), Susi Luss (Bayrisch Gmain) and Eva Geffers of the Zeitzeugenbörse (Berlin) www.zeitzeugenboerse.de/.

Professor Jim Reed, Emeritus Professor of German Language and Literature, University of Oxford, and Dr. Iain Smith, Emeritus Reader, Department of History, University of Warwick, gave expert advice on historical balance and accuracy. My wife Evelina and Susan Tiberghien of the Geneva Writers Group contributed valuable critiquing.

My special thanks go to my agent, Lorella Belli www.lorellabelliagency.com, who offered treasured guidance and support throughout the whole process from manuscript to published book.

The photos in this book all came from the author's family collection.

ENDNOTES

i.   Interview with Traudi Plesch, Northampton, 27 March 2009

ii.   Stürmer, Michael, *The German Empire 1871-1919* Phoenix, 2000, p 4

iii.   My grandfather was rejected by the Army because he was too small and spent WWI as an air raid fire warden in London.

iv.   cf Sheehan, James J., *Where have all the soldiers gone? The transformation of modern Europe*, Houghton Mifflin Harcourt, New York, 2008

v.   Mazower, Mark, *Hitler's Empire: Nazi rule in occupied Europe*, Penguin, London 2008, p 582

vi.   One picture in the *Deutsches Historisches Museum* shows so many military officers strolling around Berlin that it is entitled *Metropolis in uniform of the Guard.*

vii.   Haffner, Sebastian, *Defying Hitler: a memoir,* Phoenix, 2002, pp 18-24

viii.   www.nobelprize.org 8 June 2007

ix.   Described by my mother in a memoir hand-written in 1992, in my possession

x.   Interview with her grand-daughter, Hilde Böhme, 14 January 2012

xi.   Haffner, op.cit. pp 49-50

xii.   Zweig, Stefan, *Die Welt von Gestern: Erinnerungen eines Europäers, Fischer Taschenbuchverlag*, Frankfurt (first published 1942) p 338

xiii.   *Die Port's und ihre Geschichte*, private publication, p 59

xiv.   Judt, Tony, *Postwar: a history of Europe since 1945*, Pimlico, London, 2007 (first published 2005) p 4

xv.	Plesch, John, *János, the story of a doctor*, Gollancz, London, 1947
xvi.	Interview with Peter Plesch, Northampton,27 March 2009
xvii.	Zivier, Georg, *Das Romanische Café: Erscheinungen und Randerscheinungen rund um die Gedächtniskirche*, Haude u. Spenersche Verlagsbuchhandlung, Berlin 1954
xviii.	Plesch, János & Melanie Plesch, *Party Book 1922-1939 – Berlin and London*
xix.	Zweig, op.cit. pp 18-20
xx.	Conversation with Ingrid Lewis, 14 April 2010
xxi.	Busch, Wolf-Rüdiger (editor), *Nur aus dieser Not heraus: Geesthachter erinnern sich and die Jahre 1930-1950*, Stadtarchiv Geesthacht, p 121
xxii.	Ibid p 18
xxiii.	Interview with Peter Plesch, Northampton,27 March 2009
xxiv.	Reich-Ranicki, Marcel, *Mein Leben*, Spiegel Verlag, Hamburg, 1999, pp 78, 92
xxv.	Fussell, Paul, *Wartime: Understanding and behaviour in the Second World War*, Oxford University Press, 1989. p 251, and Fest, Joachim, *Hitler, eine Biographie*, Ullstein, 2002, first published Propyläen, 1973, p 751
xxvi.	Rees, Laurence, *The Nazis: a warning from history*, BBC books 1997
xxvii.	Fest, Joachim, I*ch nicht : Erinnerungen an eine Kindheit und Jugend*, Rowohlt, 2006
xxviii.	Plesch, op.cit. p 225-6
xxix.	Interview with Liselotte Kubitza, Berlin, 23 September 2008
xxx.	Fest, *Hitler*, op.cit, p 84
xxxi.	Her daughter Marie-Luise Plassmann keeps the *Ahnenpass* of her mother as a family record
xxxii.	Fest, *Hitler*, op.cit pp 735, 624, 700
xxxiii.	www.bbc.co.uk/news/uk 1 November 2010
xxxiv.	Kirkpatrick, Ivone, *The Inner Circle*, Macmillan, 1959, p. 135

xxxv.	Fest, *Hitler*, op.cit. p 855
xxxvi.	Zweig, *Stefan*, op.cit. pp 468-70
xxxvii.	Fest, *Hitler*, op.cit. pp 405, 407, 430
xxxviii.	Fest, *Hitler*, op.cit. pp 636, 736-43
xxxix.	Goethe, Johann Wolfgang, *Erlkönig*, Eichendorff, Joseph von, *Mondnacht*, Heine Heinrich, *Aus der Harzreise*, *Prolog*
xl.	Mill, John Stuart, *On Liberty*, John W. Parker, London, 1859 – in my family collection
xli.	Goldhagen, Daniel Jonah, *Hitler's Willing Executioners: Ordinary Germans and the Holocaust*, Vintage Books, New York, 1997 (first published 1996)
xlii.	Rost, Dankwart, *Trügerische Frühling: Bericht über eine totalitäre Jugend in Pommern*, self-published, 1996
xliii.	Interview with Peter Lorenz, Berlin, 24 September 2008
xliv.	Interview with Hans Werk, Berlin-Spandau, 24 September 2008
xlv.	Seiffert, Rachel, *The Dark Room*, Vintage, London 2001, p 338
xlvi.	Judt, op.cit. p 56
xlvii.	*Die Port's und ihre Geschichte*, op.cit.
xlviii.	Interview with my cousin, Dr Fritz Port, Ann Arbor, Michigan, 27 June 2008
xlix.	Aly, Götz, *Hitlers Volkstaat*, Fischer Taschenbuchverlag, 2005/6
l.	Interview with Traudi Plesch
li.	Zweig, op.cit. pp 485, 492
lii.	Letter of 7 December 1939 to Jeanne Küchler, in the possession of the author
liii.	Rees, Laurence, *The Nazis*, op.cit. p 59, Mazower, op.cit. p 305
liv.	Letter of 5 July 1945, in the possession of the author
lv.	Mazower, op.cit. pp 79, 87,94, 192, 216, 408-9, 548
lvi.	Davies, Norman, *Europe: a History*, Pimlico, London, 1996, p 1328
lvii.	Friedrich, Jörg, *Der Brand : Deutschland im Bombenkrieg*

1940-45, List Taschenbuch, Berlin, 2004, p 525

lviii.   Reich-Ranicki, op.cit. pp 265, 283

lix.   Mazower, op.cit. pp 163, Rees, op.cit. pp 159, 216

lx.   Werner, Herbert A., *Iron Coffins : a U-boat Commander's War 1939-1945*, Cassell, London, 1969, pp 58, 299

lxi.   Corsellis, John & Ferrar, Marcus, *Slovenia 1945: Memories of Death and Survival after World War II*, I.B.Tauris, London, 2005, p 34

lxii.   Némirovsky, Irène, *Suite Française*, Vintage, London, 2007, pp 202-8

lxiii.   As recorded by his mother in a letter to a friend in Germany.

lxiv.   Mazower, op.cit. pp 261, 271

lxv.   Aly, Götz, *Hitlers Volkstaat*, Fischer Taschenbuchverlag, 2005/6, pp 96, 118, 161, 200, 205, 219, 231, 297, 327, 333

lxvi.   Aly, op.cit. p 181; Kreuder-Sonnen, Katharina, *Ukrainische Zwangsarbeiter in Geesthacht – Zeitzeugenberichte*, Lauenburgischen Heimat, Nr. 170, 2005, p 12-3; Hastings, Max, *Armageddon: the Battle for Germany 1944-45*, Pan Books, London, 2004, p 439

lxvii.   http://nobelprize.org/alfred_nobel/industrial/articles/krummel/index.html 1 December 2009

lxviii.   Kreuder-Sonnen, op.cit.

lxix.   www.telegraph.co.uk/news/newstopics/rafbombercommand/ 8 November 2008

lxx.   Grass, Günter, *How I Spent the War*, *The New Yorker*, 31 May 2007, p 1

lxxi.   Friedrich, op.cit. pp 51-6

lxxii.   RAAF WWII casualties, compiled by Alan Storr, 2006 http://www.awm.gov.au/catalogue/research_centre/pdf/rc09125z005_1.pdf

lxxiii.   Bishop, Patrick, B*omber Boys: Fighting Back 1940-45*, Harper Perennial, London, 2007, pp 99-100, 105, 117-129

lxxiv.   Interview with Erdmute Behrendt, Berlin-Pankow, 11 June 2008

lxxv.   Bodecker, Anneliese, *Auch 'Grossi' war mal ein Kind :*

Berlin 1932-1950, self-published, pp 56, 67

lxxvi.	The Times, 8 December 2009
lxxvii.	Friedrich, op.cit. pp 113-5
lxxviii.	Kershaw, Ian, *The End: Hitler's Germany, 1944-45*, Allen Lane, London, 2001, pp 390-92
lxxix.	Interview with Ruth Kitschler, Berlin-Spandau, 24 September 2008
lxxx.	Kaack, Hans-Georg, *Ratzeburg : Geschichte einer Inselstadt*, Wachholtz Verlag, Neumünster, 1987, p 386
lxxxi.	As described by a former Reuters Chief Correspondent in Bonn, Chris Catlin, in his historical novel, *Brudersuche*, Landpresse, 2004
lxxxii.	Rost, op.cit. pp 84, 86, 106, 108
lxxxiii.	Grass, op.cit. pp 7-15
lxxxiv.	Smyser, W.R., *From Yalta to Berlin : the Cold War Struggle over Germany*, Macmillan, 1999, p 38
lxxxv.	Judt, op.cit. p 16
lxxxvi.	Anonyma, *Eine Frau in Berlin*, Hannelore Marek 2002, Eichorn 2003
lxxxvii.	Mazower, op.cit. 541
lxxxviii.	Letter of 5 July 1945, in the possession of the author
lxxxix.	Fest, *Ich nicht*, op.cit. pp 291, 342
xc.	Kaack, op.cit. p 383
xci.	Bodecker, op.cit. p 105
xcii.	Letter to my father on military service in Burma, October 1945
xciii.	Quoted by Rosenbaum, Ron, *Explaining Hitler: the Search for the Origins of his Evil*, Random House, New York, 1998, p 82
xciv.	Interview with Brigitte Hermann, Bayrisch Gmain, 3 September 2008
xcv.	Bodecker, op.cit. p 93
xcvi.	Meehan, Patricia, *A Strange Alien People*, Peter Owen Publishers, London & Chester Springs, 2001, p 165

xcvii.	Judt, op.cit. p 56
xcviii.	Meehan, op.cit. pp 103, 106
xcix.	Judt op.cit. p 60
c.	Judt, op.cit. p 98
ci.	Kaack, op.cit. p 388
cii.	Meehan, op.cit. pp 1, 40, 54
ciii.	Taylor, A.J.P. *The Course of German History*, (first published 1945), Routledge 2009, p xvii
civ.	Vansittart, Robert, *Black Record: Germans Past and Present*, 1941
cv.	Elon, Amos, *Journey Through a Haunted Land; the New Germany*, André Deutsch, London, 1967, p 174
cvi.	Meehan, op.cit. p 35
cvii.	Meehan, op.cit. pp 270, 140-1, 60,119, 232, 236
cviii.	Kaack, op.cit. p 381
cix.	Fussell, op.cit. p 281
cx.	Hastings, Max, *Armageddon : the Battle for Germany 1944-45*, Pan Books, London, 2004, pp 391-2, 431
cxi.	Bodecker, op.cit. p 104
cxii.	Meehan, pp 157, 159
cxiii.	Elon, op.cit. p 72
cxiv.	Clare, George, *Berlin Days, 1946-47*, Pan Books, London, 1989, pp 162-8
cxv.	Meehan, op.cit. pp 165, 172, 174, 178
cxvi.	Smyser, op. cit. p 77
cxvii.	Meehan, op.cit. p 257
cxviii.	Judt, op.cit. p 338
cxix.	Young, Hugo, *This Blessed Plot : Britain and Europe from Churchill to Blair*, Macmillan, 1998, pp 22, 106
cxx.	www.raf.mod/bombercommand/jan45.html
cxxi.	Smyser, op.cit. pp 78-87
cxxii.	See Snowman, Daniel, *The Hitler Emigrés*, Pimlico, London, 2003

cxxiii.   Goldhagen, op.cit. p 368

cxxiv.   Leonhard, Wolfgang, *Meine Geschichte der DDR*, Rowohlt, Berlin, 2007, p 188

cxxv.   Smyser, op.cit. p 99

cxxvi.   Judt, Tony, op.cit. p 769

cxxvii.   Knabe, Hubertus, *Gefangen in Hohenschönhausen : Stasi-Haftlinge berichten*, List, Berlin, 2007, pp 156-8, 171, 187, 266

cxxviii.   Reich-Ranicki, op.cit. p 362

cxxix.   Smyser, op.cit. p 138

cxxx.   Interview with Carl Roewer's widow, Grete, 3 July 2007

cxxxi.   Reich-Ranicki, op.cit. p 398

cxxxii.   Lorenzen, Jan N., *Erich Honecker, eine Biographie*, Rowohlt Taschenbuch Verlag, Reinbek, 2001, pp 52, 64

cxxxiii.   Smyser op.cit. pp 160-177

cxxxiv.   Roberts, Frank, *Dealing with Dictators: The Destruction & Revival of Europe 1930-70*, Weidenfeld & Nicolson, London, 1991, p 218

cxxxv.   Kellett-Long, Adam, *Frontlines : Snapshots of History*, Reuters + Pearson, 2001, pp 104-5

cxxxvi.   Geyer, David C. (editor), *Foreign Relations of the United States, 1969-1976, volume XL, Germany and Berlin, 1969-72*, United States Government Printing Office, 2008, pp 85, 104-5

cxxxvii.   FAZ.net, *Von der Idee, die Mauer zu Geld zu machen*, 7 November 2009

cxxxviii.   Interview with *Super Illi* magazine quoted on *szonline.de* 29 September 2010

cxxxix.   Hertle, Hans-Hermann + Wolle, Stefan, *Damals in der DDR*, C. Bertelsmann, Munich, 2004, p 251

cxl.   Hertle, Hans-Hermann + Wolle, Stefan, op.cit, pp 112-3, 115

cxli.   Marsh, Sarah, Reuters, 3 November 2009

cxlii.   Knabe, Hubertus, op.cit. pp 14-5

cxliii.   Hertle, Hans-Hermann + Wolle, Stefan, op.cit, p 252

cxliv.	Millar, Peter, *1989 : The Berlin Wall, My Part in Its Downfall*, Arcadia Books, London, 2009, p 114
cxlv.	Forsysth, Frederick, *Frontlines: Snapshots of history*, op.cit. p 120-5
cxlvi.	Public presentation by Ilona Rau, Dresden, 25 September 2008
cxlvii.	Remarks recorded for German ARD television, quoted by Sächsische Zeitung, sz-online.de, 19 May 2009
cxlviii.	The Economist, *Intelligent Life*, Summer 2009, pp 89-92
cxlix.	The Economist, *DNA Nation*, 25 November 2009
cl.	The Economist, 24 April 2010, p 55
cli.	Hertle, Hans-Hermann + Wolle, Stefan, op.cit. pp 166-7, 179, 185
clii.	Hertle, Hans-Hermann + Wolle, Stefan, op.cit. pp 191
cliii.	Hertle, Hans-Hermann + Wolle, Stefan, op.cit. p 221
cliv.	Hertle, Hans-Hermann + Wolle, Stefan, op.cit. pp 198, 201
clv.	Hertle, Hans-Hermann + Wolle, Stefan, op.cit. p 229
clvi.	Jirgl, Reinhard, *Abschied von den Feinden*, Deutscher Taschenbuch Verlag, 1995, p 223
clvii.	FT.com, *Failure of Imagination*, 5 November 2009
clviii.	Foreign Office, WRL 020/1, *Letter from Mr Powell to Mr Wall*, 20 January 1990
clix.	Young, Hugo, op.cit. pp 358-9, 360
clx.	Taylor, A.J.P., op.cit. p xx
clxi.	Interview with Beatrice von Mach, Geneva, 2008
clxii.	Grass, Günter, speech at "Dresdner Gespräche" 1997. *Im Krebsgang*, Deutscher Taschenbuch Verlag, 2004 (first published 2002).
clxiii.	Heym, Stefan, *Auf Sand gebaut*, 1990
clxiv.	Smyser, op.cit. p 351
clxv.	FAZ.net, 9 November 2009
clxvi.	Smyser, op.cit. pp 351-401
clxvii.	Baale, Olaf, *Abbau Ost: Lügen, Vorurteile und sozialistische Schulden*, dtv, 2008, pp 100-4

clxviii.   Berlin Charité Institut für Medizinische Physik und Biophysik Director Dietmar Lerche, quoted in *Berliner Zeitung*, 2 October 2010

clxix.   Baale, op.cit. p 145

clxx.   Expert's report to the Enquete-Kommission zur SED-Diktatur in Brandenburg, quoted by *Der Tagesspiegel*, 18 March 2011

clxxi.   Statistics quoted by The Economist, 13 March 2010, pp 14-5

clxxii.   Parchim airfield - Tribune de Genève, 8 October 2007

clxxiii.   Hilton, Christopher, *After the Berlin Wall: Putting the Two Germanys Together Again*, The History Press, 2009, pp 93-9

clxxiv.   Interview with *Super Illi magazine* quoted on *szonline.de* 29 September 2010

clxxv.   Sereny, Gitta, *Albert Speer: His Battle with Truth,* Albert A. Knopf, New York, 1995, Macmillan, London, 1995, p 465

clxxvi.   Sereny, *Speer* op.cit. pp 718-9

clxxvii.   Rosenbaum, op.cit. pp 250, 395

clxxviii.   Letter of 5 July 1945, in possession of the author

clxxix.   Hilton, op.cit. p 158. Figures for 2007

clxxx.   Patch, Harry, with van Emden, Richard, *The Last Fighting Tommy*, Bloomsbury, 2007, pp 201-2

clxxxi.   Romans XII, 18

clxxxii.   Fest, *Hitler*, op.cit. p 1058

clxxxiii.   Quoted by Hilton, op.cit. p 193

clxxxiv.   Sächsische Zeitung, 17 March 2010

SELECTED READING
IN ENGLISH

Beevor, Antony, *Berlin: The Downfall 1945*, Penguin, London, 2002

Bielenberg, Christabel, *The Past Is Myself*, Corgi, London, 1968

Bishop, Patrick, *Bomber Boys: Fighting Back 1940-1945*, Harper Perennial, London, 2007

Boyes, Roger, *From Prussia with Love: Misadventures in Rural East Germany*, Summersdale, Chichester, 2011

Bullock, Alan, *Hitler: A Study in Tyranny*, Pelican, London, 1952

Clare, George, *Berlin Days 1946-47*, Pan, London 1989

Cornwell, John, *Hitler's Pope: The Secret History of Pius XII*, Penguin, London, 1999

Davies, Norman, *Europe: a History*, Pimlico, London, 1996

Elon, Amos, *Journey through a Haunted Land: The New Germany*, Andre Deutsch, London, 1967

Fest, Joachim, *Inside Hitler's Bunker: The Last Days of the Third Reich*, Pan, London, 2002

Garton Ash, Timothy, *The File: A Personal History*, Flamingo, London, 1997

Gay, Peter, *My German Question: Growing Up in Nazi Berlin*, Yale, Newhaven & London, 1998

Goldhagen, Daniel, *Hitler's Willing Executioners*, Vintage, New York, 1997

Haffner, Sebastian, *Defying Hitler: A Memoir,* Phoenix, London, 2002

Hastings, Max, *Armageddon: The Battle for Germany 1944-45,* Pan, London, 2004

Heym, Stefan, *Uncertain Friend,* Cassell, London, 1969

Hilton, Christopher, *After the Berlin Wall: Putting the Two Germanys Back Together Again,* The History Press, Stroud, 2009

Junge, Traudl, *Until the Final Hour: Hitler's Last Secretary,* Weidenfeld & Nicolson, London, 2002

Kershaw, Ian, *Hitler,* Penguin, 2010

Kershaw, Ian, *The End: Hitler's Germany, 1944-45,* Allen Lane, London, 2011

Lebor, Adam & Boyes, Roger, *Surviving Hitler: Choices, Corruption and Compromise in the Third Reich,* Simon & Schuster, London, 2000

Mazower, Mark, *Hitler's Empire,* Penguin, London, 2008

Millar, Peter, *1989: The Berlin Wall, My Part in Its Downfall,* Arcadia Books, London, 2009

Patch, Harry, with Van Emden, Richard, *The Last Fighting Tommy: The Life of Harry Patch, the Only Surviving Veteran of the Trenches,* Bloomsbury, London, 2007

Rees, Laurence, *Auschwitz: The Nazis and the Final Solution,* BBC Books, London, 2005

Roberts, Frank, *Dealing with Dictators: The Destruction & Revival of Europe 1930-70,* Weidenfeld & Nicolson, London, 1991

Rosenbaum, Ron, *Explaining Hitler,* Harper Perennial, New York, 1998

Schwartz, Mimi, *Good Neighbours Bad Times: Echoes of My Father's German Village,* University of Nebraska, Lincoln & London, 2008

Sebald, W.G. *On the Natural History of Destruction,* Knopf Canada, 2003

Seiffert, Rachel, *The Dark Room,* Vintage, London, 2001

Sereny, Gitta, *Into That Darkness,* Vintage, New York, 1983

Sereny, Gitta, *The German Trauma: Experiences and Reflections 1938-2001,* Penguin, London, 2000

Shirer, William L. *Berlin Diary 1934-1941,* Sphere, London, 1941

Shirer, William L. *The Rise and Fall of The Third Reich,* Pan, London, 1964

Smith, Howard K. *Last Train from Berlin,* Knopf, New York,1943

Smyser, W.R. *From Yalta to Berlin: The Cold War Struggle over Germany,* Macmillan, London, 1999

Snowman, Daniel, *The Hitler Emigrés,* Pimlico, London, 2003

Stern, Fritz, *Five Germanys I Have Known,* Farrar, Strauss & Giroux, New York, 2006

Taylor, Frederick, *Dresden: Tuesday 13 February 1945,* Bloomsbury, London, 2004

Taylor, A.J.P. *The Course of German History,* Routledge Classics, London, 1945, 1961

Timms, Uwe, *In My Brother's Shadow,* Bloomsbury, London 2003

Wehner, Herbert A. *Iron Coffins: A U-boat Commander's War 1939-1945,* Cassell, London, 1969

SELECTED READING
IN GERMAN

Aly, Götz, *Hitlers Volkstaat: Raub, Rassenkkrieg und nationaler Sozialismus,* Fischer Taschenbuch Verlag, Frankfurt am Main, 2005

Baale, Olaf, *Abbau Ost: Lügen, Vorurteile und sozialistische Schulden,* Deutscher Taschenbuch Verlag, München, 2008

Bahr, Egon, *Der Deutsche Weg: Selbstverständlich und normal,* Blessing, München, 2003

Boehart, William & Busch, Wolf-Rüdiger, *Ein Traum ohne Ende: Beiträge über das Leben und Wirken Alfred Nobels aus dem Jubiläumsjahr 2001 in Geesthacht,* LIT, Münster, 2004

Busch, Wolf-Rüdiger, *"Klein Moskau" - Geesthacht 1919-1933: Kultur, Revolution, arbeitslos ...!* LIT, Hamburg, 1999

Busch, Wolf-Rüdiger, *Nur aus dieser Not heraus: Geesthachter erinnern sich an die Jahre 1930-1950,* Stadtarchiv Geesthacht, 1989

Catlin, Chris, *Brudersuche,* Verlag Landpresse, Weilerswist, 2004

Fest, Joachim, *Hitler: eine Biographie,* Ullstein, Berlin, 1973

Fest, Joachim, *Ich Nicht: Erinnerung an eine Kindheit und Jugend,* Rowohlt, Reinbek, 2006

Friedrich, Jörg, *Der Brand: Deutschland im Bombenkrieg 1940-1945,* List, Berlin, 2002

Glotz, Peter, *Die Vertreibung: Böhmen als Lehrstück,* Ullstein, Berlin, 2004

Grass, Günter, *Im Krebsgang,* Deutscher Taschenbuch Verlag, München, 2004

Haffner, Sebastian, *Anmerkungen zu Hitler,* Fischer Taschenbuch Verlag, Frankfurt am Main, 2006

Hauswald, Harald / Rathenow, Lutz, *Ost-Berlin: Leben vor dem Mauerfall,* Jaron Verlag, Berlin, 2005

Hertle, Hans-Hermann, & Wolle, Stefan, *Damals in der DDR,* C. Bertelsmann Verlag, München, 2004

Heym, Stefan, *Der König David Bericht,* Kindler, München, 1972

Hildebrandt, Alexandra, *Die Mauer. Zahlen. Daten,* Verlag Haus am Checkpoint Charlie, Berlin 2005

Jirgl, Reinhard, *Abschied von den Feinden,* Deutscher Taschenbuch Verlag, München, 1995

Jirgl, Reinhard, *Die atlantische Mauer,* Deutscher Taschenbuch Verlag, München, 2000

Knabe, Hubertus, *Gefangen in Hohenschönhausen: Stasi-Häftlinge berichten,* List, Berlin, 2007

Kreuder-Sonnen, Katharina, *Ukrainische Zwangsarbeiter in Geesthacht - Zeitzeugenberichte,* Geesthacht Museum

Künnemann, Otto, *Wir vom Jahrgang 1942,* Wartberg Verlag, Gudensberg-Gleichen, 2008

Leonhard, Wolfgang, *Meine Geschichte der DDR,* Rowohlt, Berlin, 2007

Lorenzen, Jan N. *Erich Honecker: eine Biographie,* Rowohlt, Reinbek, 2001

Menapace, Bernhard Michael, *"Klein-Moskau wird braun: Geesthacht in der Endphase der Weimarer Republik (1928-1933),* Neuer Malik Verlag, Kiel, 1991

Meyer-Rebentisch, Karen, *Grenzerfahrungen: vom Leben mit der innerdeutschen Grenze*, Thomas Helms Verlag, 2009

Stern, Carola, *Willy Brandt,* Rowohlt, Reinbek, 1988, 2002

Wolf, Christa, *Unter den Linden,* Deutscher Taschenbuch Verlag, München, 1977, 1997

Zeitzeugenbörse, *Jugend unter brauner Diktatur,* Berlin, 2003

Zeitzeugenbörse, *Ost-West Piraten,* Berlin, 2001

Zweig, Stefan, *Die Welt von Gestern: Erinnerungen eines Europäers,* Fischer Taschenbuch Verlag, Frankfurt am Main, 1942

INDEX

Subjects & places: